# Women as Therapists

**Dorothy W. Cantor, Psy.D.**, is in private practice in Westfield, New Jersey, and Director of Professional Affairs of the New Jersey Psychological Association. She is coauthor of *Divorced Parents and Their Children: A Guide for Mental Health Professionals* and coeditor of *The Psychology of Today's Woman: New Psychoanalytic Visions*.

# Women as Therapists
## A Multitheoretical Casebook

Dorothy W. Cantor, Psy.D.
Editor

𝒜

JASON ARONSON INC.
*Northvale, New Jersey*
*London*

Library of Congress Cataloging-in-Publication Data

Women as therapists: a multitheoretical casebook / Dorothy W. Cantor,
  editor.
     p.  cm.
Includes bibliographical references and indexes.
ISBN 0-87668-313-8: (pb)
   Previously ISBN 0-8261-6910-4
   1. Women psychotherapists.   2. Psychotherapy.   3. Psychotherapist
and patient. I. Cantor, Dorothy W.
RC480.5, W65   1992b
616.89'14'082—dc20                                      92-21975
                                                      CIP

Manufactured in the United States of America. Jason Aronson Inc. offers books and cassettes. For information and catalog write to Jason Aronson Inc., 230 Livingston Street, Northvale, New Jersey 07647.

First, to Laura, my daughter,
then, to Karen, my daughter-in-law,
and finally,
to my wonderful women friends and colleagues,
all of whom I love and respect.

# Contents

# Contributors

**Judith L. Alpert, Ph.D.**, is professor in the doctoral programs in school psychology and child/school psychology at New York University and is in private practice in psychoanalysis and psychotherapy in New York City. She received her Ph.D. from Columbia University and her certificate in psychotherapy and psychoanalysis from the New York University postdoctoral program in psychotherapy and psychoanalysis. Dr. Alpert is editor of several books, including *Psychoanalysis and Women: Contemporary Reappraisals*.

**Laura S. Brown, Ph.D., ABPP**, is in the private practice of feminist therapy in Seattle, and clinical associate professor of psychology at the University of Washington. She has published and presented over 60 professional articles or book chapters in a variety of areas, with special interests in lesbianism, diagnosis and assessment, victimization, and chemical dependency recovery in women.

**Sandra B. Coleman, Ph.D.**, executive director, Family Guidance Center, is a clinical and research psychologist specializing in marital and family therapy. As principal investigator of numerous large studies, Dr. Coleman has gained an international reputation for her research on families with drug and alcohol problems. Widely published, Dr. Coleman is also known for her recent book *Failures in Family Therapy*.

**Joann Paley Galst, Ph.D.**, is a senior clinical consultant at the Institute for Behavior Therapy and the staff psychologist at the Fertility Research Foundation in New York City. In her private practice of cognitive behavior therapy, she has specialized in women's behavior health, infertility, and pregnancy loss.

**Ellen Tobey Klass, Ph.D.**, is associate professor of psychology, Hunter College, City University of New York, and research associate, Center for Stress and Anxiety Disorders, State University of New York at Albany. She also is in independent practice of cognitive behavior therapy in New York City. Her clinical and research specialties are anxiety disorders, personality disorders, and dysfunctional guilt.

**Charles B. Mark, Psy.D.**, is a graduate of Rutgers University Graduate School of Applied and Professional Psychology. He is presently in private practice, Oldwick, NJ.

**Alisa S. Michaels** is currently a graduate student in clinical psychology at Catholic University of America. She received her B.A. in psychology from Clark University in 1985. Following graduation from Clark, she was a research assistant at McLean Hospital

**Lenore E. A. Walker, Ed.D.**, is a licensed psychologist in independent practice in Denver and is an adjunct member on the University of Denver's School of Professional Psychology faculty. She has recently completed a term on the board of directors of the American Psychological Association and is the current president of Division 35—The Psychology of Women. She is the author of eight books, including *The Battered Woman, The Battered Woman Syndrome,* and *Terrifying Love: Why Battered Women Kill and How Society Responds,* and editor of *Women and Mental Health Policy* and *The Handbook on Sexual Abuse of Children.* Dr. Walker is the 1987 recipient of the prestigious APA Professional Contributions in the Public Interest award for her work with battered women.

**Karen Zager, Ph.D.**, is a clinical psychologist and psychoanalyst in full-time independent practice in New York. She also serves as a consultant to a preschool educational program for handicapped and developmentally delayed children. She is active in the American Psychological Association, having served on the Public Information Committee and on the boards of directors of the Division of Psychologists in Independent Practice and the Division of Psychotherapy.

# Introduction

*Women as Therapists: A Multitheoretical Casebook* had its origins in a series of symposia sponsored by the Committee on Gender Issues of the Division of Independent Practice (Division 42) of the American Psychological Association. In 1987 and 1988, at the annual APA convention, we presented "Women Treating Women: A Case Seminar" and "Women Treating Men: A Case Seminar." We were interested in the effect of a woman therapist's theoretical orientation on how she conceptualized a case and treated a patient. The response to the symposia was so enthusiastic and so many psychologists were interested in the ideas presented that we decided to organize them into a book that would add to the growing literature on women as therapists, providing a model of how women work with their patients.

To provide a context for the case material, some questions about gender, theoretical orientation, and patient selection of therapist are presented in Part I. First, the editor looks at what has already been written about women as therapists and their work with female and male clients.

Charles B. Mark presents some cogent thoughts about how therapists come to their theoretical orientation and, particularly, the fit between their own experiences and espousement of a theoretical model.

Alisa S. Michaels reports on a research study designed to find out how women patients who work with women therapists made their choice of therapist.

The case material presented in Parts II and III looks at the interaction of the gender and theoretical orientation of the therapist with the gender of the patient.

Karen Zager presents the cases of a female and male patient; the experts respond from their own theoretical orientations and discuss how they would treat the patient. At the beginning of each discussion of the case in Part II, there is a summary of the theory behind the treatment, which is not repeated in Part III. Readers who choose to begin with the male cases in Part III are advised to read the introductory section of the companion chapter in Part II before proceeding with the discussion of the treatment.

Judith L. Alpert presents the psychoanalytic approach to the case material; Sandra B. Coleman, the family-therapy approach; Lenore E. A. Walker, the feminist-therapy approach; and Joann Paley Galst and Ellen Tobey Klass, the cognitive-behavioral approach. Readers will be fascinated by the similarities and differences among the four theoretical approaches to treatment and will be able to draw their own conclusions regarding the impact of the gender of the therapist on the course of therapy.

After reading four approaches to a single case, readers will appreciate the effect of applying different lenses to the same material and how much fuller the picture is that emerges when a variety of theoretical viewpoints is considered.

Finally, in Part IV, in contrast to the previous sections that focus on the differences among women therapists, Laura S. Brown comments on what women therapists have in common.

It is our hope that this book will advance the understanding of women who bring to their work as therapists the empathy and caring that are the cornerstone of successful treatment, regardless of their theoretical orientation.

Dorothy W. Cantor
Westfield, New Jersey

# I

## THE CONTEXT

# 1

# Women as Therapists:
# What We Already Know

## Dorothy W. Cantor

Increasingly, psychotherapists are female. For a number of years, more than half of the students admitted to graduate schools of psychology have been female. Social work and psychiatric nursing have traditionally been largely female professions. Even psychiatry is seeing a trend to increasing numbers of females (Fenton, Robinowitz, & Leaf, 1987). Only recently, though, have we begun to look at the impact of the gender of the therapist on the therapeutic process. For the early traditional psychoanalysts, the real person of the analyst was irrelevant, including gender. The transference could evolve with a therapist of either sex. This chapter will review what has been written over the last 15 years about the importance of the sex of the therapist and how the sex of the therapist influences the female-female dyad and the female-male dyad, and will look at the implications of the literature.

Samuels (1985) studied portrayals of female psychotherapists in film, fiction, and popular nonfiction, and stated, "With exceptions so rare as to be noteworthy, portrayals of female therapists are sexist, unprofessional, unethical and unbelievable" (p. 367). Yet patients must not see women therapists that way. Michaels (1990) reports that the gender of

3

the therapist was second only to her reputation as a factor in women's choice of women therapists. Samuels (1985) hypothesized that a therapist's perceived power has influenced the portrayal of women therapists in the media, because power in a women is particularly fearful and the power is diminished if she is portrayed as less than whole.

It should be noted that most of the literature pertinent to women as therapists is clinical or experientially based, with only limited research into the effects of the gender of the therapist on treatment.

## DOES THE GENDER OF THE THERAPIST MATTER?

Felton (1986) stated that an appropriate response to the question of whether a male therapist can really understand a female patient is that there are occasions in treatment when issues of gender create obstacles for the patient and the therapist, and occasions when they advance the progress of the patient. She noted that the patient's choice of a therapist of a particular gender may be indicative of what problems the patient is prepared to work through or avoid at the outset of therapy. Person (1983) has indicated that the patient's preference should be respected because it would be difficult, if not impossible, to work with a therapist of the undesired sex.

### Are Men and Women Different as Therapists?

In spite of the early belief that the gender of the therapist is irrelevant to the therapeutic process, there is concurrence in the current literature that men and women are different as therapists.

First, the role of a woman as therapist is seen as consistent with her overall socialization and role in the larger culture: always being available to nurture (Schachtel, 1986; Schlachet, 1984). Schlachet cites Chodorow's and Gilligan's work on the differences in the upbringing of boys and girls and then wonders how the resultant differences in personality and relational style influence our work as therapists. She points out that the work of listening to other people and trying to make sense of and empathize with their experience is work for which men have not been socialized. Women, on the other hand, might do the same with friends, family, and neighbors. In other words, male therapists have to learn and practice what women already have as part of their experience. She suggests that women often feel like imposters in their work as therapists because they are doing things with patients that they do in their daily lives. Because the relational context is so crucial to the work, women therapists may feel less valid than women who are, for example, dentists or gynecologists.

Schachtel (1986) speaks of the interaction of gender role and analytic role. Female identity is defined by being empathic and caring, not hurting others, and remaining attached. Masculine identity is defined by separation and threatened by intimacy. The female role is associated with the mother's expressive functions, and the male role is characterized as representing instrumental functions. Schachtel points out that because women have been trained to respond by doing something to and for the other person, a female therapist needs to monitor a lifelong gender role: to "make it better," a responsibility that male therapists are not likely to feel and that is not actually the task. For example, she states that "the patient's anger and resistance in the face of nonnurturance may evoke in the female analysts feelings of being 'bad'—and of not understanding" (p. 249). Schachtel believes that when the male analyst is seen as a "bad mother," he will feel less bad than his female counterpart.

Schachtel (1986) discusses male socialization, which has stressed separateness and repression of feelings, particularly early ones. She has found that women in training as analysts have an easier time being a receptor of feeling than their male counterparts, who may "stonewall" the feelings. The danger for males is that feelings will break through the boundaries of control.

The question of the relative status and authority of male and female therapists has been considered by several writers (Brodsky, 1976; Cooke & Kipnis, 1986; Kaplan, 1985). Cooke and Kipnis (1986) did a study of the process of psychotherapy in the context of social-power theory. They were interested in the therapists' attempts to "influence" their clients—any attempt to change a client's behavior, cognitions, or feelings. One of the questions they raised was whether the therapist's and/or the client's gender affect the frequency of use or strength of influence tactics. The sample was small (an analysis of 22 tapes provided by five females and six male therapists), but the results were most interesting. Among the findings were that male therapists attempted more influence acts and interrupted their clients more frequently than did female therapists. Women therapists spent more of the therapy session listening to their clients. Although Cooke and Kipnis interpret this as an indication of female passivity, it can also be seen in terms of the previously discussed socialization of females to be listeners. It is noteworthy, too, that the study found that both male and female therapists make more frequent and stronger attempts to influence female clients.

Brodsky (1976) stated that she intuitively felt that female therapists have less sense of omnipotence about their role in the therapy process than men. It would seem that her intuition was borne out by the Cooke and Kipnis study.

Kaplan (1985) looked at Gilligan's (1982) formulation of the sense of self, in which women typically portray the self as a relational being while men reflect an autonomous and separate sense of self. She then suggested that a woman therapist might be especially sensitive to the dangers of overstepping the boundaries of her authority and concerned about making arbitrary or capricious decisions for her client. A male therapist would be more comfortable with the dominant aspects of the therapist's roles, less apt to worry about overstepping boundaries, and less likely to weigh his decision-making process in terms of his client's reaction.

Male and female therapists' responses (verbal replies, affective reactions, and clinical judgments) to audiotapes of client sexual material were studied by Schover (1981). Thirty-six male and 36 female therapists, equal numbers of M.S.W.-level social workers, Ph.D.-level clinical psychologists, and postresidency psychiatrists participated in the study. The results of the study were that female therapists seemed to make relatively fewer therapeutic errors, whereas male therapists showed both over- and underemphasis of sexual material. Female therapists seemed better able to turn a client's sexual inquiries back to the client's emotional experience, rather than being self-disclosing. Overall, female therapists were more comfortable than males with client sexual material.

In a study of male and female psychiatrists and their patients based on data from a national survey, Fenton, Robinowitz, and Leaf (1987) found that female psychiatrists were as likely to diagnose female patients as neurotic as their male colleagues. Similarly, medication was prescribed at about the same rate by male and female psychiatrists. On these dimensions, then, the gender of the therapist was not significant.

Finally, Cavenar and Werman (1983) reviewed the literature and concluded that the determining factor in whether the gender of the therapist was significant to psychotherapy was whether the therapy was supportive or insight-oriented. They stated that in supportive therapies, one attempts to strengthen defenses, encourage repression, and provide symptom relief. Identification with the therapist is encouraged, and the therapist takes an active role in helping the patient seek solutions. Therefore, the real qualities of the therapist, including gender, are important in encouraging identification. On the other hand, insight-oriented therapies whose goal is to make the unconscious conscious and to help the patient achieve greater self-understanding are less dependent on the real qualities of the therapist and can proceed to a satisfactory conclusion regardless of the sex of the therapist.

It would seem that no one is arguing that only one gender is capable of successful treatment but that therapists need to be aware of the qualities their socialization and sex roles bring to their role as therapists so that they can interfere as little as possible with the work at hand.

## What Impact Does the Therapist's Gender Have on Psychotherapy Outcome?

A relatively early study by Orlinsky and Howard (1976) addressed the effect of the sex of the therapist on the therapeutic experiences of women. They reanalyzed data collected in 1964 when they had not been concerned with whether the therapist was male or female. They had data from 118 women in outpatient psychotherapy; 78 had male therapists, and 40 had female therapists. They concluded that female patients who were young and single were most ambivalently reactive to male therapists and most satisfied with female therapists. In addition, patients diagnosed as depressive reactions were most strongly responsive to therapist gender, while those diagnosed as personality disorders were least reactive. Depressed patients who had women therapists felt that they got more encouragement, felt less inhibited, and had fewer concerns about identity, sex, and guilt. The authors concluded that whether the therapist is able and sensitive may be less important than what the therapist's gender means to the patient.

Jones and Zoppel (1982) reported on two studies of the impact of client and therapist gender on psychotherapy process and outcome. In the first study, therapists rated outcome for 160 former clients. In the second study, 99 former therapy clients who had been seen for an average of 7.6 sessions were interviewed about their experience in therapy and therapy effectiveness. Women therapists rated themselves more successful, particularly with female clients. Women therapists displayed more "unconditional positive regard." Clients, regardless of gender, agreed that women therapists formed a more effective therapeutic alliance than did male therapists. However, both male and female clients of male therapists reported significant improvement.

Jones and Zoppel concluded that there are differences between men and women therapists in abilities or behavioral skills and emotional capacities as well as attitudes. However, they believe that the term *sex bias* does not do justice to the complexity of the impact of gender in psychotherapy.

## Gender Effects in Various Therapeutic Modalities

### Brief Psychotherapy

Kirshner, Genack, and Hauser (1978) reported on a study in which 92 male and 97 female patients and their psychotherapists at a university health service were asked to self-rate their treatment after individual short-term therapy. They found both a "patient gender effect" and a "therapist gender effect." Female patients were more responsive to psychotherapy and showed greater improvement than males on attitudes toward career, academic motivation, academic performance, and family relations. Patients of female therapists reported greater improvement in the main problem, greater satisfaction with treatment, and more congruence with the therapist's ratings. This female-therapist effect held when therapist experience (junior-senior) was statistically controlled. The researchers, all men, concluded that an empirical "gender effect is supported by our findings, adding weight to the major trends of previous studies: women appear to be both more responsive and effective in psychotherapy than men" (p. 167).

More recently, Jones, Krupnick and Kerig (1987) reported on two studies of gender effects in brief psychotherapy. The first study attempted to replicate the finding of gender effects in psychotherapy by determining whether women patients achieve superior outcomes when treated by female therapists in a 12-session psychodynamic therapy. The second study explored how patient characteristics influence therapeutic processes. For Study 1, 60 women were selected, half of whom had been treated by males and half by females. For Study 2, the sample was a subset of 40 of the women for whom audiotapes were available.

The researchers found that female therapists were "more assured and comfortable as well as more clear and direct in their comments to their patients. In turn, their clients appeared more trusting and secure, more familiar with what was expected of them in therapy, and struggled less with concerns about how the therapist would respond to them" (p. 346). Patients of male therapists experienced more negative affect and struggles to manage or maintain control over those emotions. Their attitude toward their therapists was characterized as more ambivalent, conflicted, and wary. They worried about being judged. It should be noted that the researchers found that patient pretherapy level of distress was clearly the factor most predictive of outcome and that the age of the patient also had an important predictive role, accounting for almost twice as much outcome variance as therapist gender. Thus, the impact of the gender of the therapist on outcome must be seen in the context of the patient's initial adequacy of personality functioning and age.

## Hypnotherapy

McCabe, Collins, Jupp, Walker, and Sutton (1983) looked at whether the gender of the therapist would influence the outcome of a 10-session hypnotherapy program with obese female patients. The assumption that effectiveness of therapy via rapport would be enhanced with a same-sex therapist was not supported. Since hypnotherapy does not involve the listening and empathic components that psychotherapy does, the results are not surprising.

## Psychoanalysis

Kulish (1984, 1986, 1989) has written quite extensively on the effect of the sex of the analyst on the transference.

First, she reviewed the literature on the effect of sex on transference (Kulish, 1984). She noted that the most extensive discussions have centered on the assignment of patients to therapists of a particular gender. The situations in which gender affects transference are "(1) situations that provoke strong initial resistances (2) situations that facilitate transference (3) situations that involve patients whose histories include the death of a parent" (p. 97). When a patient picks an analyst, the analyst's sex is often part of the transference and should be distinguished from the actual effects of the analyst's sex on the therapeutic process. Historically, male therapists were chosen because they were perceived as more competent and authoritative. Female therapists were viewed more negatively in studies Kulish reviewed. Patients saw female therapists as more empathic but could more readily accept male therapists' authoritative behavior than female therapists' empathic behavior. The most frequently mentioned effect of the sex of the analyst on the transference was its influence on the the order in which crucial psychosexual conflicts emerged during the course of treatment. Kulish noted that even the early writers, such as Kubie, Glover, and Blum, who tended to reject any influence of the sex of the therapist, would state that the order the material was presented was frequently affected by that factor. She also found that while sustained maternal transferences toward male analysts have been reported frequently, sustained paternal transferences to women have not. Kulish concluded that there was "little information of firm substance" (p. 108) regarding the effect of the sex of the analyst on the transference.

In her 1986 paper, Kulish stated her feeling that "gender can be a major organizing factor both for the patient and for the analyst" (p. 394). She investigated further the question of whether women analysts evoke a paternal transference. She found that if they did, it was described as "more subtle," "less frequent," or "not sustained" (p. 395). Kulish explained this from the patient's side in terms of the early experience with the mother or the idea that "maleness" is more tied to reality and therefore less likely to be superimposed on a female analyst. From the analyst's point of view, she suggested that it may be particularly difficult for women to view themselves in masculine terms or that women may too readily focus on the early maternal material. Another area of difference between male and female analysts is the eroticized transference. Kulish pointed out that there are "virtually no published reports of strongly and sustained erotic or eroticized transferences of male patients toward female analysts, in contrast to the common story of the female falling deeply in 'love' with her male analyst, or into a wildly unmanageable erotic transference" (p. 397). If erotic transferences exist toward women analysts, Kulish concluded, they aren't appearing in the literature. Kulish put forth the notion that the therapist's gender may organize and limit the patient's fantasies, just as the form of a Rorschach blot sets limits on the fantasies projected on it.

In her most recent paper, Kulish (1989) reported on interviews with 17 senior female analysts to find out whether gender affected the transference, sequence, referral choice, erotic or eroticized transferences, and oedipal transferences. Her conclusion was that the sex of the therapist had more bearing on the transference than has been appreciated or acknowledged in the literature. Several respondents felt that the effect of gender is greatest initially and would fall away over the long run. Several felt that female analysts might pull pre-oedipal issues sooner than a male analyst. A number commented on the need to consider the analyst's gender in assigning adolescents to treatment. The respondents were less in agreement over the appearance of paternal transferences. In general, they suggested that the development of an intensely erotic transference of a male patient with a female analyst was blocked by inhibitions from both patient and analyst. Kulish concluded that "gender may serve as a basic, unconscious organizing factor around which the clinical material is experienced, processed, understood, and interpreted" (p. 70).

## Family and Couples Therapy

Okun (1989) stated that in couples and family work, there is safety in numbers and that the focus is on the intracouple and intrafamilial interactions and dynamics, which take precedence over the therapist-family interaction. Nevertheless, the female couples therapist must be aware of the model of couples relationships that she has; for instance, whether she believes in equal power in relationships or defers to males. In couples therapy with heterosexual couples, there are two of one gender and one of the other. With a women therapist, the male with two females is in a nondominant position, regardless of the therapist's views, and the therapist needs to appreciate that position.

Okun noted that women therapists have typically found it difficult to assume powerful, active roles with families and have either avoided confronting males in the system or have entered the system too aggressively. She warned that female therapists have to avoid their acculturation as a nondominant female in a dominant male world. They have the opportunity to teach couples mutual empathy, empowerment, and enhancement by equally valuing both genders and modeling respectful attachment behaviors.

Finally, Okun stated that it is critical for women family and couples therapists to meet their own needs for closeness and relationships outside work, to avoid jealousy, resentment, and voyeuristic feeling in their therapeutic experience.

## Feminist Therapy

Cammaert and Larsen (1988) discussed the feminist frameworks of psychotherapy. They noted that feminist therapy evolved from a philosophical system and that its core concept is that the therapist respects the woman and honors the perception of her world. The therapist, who must be a woman, presents herself as a role model, modeling supportive, helpful behavior and involvement with others as well as her own intellectual and professional growth, involvement in political issues, and economic self-interest.

Feminist therapists see the female-female therapeutic dyad as removing the power effect of a male therapist's working with a female client. However, they are aware that an egalitarian relationship between therapist and client is more an ideal than a reality because the power of the expert cannot be eradicated by having a same-sex therapist. The recommendation Cammaert and Larsen cite Douglas as having made is to define the therapeutic relationship as one of temporary inequality and to make the inequality as little disparate as possible.

Feminist therapists use appropriate self-disclosure as a means of developing the potential bond that arises out of the communality of women's experiences. They no longer espouse immediate self-disclosure because research has found that clients at times felt intimidated or coerced by the therapist's values.

## THE FEMALE-FEMALE DYAD

Not surprisingly, most of what is reported in the literature about the relationship between patient and therapist is written from a psychoanalytic perspective since it is psychoanalysis that relies on analysis of transference and understanding of countertransference as a cornerstone of treatment. Additionally, feminist therapists write about the dyad because they see it as crucial to successful therapy for women.

The focus on whether women make better therapists for women clients developed with the women's movement. Tanney and Birk (1976), reviewing the literature to that date, quoted Fabrikant's observation that there had been some exploration of the relative advantage of the sex of a therapist corresponding to the sex of the parent who was considered the focus of difficulty. They found that by 1976, there was only sparse empirical evidence of female clients' preferences and that the results of research were often contradictory. Far more attention had been paid to therapists' attitudes about sex-role stereotypes. Following the classic Broverman study of 1970, which demonstrated that clinicians' judgments about the mental health of individuals differed as a function of the sex of the person evaluated, the assumption was made that women clients needed women therapists. However, Tanney and Birk did not find at that time that the research was sufficient to describe clearly the impact of the gender of the therapist on women clients.

Some years later, Kaplan (1985) reached the same conclusion as she reviewed psychotherapy research, noting that the sex of the patient and the therapist was but one of many factors that influenced the process of therapy. She wondered, however, whether the absence of replicable gender effects in therapy might be more a function of method than a real absence of potentially discernible effects. Nonetheless, to date there has been no research published that provides clear, replicable evidence of a strong, specific gender effect.

Goz (1973) looked at what the choice of a woman therapist by a women meant when it was couched in "the current phraseology of women's liberation" (p. 298). Her hypothesis was that "the request for a woman therapist by a woman patient is in some major form or other nearly always a disguised request by the patient to duplicate, review, reinstate, reenact, repair, and recreate some powerful unresolved tensions in her relationship to her mother in particular, and the realistic presence of a female therapist before her very eyes in short-term psychotherapy enhances the likelihood that this may occur" (p. 299). Goz suggested that issues of pregnancy, symbiosis and homosexuality could be worked on to special advantage by women patients with women therapists.

Person (1983) wondered why women were seeking women therapists when the mother problem had always existed. The explanations given, which are the conscious reasons women cite, were: fear that men will hold sexist values; a belief that it is too easy to fool a male and avoid problems; the wish to avoid erotic transferences and countertransferences; the desire to have a strong woman with whom to identify. The first three reasons involve avoidance of a male, either because he is viewed as biased or because of fear that the relationship is intrinsically subject to distortion. The fourth reason, wanting a role model, implies that the therapist is sought as a stand-in for the mother. In this role, according to Person, the female therapist is sought to give the patient permission to compete and achieve in order to avoid unconscious conflicts centering around mother-daughter competition. In longer-term female-female psychoanalysis, the rivalrous oedipal material will emerge, and the patient will fear loss of love, starvation, and annihilation. In short-term therapies, the permission may lead to a transference "cure."

Shainess (1983) wrote of some of the pitfalls of being a role model to the patient. For example, since competent females are still looked on with distrust, the patient is likely to bring doubt and distrust to the same therapist she looks to as a role model. Some patients have a preconceived fantasy of the role model and are disappointed in the reality of the woman they encounter.

Shainess found that patients generally avoid the therapist who reflects the sex of the more damaging parent, although some choose to become directly involved in spite of fears. In the latter case, the outset of the therapy may be very difficult, bringing the transference into play more immediately. Shainess's conclusion was that "women patients are more likely to be helped to be autonomous, self-reliant people with competent women therapists, who have reason to be alert to gender problems and gender role stereotypes out of their own experience (p. 216).

Feminist therapy is seen as a way of implementing feminist policy into practice (Rosewater, 1988). Feminist therapists do not think of their clients as "sick," but rather that an individual's problem behavior is a function of being confused. The feminist therapist recognizes her own competence but appreciates her client's ability to teach her. Rosewater sees that as a logical outgrowth of the grass-roots development of feminist therapy, which began as women helping women. The therapist's role is "a model and guide, helping other women explore familiar terrain with a positive belief about recovery from oppression" (p. 152).

## Lesbian Clients

Some attention should be given to the work of female therapists with lesbian clients. Eisenbud (1986), a psychoanalyst, stated that in working with a woman who had made a truly primary lesbian choice, the analyst is dealing with transference from a pre-oedipal time. The early strong erotic turn-on has resulted in a permanent erotic inner construction toward a female, which, if invalidated, leads to humiliation, hopelessness, deprivation, and rage. With a female therapist, Eisenbud describes three different patterns in the transference. The most direct is an overt demand for proof of special love and inclusion in the woman analyst's life. In the second, the patient interprets analytic acceptance as seduction. And in the third, the transference revolves around a fierce struggle for control. Eisenbud stated that "transference interpretation, respect and empathy, and firm limit setting encourage new individuation."

Feminist therapy perceives the variability in sexual orientations in human beings as a simple fact rather than a matter for concern or intervention, or pathological per se (Brown, 1988). A feminist therapist working with a lesbian client will be more likely to explore sociocultural issues, especially homophobia in the culture and its resultant self-devaluation. Brown described one task of the feminist therapist as helping lesbian clients understand how they participated in their own oppression by having internalized the societal oppression. Other tasks are to challenge constantly the lesbian's own homophobia, to deal with problems associated with noncompliance with gender roles, and to explore sexual dysfunction in the same-sex couple. Brown's experience as a referral source is that almost all prospective lesbian clients request a feminist therapist, like herself, and sees that as the best match.

## Countertransference

Ruderman (1986) has studied the countertransference themes of women therapists working with women. Most striking was the profound resonance, going beyond empathy, that the therapists experience, especially on issues of midlife: menopause and premenopause. Then she noted that unacknowledged and unmanaged countertransference can be countertherapeutic as well as mirroring oppressive sociocultural values.

Similarly, Levy (1982) sounded a note of warning that a female therapist's overidentification with a client can obstruct empathic processes. "Longstanding female identification processes, rooted in the early mother/daughter relationship, produce a situation wherein both female therapists and their female clients will most likely struggle with intense issues around identification and nurturance" (p. 38). The challenge to the female therapist is to produce an overt recognition of the relational struggle, so that the therapy does not become a recapitulation of the patient's earlier experiences with her mother.

A third finding of Ruderman's study was that 18 of the 20 women therapists interviewed undervalued their obviously excellent therapeutic skills. At the same time, they showed immeasurable respect for their women patients, allowing them the "widest latitude to make their own choices and unfold in their own way" (p. 21).

## FEMALE-MALE DYAD

Women therapists, although they certainly treated male patients before the 1980s, didn't begin to write of their experiences until then. Gilligan (1982) noted that woman's place in man's life cycle has been that of nurturer, caretaker, and helpmate. Women as therapists to men are therefore not incongruous. Yet, as Gornick (1986) pointed out, men's fears of merging with mother, or of the threat that women pose to masculinity, make the female-male dyad less assured of a smooth course than might be expected.

Two of the earlier writers (Guttman, 1984; Zickerman, 1984) focused on the emergence of sexual feeling between male patients and their therapists. Guttman first described the asexual transference images that a male patient may have, noting (1) "the nurturant mother, the 'good breast,' the mirror, the asexual madonna" (p. 188), the fundamental symbols of basic trust; (2) "the suffocating, merging, engulfing female" (p. 189) who does not permit differentiation; (3) "the withholding, inattentive mother, the 'bad breast,' the self-sacrificing martyr" (p. 189) who exacts a high price for her gifts. These asexual images are pre-oedipal but according to Guttman, are usually combined with more sexualized feeling because men have a tendency to deny their dependency. Additionally Zickerman noted that "a male patient engaged in therapy with a female faces cultural pressures that are not simply the converse of those experienced in the traditional female patient–male therapist paradigms" (p. 546). Seeking help from a female puts a man in a powerless, somewhat inferior position, which many men cannot tolerate.

Zickerman noted that the male patient–female therapist dyad discourages those sexual feelings that are psychologically difficult and socially awkward. However, Guttman described positive and negative images of the therapist as sexual object. If the therapist is seen as attractive, the patient may have to deal with the problem of divulging sexual feelings to a "lady" or the problem of having sexual feelings in a situation where the woman is dominant. The converse image is the therapist as a sexually tantalizing, frustrating, potentially dangerous object. Guttman hypothesized that the female therapist–male patient dyad must overcome many social customs and taboos in order to address sexual issues freely.

Felton (1986) looked at the reluctance of women therapists to push for sexual fantasies and feelings, and the effect that has on leaving power issues out of the therapy. In order to be successful with male patients, she stated, women need to be comfortable with their own aggressiveness and competitiveness. Felton believes that the female therapist must look at her own countertransference and not blame the desexualization of her by a male patient as all his doing.

Gornick (1986) discussed four transference themes common to the male patient–female therapist dyad: pre-oedipal maternal transference, feelings of shame in response to the therapist's authority, erotic transference, and hostile transference. Gornick, who interviewed female therapists, found that the maternal transference occurred at the outset of the treatment. Erotic transferences may evolve later as a solution to the dilemma of feeling inferior to the therapist. The development of the erotic transference may, in fantasy, restore the man to the dominant position. Gornick found that women therapists frequently pointed to the intensity of the hostility of their male patients. The issues then involved included the fear of annihilating the source of basic needs, the cultural prescription that men should protect and take care of women, and the assumption that men could physically harm women. Gornick concluded that in examining the transference themes of male patients toward their female therapists, we get a look at male development, particularly the relationship of boys and their mothers.

Feminist therapists at times work with men because they have redefined the norms for mental health of both the adult male and adult female and have asserted that the norms are the same for both (Ganley, 1988). Feminist therapists help men to value relationships as well as achievement; to increase intimacy in a variety of relations; to become comfortable with self-disclosure, insight, and empathy; to identify all emotions rather than using anger to mask feelings; to improve communication skills to be more comfortable and less coercive in relationships; to nurture the self and others; to value consensual sex and accept a negative response. Ganley noted that there were certain process issues that have to be reconsidered by feminist therapists working with male clients. For example, while the therapist can model specific skills, she cannot serve as a role model as she does with female clients. Power issues need to be seen differently since male clients will often assume a position of power, and therapists must deal with their own concerns about having power over men.

## IMPLICATIONS OF THE LITERATURE

It seems clear that the gender of the therapist affects the therapeutic process. We know more about the form of the therapeutic dyad than we do about the impact on outcome. More research into gender effects on outcome of treatment needs to be done in the future.

Women therapists need to be cognizant of the impact of the reality of their gender on treatment because denial of it will create blind spots in the therapy. Brodsky (1976) has suggested that training to conduct therapy with the opposite sex is not complete until there is experience with a supervisor of the opposite sex. Earlier in training, graduate study should include a focus on gender issues for the clinician. The era of men's writing women's histories is past. The more that women therapists discuss and write about how they work with both female and male clients, the more that other women therapists will have to draw upon to make their work more effective.

## ACKNOWLEDGMENT

The author wishes to thank Christina Russell for her invaluable research assistance.

## REFERENCES

Brodsky, A. (1976). Countertransference issues and the woman therapist. In G. Gottshegen (Chair), *Countertransference issues in women therapists*. Symposium presented at the annual convention of the American Psychological Association, Washington, DC.

Brown, L. S. (1988). Feminist therapy with lesbians and gay men. In M. A. Dutton-Douglas & L. E. Walker (Eds.), *Feminist psychotherapies: Integration of therapeutic and feminist systems*. (pp. 206–227) Norwood, NJ: Ablex.

Cammaert, L. P., & Larsen, C. C. (1988). Feminist frameworks of psychotherapy. In M. A. Dutton-Douglas & L. E. Walker (Eds.), *Feminist psychotherapies: Integration of therapeutic and feminist systems* (pp. 12–36). Norwood, NJ: Ablex.

Cavenar, J. O., Jr., & Werman, D. S. (1983). The sex of the psychotherapist. *American Journal of Psychiatry, 140*(1), 85–87.

Cooke, M., & Kipnis D. (1986). Influence tactics in psychotherapy. *Journal of Consulting and Clinical Psychology, 54*(1), 22–26.

Eisenbud, R. (1986). Women feminist patients and a feminist woman analyst. In T. Bernay & D. W. Cantor (Eds.), *The psychology of today's woman: New psychoanalytic visions* (pp. 273–290). Hillsdale, NJ: Analytic Press.

Felton, J. R. (1986). Sex makes a difference: How gender affects the therapeutic relationship. *Clinical Social Work Journal, 14*(2), 127–136.

Fenton, W. S., Robinowitz, C. B., & Leaf, P. J. (1987). Male and female psychiatrists and their patients. *American Journal of Psychiatry, 144*(3), 358–361.

Ganley, A. L. (1988). Feminist therapy with male clients. In M. A. Dutton-Douglas & L. E. Walker, (Eds.), *Feminist psychotherapies: Integration of therapeutic and feminist systems* (pp. 186–205). Norwood, NJ: Ablex.

Gilligan, C. (1982). *In a different voice*. Cambridge, MA: Harvard University Press.

Gornick, L. K. (1986). Developing a new narrative: The woman therapist and the male patient. *Psychoanalytic Psychology, 3*(4), 299–325.

Goz, R. (1973). Women patients and women therapists: Some issues that come up in psychotherapy. *International Journal of Psychoanalytic Psychotherapy, 2*(3), 298–319.

Guttman, H. A. (1984). Sexual issues in the transference and countertransference between female therapist and male patient. *Journal of the American Academy of Psychoanalysis, 12*(2), 187–197.

Jones, E. E., Krupnick, J. L., & Kerig, P. K. (1987). Some gender effects in brief psychotherapy. *Psychotherapy, 24*(3), 336–352.

Jones, E. E., & Zoppel, C. L. (1982). Impact of client and therapist gender on psychotherapy process and outcome. *Journal of Counseling and Clinical Psychology, 50*(2), 259–272.

Kaplan, A. G. (1985). Female or male therapists for women patients: New formulations. *Psychiatry, 48*, 111–120.

Kirshner, L. A., Genack, A., & Hauser, S. T. (1978). Effects of gender on short-term psychotherapy. *Psychotherapy: Theory, Research and Practice, 15*(2), 158–167.

Kulish, N. M. (1984). The effect of the sex of the analyst on transference: A review of the literature. *Bulletin of the Menninger Clinic, 48*(2), 95–110.

Kulish, N. M. (1986). Gender and transferences: The screen of the phallic mother. *International Review of Psychoanalysis, 13*, 393–404.

Kulish, N. M. (1989). Gender and transference: Conversations with female analysts. *Psychoanalytic Psychology, 61*(2), 59–71.

Levy, S. B. (1982). Toward a consideration of intimacy in the female/female therapy relationship. *Women and Therapy, 1*(2), 35–44.

McCabe, M. P., Collins, J. K., Jupp, J. J., Walker, W., & Sutton, J. E. (1983). The role of the sex of therapist and group versus individual therapy in treatment outcome using hypnosis with obese female patients: A research note. *American Journal of Clinical and Experimental Hypnosis, 11*(2), 107–109.

Michaels, A. S. (1990). How women patients choose women therapists. In D. W. Cantor (Ed.), *Women as therapists: A multitheoretical casebook* (pp. 20–32). New York: Springer Publishing Co.

Okun, B. F. (1989). The experience of the woman therapist in different modalities. In D. W. Cantor (Chair), *Treating Men; Treating Women: The Experience of Women Therapists.* Symposium presented at the annual meeting of the American Psychological Association, New Orleans.

Orlinsky, D., & Howard, K. (1976). The effects of sex of therapist on the therapeutic experiences of women. *Psychotherapy: Theory, Research and Practice, 13*(1), 82–88.

Person, E. S. (1983). Women in therapy: Therapist gender as a variable. *International Review of Psychoanalysis, 10*, 193–204.

Rosewater, L. B. (1988). Feminist therapies with women. In M. A. Dutton-Douglas & L. E. Walker (Eds.), *Feminist psychotherapies: Integration of therapeutic and feminist systems* (pp. 137–156). Norwood, NJ: Ablex.

Ruderman, E. G. (1986). Gender related themes of women psychotherapists in their treatment of women patients: The creative and reparative use of countertransference as a mutual growth experience. *Clinical Social Work Journal, 14*(2), 103–126.

Samuels, L. (1985). Female psychotherapists as portrayed in film, fiction, and nonfiction. *Journal of the American Academy of Psychoanalysis, 13*(3), 367–378.

Schachtel, Z. (1986). The "impossible profession" considered from a gender perspective. In J. L. Alpert (Ed.), *Psychoanalysis and women: Contemporary reappraisals* (pp. 237–257). Hillsdale, NJ: Analytic Press.

Schlachet, B. C. (1984). Female role socialization: The analyst and the analyses. In C. M. Brody (Ed.), *Women therapists working with women: New theory and process of feminist therapy.* New York: Springer Publishing Co.

Schover, L. R. (1981). Male and female therapists' responses to male and female client sexual material: An analogue study. *Archives of Sexual Behavior, 10*(6), 477–492.

Shainess, N. (1983). Significance of match in sex of analyst and patient. *American Journal of Psychoanalysis, 43*(3), 205–217.

Tanney, M. F., & Birk, J. M. (1976). Women counselors for women clients? A review of the research. *The Counseling Psychologist, 6*(2), 28–32.

Zickerman, V. (1984). Sociocultural considerations in the emergence of sexual feelings in male patients seeing female therapists. *Journal of the American Academy of Psychoanalysis, 12*(4), 545–551.

# 2

# How Women Patients Choose Women Therapists

## Alisa S. Michaels

## INTRODUCTION

Night after night, Angela awoke at 4:00 in the morning, soaked in sweat from head to toe. Agitated and restless, she would dress quickly and randomly, bursting out into the cold autumn air, finding solace only by roaming the dangerous maze of East-Side streets until sunrise. Faced with seemingly insurmountable stressors, Angela wondered how she was going to cope. The thought of seeing a therapist had become a viable option in her mind. Angela felt she was at a crossroads. She undoubtedly needed psychological support.

How do Angela and women like her determine who to turn to? What can be said that is general and true about how women select a therapist? Do they flip through the yellow pages as they would for an Italian or Chinese restaurant? Do they allow a friend or an internist to select one as they would a blind date? Alternatively, is the selection of a therapist a well-thought-out decision, based on specific qualities of the therapist? What influences patients' decisions to begin therapy with a particular therapist?

There are many ways to discover how female patients choose female therapists. In popular literature, characters frequently enter therapy after facing a crisis. Can we, however, generalize what we read in stories such as biographies and novels to answer questions about how people choose a therapist? A basic premise in research is that conclusions should not be based on a single or even a few events.

## PREVIOUS RESEARCH

There has not been much research addressing which factors are important in a patient's choice of a therapist. Researchers have devised experimental paradigms designed to simulate isolated aspects of the complex process of therapist selection. It is important to note, however, that most of these studies are analog designs using college students as subjects (Boulware & Holmes, 1970; Cashen, 1979; Coursol & Sipps, 1986; Good, 1975; Holen & Kinsey, 1975; Knudson & Carskadon, 1978; Kowitt & Garske, 1978; Schroeder & Bloom, 1979; Simon, 1973; Stuehm, Cashen, & Johnson, 1977; Trautt & Bloom, 1982; Trautt, Finer, & Calisher, 1980). Most of the research examining how patients select a therapist has used therapists, asking them how they chose their own therapists. No research studies have been done to examine how women patients in particular select a therapist. In light of this, an original study was undertaken by the author to determine what variables contributed to female patients' selection of their female therapists.

## SUBJECTS' PREFERENCES FOR
## THEORETICAL ORIENTATION

Researchers have generated a plethora of research examining whether theoretical orientation of the therapist is important in the choice of a therapist. Some of the commonly researched theoretical orientations include psychoanalytic-psychodynamic, behavior, gestalt, and client-centered. Psychoanalytic theory is based on the notion that current problems can be eased by resolving conflicts, which arise from early experiences. Similar to the psychoanalytic approach, the psychodynamic approach focuses on unconscious motives and conflicts, emphasizing past experience (Corsini, 1984). Behavior therapists focus upon observable, measurable behaviors and the relationships between these behaviors and the antecedent and consequential events that maintain them (Mischel, 1986). Gestalt therapy attempts to increase the awareness of oneself, focusing on feelings and creative potential (Mischel, 1986). Cli-

ent-centered therapy provides an accepting, nonjudgmental environment that enables one to deal with current relationships and feelings
(Mischel, 1986).

Some studies have shown that simulated clients prefer one or another
of the therapies. Holen and Kinsey (1975) conducted a study that examined whether undergraduate subjects preferred behavioral, client-centered, or psychoanalytic theory. Subjects listened to three tapes of
simulated counseling sessions representing the three forms of therapy.
In sum, the subjects preferred the behavioral approach, feeling it was
the most effective. As the authors note, it is still possible that a subject's
preference for an approach may be related to factors other than therapeutic technique, such as the particulars of the client problem.

A patient's preference regarding theoretical orientation may be influenced by personality factors in the patient. In particular, Stuehm et al.
(1977) speculated that subjects' locus of control was related to their theoretical preference. Locus of control is the source to which one attributes control of events. It can be internal (i.e., caused by the person) or
external (i.e., caused by the situation or chance) (Mischel, 1986). According to Rotter's locus-of-control theory, people with an external locus
of control tend to comply in circumstances of overt influence, whereas
people with an internal locus of control seem to object to such influence. Thus, Stuehm et al. hypothesized that undergraduate subjects
with an internal locus of control would prefer a client-centered (humanistic) approach, whereas subjects with an external locus of control
would prefer a more directive (behavioral) approach. All subjects
viewed videotapes of initial counseling sessions representing psychoanalytic, humanistic, and behavioristic approaches. The researchers found
that all subjects, regardless of locus of control, preferred the behavioral
approach. Stuehm et al. explained that subjects preferred the behavioral
approach because of the "structure" of the approach. Like Holen and
Kinsey (1975), these researchers concluded that subjects' preference for
the behavioral approach may be a function of factors such as client problem, sex of client or counselor, and age, rather than the therapeutic approach itself.

Schroeder and Bloom (1979) conducted a study that considered
whether there were differences in undergraduate subjects' perceptions
of therapist attractiveness and credibility as a function of therapy orientation. Subjects read unlabeled descriptions of the various approaches,
then viewed videotapes of simulated therapy sessions illustrating the
techniques. In contrast to Holen and Kinsey's (1975) and Stuehm et al.'s
(1977) findings, Schroeder and Bloom found that subjects rated psychoanalytic therapy as most attractive and credible. Gestalt therapy was

rated next highest, followed by behavioral and client-centered modalities.

Schroeder and Bloom went a step further and examined which therapist variables in particular were contributing to subjects' theoretical preference. Interestingly, interviews revealed that subjects tended not to focus on specific techniques; rather, they were influenced by three distinct personal qualities of the therapist. The most frequently reported variable was the extent to which the subject felt the therapist was personally involved with and concerned for the client. Second, characteristics of the therapist—including empathy, warmth, and sensitivity—emerged as important variables. Subjects' feelings about the therapists' degree of competence, expertise, and professionalism appeared as a third group of influential factors. Echoing earlier studies, Schroeder and Bloom concluded that subjects' theoretical preferences were most likely related to the personal qualities of the therapist rather than to the theoretical rationale or the actual process.

Like Schroeder and Bloom, Cashen (1979) sought to understand factors that contributed to clients' preferences for a specific theoretical orientation. However, Cashen proposed that gender of the therapist could be related to clients' preferences. Based on earlier studies (Apfelbaum, 1958; Tinsley & Harris, 1976), Cashen hypothesized that a client-centered approach would be preferred by females and that a more directive approach would be preferred by males. Undergraduate subjects viewed two audiovisual tapes of simulated first sessions that illustrated client-centered and behavioral techniques. Results indicated that gender of the therapist was not a significant factor contributing to clients' preferences. Contrary to Cashen's hypothesis, both males and females preferred behavioral counseling. Again, the subjects' preference for the behavioral approach appeared to be related to the "structure" provided by the behavioral orientation. Cashen concluded that future research must focus on the interaction between theoretical preferences and factors such as gender of the therapist, client's presenting problem, and expectations about therapy.

## Characteristics of the Therapist

Do the specific qualities (e.g., gender, age) of the therapist influence patients' selections? Boulware and Holmes (1970) explored how therapist variables are related to subjects' preferences for a therapist. Undergraduate subjects were shown slides of faces of different types of therapists (e.g., older, younger) and were asked to select whom they would like to talk to if they had a personal or a vocational problem. Additionally, subjects were asked to discuss what they thought each therapist was like as a person. An older male was most commonly selected by males as the choice for both vocational and personal problems. Females chose an older male therapist for vocational problems. Interestingly, females with personal problems preferred an older female. Overall, the researchers found that the most influential factor in determining preference was the extent to which the subject believed the therapist would understand his or her problem.

Simon (1973) hypothesized that the therapist's age, gender, and title were important factors. Subjects were instructed to imagine they had a personal problem they wanted to discuss with a therapist. First, subjects were given a choice of therapists with varied titles (e.g., behaviorist, emotional counselor, psychologist, psychiatrist, psychoanalyst, social worker). They were then asked to rank-order their preferences. Second, they were provided with information regarding age and sex (e.g., 25-year-old woman or man, 40-year-old woman or man, 55-year-old woman or man) and were again asked to rank their preferences. In general, subjects preferred psychologists and psychiatrists to the other titles. However, subjects under 22 years of age preferred an emotional counselor. Male therapists were more frequently selected than female therapists, and forty-year-old therapists were most often chosen. Simon concluded that a more in-depth study was needed to understand why age, sex, and title influenced subjects' preferences.

What can be said about the factors that determine how therapists select a therapist for themselves? Grunebaum (1983) examined factors contributing to therapists' choice of a therapist. Subjects consisted of 23 experienced psychotherapists who had undergone treatment. They were asked to recall which factors were important when they selected their therapists. The most prominent factor was competence. Subjects explained that they were able to find a competent therapist based on the therapist's reputation and recommendations from friends and colleagues. It was also important that the therapist was not in the patient's professional and social network. Two other important factors were related to the personal characteristics of the therapist. One was that the therapist was "warm," "liked," "caring," and "supportive"; related to this first factor was that they felt appreciated, validated, and respected. A second prominent feature was that the therapist spoke during the session rather than simply being silent. Other therapist characteristics of importance included lack of criticism, openness, and flexibility. Finally, about 25% of the therapist-patients noted that they did not want a therapist who attributed everything to transference!

A related study by Norcross, Strausser, and Faltus (1988) examined aspects of the decision-making process of therapists who were selecting a therapist for themselves. Subjects were instructed to rate 16 variables that influenced their decision. The four therapist qualities that most strongly predicted psychotherapist selection were perceived competence, clinical experience, professional reputation, and interpersonal warmth.

## Characteristics of the Patient and the Therapist

It makes sense that interaction variables would be important, perhaps more so than the patient and therapist variables alone. Good (1975) hypothesized that attitude similarity between client and therapist may result in higher ratings of the therapist by the client. To test this hypothesis, Good examined the preferences of undergraduate subjects, using simulated case scenarios of therapeutic interactions. Good found that clients rated therapists higher in many respects when they were perceived as similar in attitude (e.g., openminded, understanding of people).

Further support for Good's findings was observed by Trautt et al. (1980), who examined whether the degree of attitude similarity between the therapist and subject would influence subjects' perceptions of the therapist. This study sought to determine whether attitude similarity could be considered a "therapeugenic factor." Bloom, Weigel, and Trautt (1977) define a therapeugenic factor as "factors independent of specific therapeutic techniques that potentiate psychotherapeutic effects" (p. 867). The researchers found that undergraduate subjects rated therapists with similar attitudes higher regarding interpersonal attraction, willingness to recommend to a friend, and likelihood of seeking therapy from the therapist. Subjects were also more likely to rate therapists with similar attitudes as more qualified and more likeable. Trautt et al. concluded that the degree of attitude similarity between a client and therapist may function as a "therapeugenic factor."

Trautt et al. also examined whether the sex of the therapist altered subjects' perceptions of the therapist. In contrast to the findings of Simon (1973), there were no significant findings related to the sex of the client or therapist, with the exception of the interaction between the sex of subject and attitude similarity. Male subjects were more strongly influenced by the degree of attitude similarity than female subjects. From this study, the importance of gender effects cannot be ruled out. However, Trautt et al. concluded that gender differences may be minimized by subjects' perceptions of the degree of attitude similarity.

Clopton and Haydel (1982) examined factors they postulated would influence therapists' referral patterns to colleagues. Specifically, they wanted to know whether sex-role expectations were influential in deciding upon a referral. The researchers observed that psychologists most often referred the client to a therapist of the same gender, especially when the client was the same sex as the referring therapist. Interestingly, both women and children were referred to women therapists much more frequently than would be expected based on the disproportionate numbers of male therapists (75% male vs. 25% female) when this study was conducted. Adult male clients were almost always referred to male therapists.

## Summary of the Research

In almost all of the studies that have been reviewed, simulated material has been used to examine factors related to therapist selection. One consequence of using simulated material is that the generalizability of the results is limited. Support for this limitation was found by Coursol and Sipps (1986), who examined the influence of stimulus context (e.g., therapy session vs. therapy description) and stimulus medium (e.g., audiovisual vs. written) on subjects' selection of theoretical orientation. The researchers found that subjects preferred the behavioral orientation as opposed to the person-centered orientation when the stimulus was presented audiovisually as a therapy session. In contrast, person-centered therapy was preferred when the stimulus was presented in a written fashion. Coursol and Sipps concluded that previous findings regarding orientation preference may be greatly confounded by methodological flaws.

The present survey was undertaken to augment previous research by studying how women patients choose women therapists, using real patients.

## THE PRESENT STUDY
## Survey of Patients

In order to understand how female patients choose women therapists, a questionnaire was constructed to assess factors believed to influence a patient's decision to enter treatment with a particular therapist. Each patient was asked to indicate whether she knew her therapist's primary theoretical orientation when selecting her. If she did not know the therapist's theoretical orientation initially, the patient was asked whether she knew this information at the time she completed the questionnaire for the present study. Information was collected regarding how patients found out about their therapist (e.g., family member, friend) and whether they interviewed other therapists before making a decision. Patients were also asked whether they had undergone treatment prior to their current therapy. If so, they were asked to indicate how long they had been in treatment, the gender of their prior therapist, and their prior therapist's theoretical orientation.

Patients were instructed to indicate personal factors that were important to them when they selected their therapist. The variables included age, area of expertise, availability, academic degree, fee, gender, geographic location, race, religion, reputation, sexual orientation, theoretical orientation, training, and "other." Patients were then asked to indicate which of these factors would be important to them if they were to go to another therapist in the future.

## Procedure

A cover letter, the questionnaire, consent forms, and stamped return envelopes were mailed to six clinical psychologists representing various theoretical orientations, including psychodynamic, cognitive-behavioral, family systems, and feminist perspectives. Each of the six psychologists was instructed to distribute the questionnaire and consent form to six patients currently in treatment. Of the 48 questionnaires distributed, 40 were returned. One of the six therapists felt that it would not be appropriate to distribute the questionnaire to her patients because as an analyst she felt that the content of the measure would compound the transference. This therapist distributed the questionnaire to other therapists, who agreed to give the measure to their patients. Two of the returned questionnaires were not included in the sample because they involved male therapists. Thus, the final sample contained 38 subjects. The response rate of 83% was much better than the average return rate of 46% for a single mailing (Heberlin & Baumgartner, 1978).

## Characteristics of the Sample

Of the 38 responding patients, 37% knew the theoretical orientation of their therapist when they selected her. An additional 40% reported that they knew the theoretical orientation at the time they completed the questionnaire for this study. Of the 77% who reported that they knew their therapist's theoretical orientation, 97% reported accurate information.

The respondents represented a variety of theoretical orientations, including psychodynamic (32%), cognitive-behavioral (26%), family systems (11%), and feminist perspectives (18%). An additional 13% were distributed among patients to which the theoretical orientation of the therapist was unknown.

More than one-third of the subjects (37%) were referred to the therapist by friends. Consistent with this finding, Norcross, Strausser-Kirtland, and Missar (1988) found that 40% of psychotherapists heard about the therapist they had selected from a friend. In the current survey, 24% of patients were referred to their therapist by another therapist. Interestingly, 10% were referred to their current therapist by a person who was both a friend and a therapist. Thus, the categories of friend and therapist contributed a total of 71% to the referrals. Other referrals came from professionals such as lawyers and physicians (13%) and family members (5%). The remaining 11% of the referrals came from a family member who was also a therapist, the yellow pages, or the identified patient herself.

Almost one-quarter of the patients (24%) in this study reported interviewing more than one therapist before deciding to enter treatment with a particular therapist. Over half of the patients (58%) reported being in therapy prior to their current treatment. Of these, 21% reported being in therapy more than once before. The length of time that patients reported being in prior treatment was varied. Fifteen percent reported that their treatment lasted less than 6 months. Fifty-five percent were in therapy from 1 to 4 years. The remaining 30% reported being in therapy anywhere from 6 to 10 or more years. It is important to note that patients did not specify whether treatment was ongoing or sporadic.

Of those reporting prior therapy, 52% reported that they had been in treatment with a female therapist. Twenty-nine percent had been in treatment with a male therapist. The remaining 19% had been in treatment at different times with a variety of therapists (e.g., one male and one female, two females).

Patients were asked to indicate the most important factors in the selection of their therapist (see Table 2.1). The three therapist variables most prevalent among this sample were reputation (45.9%), gender (42.9%), and area of expertise (32.4%). The three least important factors were race, religion, and sexual orientation. Patients were also asked to indicate factors that would be important if they were to select another therapist in the future. Interestingly, the most prevalent factor, area of expertise, was selected by 57.6% of the patients. Theoretical orientation and reputation were also important factors, being selected 47.2% and 42.9% of the time, respectively. Again, the least commonly selected variables included race, religion, and sexual orientation.

## Discussion

The profile of the patients in this survey revealed that the typical patient sought the advice of a friend, therapist, or friend-therapist. Based on the finding that 71% of the referrals came from more personal sources, it is understandable that the most prevalent factor would be the thera-

Table 2.1 Factors Influencing How Women Patients Choose Women Therapists

|  | Factors of importance at beginning of therapy vs. future factors | |
|---|---|---|
|  | Initially | Future |
| Age | 14.3% | 11.4% |
| Area Expertise | 32.4 | 57.6 |
| Availability | 11.4 | 5.9 |
| Degree | 11.1 | 11.4 |
| Fee | 20.0 | 8.6 |
| Gender | 42.9 | 36.1 |
| Geographic Location | 25.0 | 41.7 |
| Race | 0.0 | 0.0 |
| Religion | 0.0 | 5.3 |
| Reputation | 45.9 | 42.9 |
| Sexual Orientation | 2.6 | 2.6 |
| Theoretical Orientation | 25.0 | 47.2 |
| Training | 5.9 | 14.7 |

pist's reputation. One can speculate that when a woman is in crisis, she will turn to a friend and ask where she can get help.

In the current study, the most frequently selected variable was "reputation." This study did not expand upon the factors included in the notion of reputation. For example, did those people who selected reputation hear that the therapist was warm and empathic? Had they heard that patients improved quickly? Or that the therapist had a good sense of humor? It would be beneficial to explore the question further.

When therapists make referrals, they often ask whether the patient would prefer to see a male or female. Indeed, gender was one of the three most prevalent factors in the patients' initial therapist selection. However, it was not one of the three most prevalent factors they would use in the future. Previous research may provide some insight to understanding this pattern. Research findings indicate that personal characteristics of the therapist (e.g., warmth) are very important to patients. A related variable of considerable magnitude is that patients want to feel that the therapist can understand their problem. In the current study, the most frequently selected future variable was the therapist's area of expertise. What is implicit under the subheading of area of expertise is that the therapist is an expert at dealing with particular problems. In other words, these patients perceive that a therapist who specializes in an area will be more likely to understand their problem. One reason why area of expertise may not have been as important at the time patients initially selected their therapist is that they may not have known exactly what their difficulties were.

Seventy-seven percent of the patients knew their therapist's theoretical orientation either when they chose their therapist or when they filled out the questionnaire. Theoretical orientation, however, was not one of the most prevalent factors in patients' initial choice. Although many of the patients were cognizant of the therapist's theoretical orientation, the fact that the therapist had a solid reputation appeared to carry more weight. Interestingly, when selecting future factors, the prevalence of theoretical orientation had almost doubled compared with initial ratings. One possible reason for this shift is that over time, patients develop a more sophisticated understanding of the meaning of their therapist's theoretical orientation. One can speculate that if this survey had been given exclusively to analytic patients, theoretical orientation of the therapist may have been a more important initial factor, due to the enormous commitment (e.g., time, money) required of analytic patients.

## CONCLUSION

The current study was an initial exploration of the process by which patients select a therapist. Although the use of actual patients was an improvement over previous research, there was a bias in the selection of the sample. Therapists were instructed to distribute the questionnaire to patients who they felt would be willing to participate. We may wonder if patients' responses would have been different if a group of "less compliant" patients was asked to fill out the questionnaire. Although a range of theoretical orientations was represented, all therapists were clinical psychologists, and all patients were private psychotherapy patients.

In sum, there has been a growing interest in understanding the factors involved in therapist selection. Research in this area has focused on subjects' preference for theoretical orientation and influential qualities of the therapist. Results regarding preference for theoretical orientation and gender have been inconsistent. However, it does appear that personal qualities of the therapist (e.g., personal involvement, warmth, attitude similarity, competence) are influential factors. In almost every study in which theoretical orientation was found to be important, researchers cautioned that other factors, such as characteristics of the therapist, must be studied further before conclusions could be drawn regarding preferences. All studies that have been reviewed have been limited by a selection bias. With the exception of the Grunebaum (1983) and Norcross et al. (1988) studies, virtually no studies have been done with actual patients in psychotherapy. It is important to note, however, that the generalizability of the Grunebaum (1983) and Norcross et al. (1988) studies are limited because they used therapist-patients to study the selection process.

It is quite clear that more research about how patients choose therapists needs to be done. Ideally, the way to proceed in the future would be to do a longitudinal study in which patients' preferences are assessed both prospectively and retrospectively. For example, when patients arrive for their first therapy session, data could be collected that assess therapist-selection criteria. A follow-up study could be conducted to determine whether patients' initial selection criteria matched what they had anticipated. Patients could be assessed at termination regarding their feelings about the effectiveness of treatment.

In the meantime, results of this pilot study shed light on the process by which women patients choose female therapists. Therapists can be cognizant of the fact that it is their reputation rather than gender or theoretical orientation that brings them new patients. Based on the recommendation of friends or other therapists, patients seek a relationship with a therapist whom they can trust to help them with their difficulties.

## ACKNOWLEDGMENT

The author wishes to thank Dr. Diane Arnkoff and Dr. David Jobes for their helpful comments on the questionnaire. The author is also grateful to Dr. Michael Robinson and Sheila Woody for their constructive comments concerning the manuscript.

## REFERENCES

Apfelbaum, D. (1958). *Dimensions of transference in psychotherapy*. Berkeley: University of California Press.

Bloom, L. J., Weigel, R. G., & Trautt, G. M. (1977) "Therapeugenic" factors in psychotherapy: Effects of office decor and subject–therapist pairing on the perception of credibility. *Journal of Consulting and Clinical Psychology, 45*(5), 867–873.

Boulware, D. W., & Holmes, D. S. (1970). Preferences for therapists and related expectancies. *Journal of Consulting and Clinical Psychology, 35*(2), 269–277.

Cashen, V. M. (1979). Sex of client as a factor in preference for an approach to counseling. *Journal of Clinical Psychology, 35*(3), 680–682.

Clopton, J. R., & Haydel, J. (1982). Psychotherapy referral patterns as influenced by sex of the referring therapist and sex and age of the client. *Journal of Consulting and Clinical Psychology, 50*(1), 156–157.

Corsini, R. J. (1984). *Current Psychotherapies*. Itasca, IL: F. E. Peacock Publishers.

Coursol, A., & Sipps G. J. (1986). Examination of the unintentional effect of stimulus medium and context on preference for psychotherapy. *Journal of Clinical Psychology, 42*(2), 280–286.

Good, L. R. (1975). Attitude similarity and attraction to a therapist. *Journal of Clinical Psychology, 31*, 707–709.

Grunebaum, H. (1983). A study of therapists' choice of a therapist. *American Journal of Psychiatry, 140*(10), 1336–1339.

Heberlin, R. A., & Baumgartner, R. (1978). Factors affecting response rates to mailed questionnaires: A quantitative analysis of the published literature. *American Sociological Review*, 447–462.

Holen, M. C., & Kinsey, W. M. (1975). Preferences for three theoretically derived counseling approaches. *Journal of Counseling Psychology, 22*, 21–23.

Knudson, M. L., & Carskadon, T. G. (1978). Psychotherapy preferences as a function of subjects' conceptual systems. *Journal of Clinical Psychology, 34*(3), 748–750.

Kowitt, M. R., & Garske, J. P. (1978). Modality, self-disclosure, and gender as determinants of psychotherapeutic attraction. *Journal of Consulting and Clinical Psychology, 46*(1), 173–174.

Mischel, W. (1986). *Introduction to personality*. New York: Holt, Rinehart and Winston.

Norcross, J. C., Strausser, D. J., & Faltus, F. J. (1988). The therapist's therapist. *American Journal of Psychotherapy, 42*(1), 53–66.

Norcross, J. C., Strausser-Kirtland, D., & Missar, C. D. (1988). The processes and outcomes of psychotherapists' personal treatment experiences. *Psychotherapy, 25*(1), 36–43.

Schroeder, D. H., & Bloom, L. J. (1979). Attraction to therapy and therapist credibility as a function of therapy orientation. *Journal of Clinical Psychology, 35*(3), 682–686.

Simon, W. E. (1973). Age, sex, and title of therapist as determinants of patients' preferences. *The Journal of Psychology, 83*, 145–149.

Stuehm, M. H., Cashen, V. M., & Johnson, J. J. (1977). Preference for an approach to counseling. *Psychological Reports, 42*, 124–126.

Tinsley, E., & Harris, J. (1976). Client expectations for counseling. *Journal of Counseling Psychology, 3*, 173–177.

Trautt, G. M., & Bloom, L. J. (1982). Therapeugenic factors in psychotherapy: The effects of fee and title on credibility and attraction. *Journal of Clinical Psychology, 38*(2), 274–279.

Trautt, G. M., Finer, W. D., & Calisher, S. B. (1980). Therapeugenic factors in psychotherapy: The effect of attitude similarity on therapist credibility and attraction. *Journal of Clinical Psychology, 36*(3), 743–747.

# 3

# The Personal Relationship between Therapists and Their Theoretical Orientation

## Charles B. Mark

Clinical psychology is a divided profession. Each theoretical orientation offers clearly delineated explanations of human behavior, motivation, and methods to solve psychological problems. These explanations, however, grow out of divergent assumptions about the nature of human functioning. Although the major orientations overlap, they approach treatment in very different, often opposing ways. Practitioners hold their clinical views with a great deal of conviction. At times, their conviction appears to go much deeper than the rational or scientific outlook in which it is cloaked. The defense of one's clinical orientation sometimes becomes emotional or even personal. What is it that allows highly trained clinicians to observe the same clinical event, yet fervently describe entirely different or opposing clinical explanations?

In clinical training we spend most of the time studying, being supervised, undergoing personal therapy, and otherwise being occupied with the massive personal and professional task of learning to practice one's chosen field. In the course of events, the practitioner may be exposed to various theoretical orientations. For the committed practitioner this connection between theory and clinician is deep-seated. Yet in formal training, this crucial link is all but ignored (perhaps addressed only within the clinician's personal therapy); instead, the focus is on the relative veracity of the various theoretical ideas. It seems that this complex decision is usually left to fate and unconscious motivations. Clinical training tends to focus almost exclusively upon developing expertise within a given framework.

This chapter will look at the psychoanalytic, behavioral, and family-systems approaches, endeavoring to illustrate the intimate relationships between therapists as people and their theoretical approach to treatment. The brief case studies serve to illustrate the incredible complexity of the connection. In the end, it is the unique personal tie to one's approach that gives the treatment its power, its authenticity, its effectiveness.

## RESEARCH

The research into the link between clinical technique and clinician is extremely diverse. The most straightforward research suggests certain major influences on theoretical choice: exposure to training of one orientation or another (Cummings & Lucchesc, 1978; Herron, 1978); direct clinical experience and supervision (Henry, Sims, & Spray, 1975); one's own therapist, course work, and readings (Steiner, 1978). Surely, these present a substantial influence. An impressive or personally influential mentor is likely a part of any student's past. A thoughtful theoretical paper or presentation can affect the way a person works. Who could deny that personal experience in therapy is a significant influence upon how therapists practice or how they view themselves? Last, it is impossible to become a sophisticated practitioner of a particular approach if the opportunity to study existing literature or work with senior clinicians is not available. These are certainly influential factors.

To gain the most complete portrayal of this intricate relationship, we must turn to the realm of personality. Although this perspective leaves no sound answers, it allows for appreciation of the complex, configural relationship between therapist and theory. One study, comparing the variables of personality and opportunity (Chaust, 1978), found that most psychologists recognized their personality as more influential than their theoretical approach to treatment. One might observe that when therapists make a referral to another clinician, they are most likely to call on colleagues with an orientation similar to their own. Further, it is often the personality of the practitioner that they have in mind when they make the recommendation. Within a theoretical framework, the clinical outlook is held relatively constant. It is the way that the clinician's personality relates to the theory that creates the variation in technique. Alexander (1963) has suggested that therapists do not always practice as they would describe their work publicly. All respected psychotherapists learn the standard vocabulary to describe their therapy. The therapist's personality and style may have the greatest impact on how the treatment is actually carried out. The personality of the therapist may reflect itself in what issues he chooses to address with a given patient and in who become his patients.

Although Herron (1978) also feels that exposure to a given theoretical approach is important, he develops the concept of "adaptability factor". Here he refers to the degree to which a theoretical approach allows for adjustment to fit the unique perspective of the therapist's personality needs. In this sense, an interactive and complementary relationship develops between therapist and approach. This is somewhat similar to Walton's (1978) view. He studied the "self-concept" of practitioners from varying orientations. Psychodynamic clinicians saw themselves as serious and complex. He found that rational-emotive therapists saw themselves as more simple and humorous.

Some of the most interesting research in this area stems from "psychobiographical" studies, notably the work of Stolorow and Atwood (1976, 1979). They sought to gain insight into various psychological theorists by determining how that person's ideas related to her unique psychological makeup. They attempted to portray what they call resonance. This notion asserts that the theorists' "pre-theoretical" values, interests, conflicts, and overall personality makeup interact with the environment to create a predisposed tendency toward certain interests and styles of exploration. In an earlier but similar approach, Creelan (1974) drew analogies between John Watson's intense interest in behavioristic analysis of human behavior and an extreme effort to rid himself of the Calvinistic doctrine in which he was raised. Similarly, Atwood & Stolorow (1977) have explored connections between events in the early life of Wilhelm Reich and his later development of a metapsychological conception of sexuality. (See also Atwood & Stolorow, 1978; Stolorow & Atwood, 1976; Stolorow & Atwood 1978, for other examples with regard to Freud, Rank, and Jung.)

Pretheoretical life themes produce not only an attraction to certain ideas, theories and practices but also allow a working-through and ultimately a healthful sublimation of these realms. Theories, especially psychological ones, are statements about an outlook on the world. In a similar fashion, psychological theory as it is held and applied by the clinician serves a purpose psychologically and existentially. For the clinician, all psychological theories or methodologies are grounded in assumptions about human nature and a world view. A thorough inspection of a theoretical approach and its origins reveals the central values that are embedded within it. Accordingly, it is these *implicit* value statements that serve as a source of "resonance" to that particular orientation.

# THE PSYCHOANALYTIC PERSPECTIVE
## Theoretical Considerations

Let us use a very broad definition of *psychoanalytic therapy*. I do not refer to a particular subschool of this theory but a range of related treatment approaches that tend to address the influence of unconscious concerns and personal history, and transference as a primary therapeutic tool. Although at times I will be referring to classical approaches and their present derivatives, I intend to focus on psychoanalysis as a phenomenon, an approach, and a way of thinking. It is therefore not necessary to limit discussion to specific theories.

Psychoanalysis seems to use different approaches simultaneously. First, there is the positivist, rational, and scientific frame of reference. Here the analyst's direct observations are combined with rational thinking to form and test hypotheses about the nature of the phenomenon in question. Numerous sources combine to comprise the analyst's rational conceptualization of the patient. In this regard, the thinking is not unlike the behavior therapist's. Both are positivistic, empirical (based on direct observation), and concerned with building a complete view of the person's experience. The second element of psychoanalytic thinking stands in clear contrast to the behavioral perspective. Here the emphasis is intuitive, subjective, introspective, and idealistic. Qualitative variables become paramount. This portion is firmly planted in a Cartesian model of thinking or a Kantian phenomenological approach. Hypotheses are based on inference, analogy, self-evidence, and metaphor. The objective reality of the clinical relationship is considered second to the psychic reality. Introspection and subjective observation of free associations are considered valid observational approaches on which to base clinical theory and practice.

Psychoanalytic theory grew out of a period of tremendous change. Mosse (1974) saw Freudian psychology as part of a great new wave of thinking that was developing within the culture. He points out Proust's look into the unconscious, the rise of expressionistic art, and Nietzsche's attraction to the primeval. All looked deeply into the soul for their answers. In this perspective, Freud's life itself demonstrated the conflict between the subjective and the positivistic, materialistic position. Freud kept a bourgeois lifestyle and maintained a strong faith in science as the key to better life (partly as a means of gaining generalized acceptance of his theories). Yet in contradiction to this, he sought to study the unconscious, a central element of subjective human experience.

The unique combination of a hearty interest in the phenomena of the mind and a continued acceptance of positivistic rationalism created an unwieldy but workable approach. The metaphysical notions of the unconscious are scrutinized with the discerning intensity of the scientist and the expansiveness of the artist. Given these origins, it is not surprising that psychoanalytic theory is a theory of conflict, a study of opposites. The human psyche is viewed as struggling with itself. Freud pursued human contradiction with a focus on suffering, conflict, and the paradoxical twists of the individual's perspective. The weltanschauung of psychoanalysis reflects a "tragic" and "ironic" vision of reality with its accompanying ambiguity, complexity, interest in recognizing the depths of the inner world, and appreciation for suffering (Schafer, 1976). The theory itself and this resultant image of humanity is a tangible indication of the disunion from which psychoanalysis grew. Psychoanalytic theory, according to Schafer, does not attempt to determine truth (as it might propose to do) but reflects a valuing of and inclination toward the process of investigation, with all its inherent complexities and conflicts. It is the process of the search for truth and understanding of the apparent contradictions that is considered to be the curative element.

Psychoanalytic theory proposes a struggle between opposing forces of reasoning (Reiff, 1964; Rychlak, 1968). Holt (1972) uses the terms *humanistic* and *mechanistic* to define these two cognitive modes. The mechanistic mode is that branch that stems from the natural sciences of the day. The terms *energy, psychic apparatus*, and conflicting *forces* all bring to mind nineteenth-century physics and chemistry. The "humanistic" image is revealed by Freud's nonacademic activities. His writing was broad and speculative. He was well versed in classical literature and the fine arts. The case study of Dr. O (to follow) suggests these two conflicting forces—one personified as father, the other as mother.

It seems that the values of introspection, understanding, and interpersonal relationships are primary. As these values stem from divergent methods of investigation, ranging from the highly intuitive to more objective observation, we might expect individual practitioners to resonate to differing elements of the approach. For example, introspection is on the one hand a subjective experience of the self but may be combined with "understanding," which is taken to be a more intellectual process of knowing the origins of emotions. Similarly, interpersonal relations are both an objective reflection through which to understand intrapsychic functioning and a phenomenological event that should be experienced without block, inhibition, or deficit. In the end, the patient adopts an unusual combination of determinism and free will.

The idiosyncratic way an analyst assimilates psychoanalytic theory will reflect that clinician's personal values and personal spheres of conflict. Some practitioners will resonate to the objective cluster of values. Others, who maintain a more phenomenological system of personal values, will personalize their relationship with the subjective cluster. Each branch of theory attends in varying degrees to differing values within the perspective. The psychoanalyst will likely express some combination of concerns with the above stated themes.

## Case Study: The Highly Committed Psychoanalyst

Note: The case study of Dr. O is condensed from this author's doctoral dissertation (Mark, 1981). The case study of a behavior therapist and a family therapist are based on interviews with this writer carried out in 1989.

The origins of Dr. O's interest in psychoanalysis can be traced back to several central childhood experiences. She has memories as a very young child of being generally happy, of having a kindhearted mother. Dr. O describes being a good student and maintaining close friendships. After a period of illness, her mother died. This loss still reverberates in Dr. O's life. Memories of her mother drifted into the past and became idealized as extremely benevolent, caring, and ceaselessly empathic.

> I remember from very, very young, coming home upset about something and she (mother) would sit me down and say, "Well let's figure out why a person would have done that. . . ." I think I was socialized to wonder about people. It also carried a burden of "you should always forgive."

Her father is remembered as a good person but at times rather ill-tempered, a loud and sometimes frightening figure. Politically and socially conservative, he stressed the virtues of "education," "good food," "moderation," and "honesty." The effort to balance and assimilate the recollection of mother and the reality of father became a central psychological theme. Father became viewed as powerful and mother as idealized but "weak" (and vulnerable). She states:

I thought of him as exceptionally powerful. And with mother dying and my father such a powerful force, it made me think that men were very, very powerful and women weak and in danger of dying. . . . I had a very compensating type of identification with male power. . . . I thought of my own strength as my masculine side. . . . Every time I did something assertive or theoretical or strong that could be expressing a woman, I connected power and masculinity. I thought of women as basically weak and going to die.

Balancing this dilemma became an important task of adolescence. Though developing a strong interest in "collecting boyfriends," she also took on a tomboyish quality. Attention from boys was a valuable source of self-esteem. "I wanted their love because I wanted to be accepted by these powerful male creatures." An inverse expression of this conflict was acted out during summers at camp. In this environment she related almost entirely to girls. At camp, she acted on her feminine interests, often idealizing an attractive or capable older girl.

As Dr. O revealed her life history, it became increasingly clear that conflicts about personal identify and self-esteem were central. On the one hand, the mother was idealized for her warmth, empathy, and caring—all positive "feminine" qualities. On the other hand, she viewed women as tremendously vulnerable. This stood in contrast to the apparent power of her father and his seemingly irrational temper. Balancing these influences was very problematic.

As adolescence progressed, she became aware, at least intellectually, of how in some ways females are safer than males. Females do not have to go to war. The realization that men and boys, envisioned as a source of strength, die earlier than women became troublesome as well. This ever-active dynamic conflict seemed to form some of the early interests in becoming a psychoanalyst. The identification with mother helped serve as a model for goodness, kindness, and helping others. The father became associated with the theoretical mind, the thinker, the intellectual.

I think I was destined to become a psychologist. My mother was a kind of a do-gooder. I was brought up to be one. . . . I idealized and identified with an idealized image of her. . . . I was always interested in human psychology. I can't remember a time that I wasn't.

Like her father, Dr. O developed strong political convictions. As with mother, these usually centered around humanistic social causes. Several responses to Thematic Apperception Test (TAT) cards imply the struggle between these two polarities. It is first seen on card 2. This card shows a farm scene. A man operates a horse drawn plow while a woman leans against a tree. In the foreground a younger female holds books and stares in the opposite direction. (Dr. O. was pregnant at the time of this interview and struggling with career-versus-family conflicts.)

> The mother appears to me to be trying to convey an attitude toward the daughter—that she'll be fine, that she can manage, that the daughter should go ahead and do what she wants to, but the daughter suspects that is not really true; that the mother could really use her and won't be able to manage to well. She's going to go away to school, but with some guilt, with some feeling that she could have been in two places at once, helping her family out and pursuing her own interests.

This issue is expanded by her response to card 9GF. This TAT card shows two girls or young women. One peers from behind a tree looking down as the other moves below. Here, Dr. O told of two sisters. One is very well behaved and obedient, the other defiant of family expectations. The story concludes that some defiance is necessary:

> The younger (defiant sister) is going to do fine. She's going to hit the jackpot and buy a new dress with the money. I guess things are going to come out allright. I'm seeing the younger one as looking like she will be getting into trouble, but she's in better shape than the older one.

Her response to card 11 seems to work toward an integration of strength and empathic relating. TAT card 11 is dark and indistinct. It shows some sort of insect shaped creature near an arched bridge. A lizard or dragonlike head extends out above a rocky rubble.

> I am identifying here with this small creature that looks almost like a big insect on the top of bridge in some kind of subterranean canyon. I see it as being very frightened by a serpent that has pierced the wall. It's going to try to make friends with the serpent. It's frightened, but it feels the smart move would be not to antagonize the creature, and it will probably succeed and be friendly and find out that a powerful ally is a handy thing to have.

In many respects, being a psychoanalyst is both an expression of these central issues and a solution. Dr. O explained that during her work she is able to develop a special and intense form of intimacy, and yet still have some degree of intellectual privacy,

> to be close and distant from a patient at the same time. . . . I think consciously of myself a as person who likes to be very close to people. But its painfully evident to me as I get (to) know myself better that the other side of that is also there. I like to have a certain private space. . . . I get worried if I get really close to someone that they're going to die or leave me or control or criticize me.

As an analyst, Dr. O can be aloof and intimate at the same time: she can express her strong need for intimacy, utilize her highly valued emotional sensitivity, yet simultaneously maintain privacy and personal territory in the relationship. She highly values the intensity of the therapeutic relationship, preferring to see patients on a frequent basis (two, three, or four times per week). Dr. O also encourages patients to bring in dreams. She states, "I like analyzing dreams—the combination of my intellectual fascination of the dream and the power of the experience to a client of a sense of discovery that you get." In keeping with the analytic tradition, she holds a historical perspective of the problems that she works with. Similarly, she naturally sees her own life as something that is not happening only in the present but constantly carrying the traces of previous experience with it. The interviews with Dr. O had the feel of weaving as she moved gracefully between memories of her childhood and articulate statements about how she sees her work today.

Dr. O's personal values and experience intersect to produce a strong concern for understanding the origins of personal lives. Her profound interest in "understanding why people do things" may be viewed as one way of recapturing the benevolent attitudes of her mother, as a reaffirmation of both herself and mother as good, alive, and well. There may be a need to recover the strength and protection of the caring mother, a time when questions about her identity and fortitude as a woman were not yet called into question. Dr. O has found strength by reliving and reexperiencing her early memories. It seems likely that the resonance to psychoanalysis also hinges upon its commitment to the search for origins.

## THE BEHAVIORAL PERSPECTIVE
### Theoretical Considerations

We have seen how the values inherent in psychoanalytic therapy can be traced from the manner and process by which techniques were formulated to its concept of ideal human functioning. Similarly, the methods by which behaviorally oriented therapy were invented are directly related to the concept of ideal functioning proposed by the theory. A look at behavior therapy necessitates a brief survey of its philosophical origins in behaviorism.

Defining behavior therapy is difficult because some of the earlier definitions emphasize only the clinical application of experimentally derived techniques. For example, Yates (1975, p. 4) defines behavior therapy as

the attempt to utilize systematically that body of knowledge which has resulted from the application of experimental method in psychology and its closely related disciplines . . . in order to explain the genesis and maintenance of abnormal patterns of behavior; and to apply that knowledge to the treatment and prevention of abnormalities by means of controlled experimental studies of the single case, both descriptive and remedial.

Definitions by Eysenck (in Yates, 1975) and Wolpe (in Franks & Wilson, 1974) are very similar. The rubric of behavioral therapy has widened greatly in recently years. These advances leave older definitions somewhat narrow. The cognitive behavioral approaches, which dominate the field, go beyond the practical limitations of learning theory. Ostensibly, these techniques are incorporated into behavioral therapy because they have shown their effectiveness. Many behavior therapists are less and less *behavioral* in the strict sense of the word. Nevertheless, they still accept the behavioral principle that changes in behavior (covert and overt) produces a change in personal outlook and self-concept.

As originally conceived, in the early Skinnerian sense, behavior therapy denied the importance of mental events altogether, adhering strictly to the principles of determinism, empiricism, and logical positivism. Contemporary behavioral treatment allows a focus on consciousness as much as any other psychological therapy. Modern behavioral therapy does encompass essential elements of its origins, however, Effectiveness, as shown by controlled observation, remains the most common means by which a technique is accepted into use as customary treatment. Early in clinical development of "broad-band" techniques, Mahoney, Kazdin, and Lesswing (in Franks & Wilson, 1974) state, in keeping with the tradition of British empiricism, "In its present state of development behavior therapy must be evaluated in terms of therapeutic efficacy rather than dismissed on the basis of incompletely theoretical explication or rationale" (p. 19). This stands in stark contrast to psychoanalytic and family-therapy approaches, where coherent application of theory can stand as a self-evident rationale for treatment practices. Although the objects of study within behavioral treatments go far beyond those envisioned by early behavioral therapists, behavior therapy has maintained much of the rigorous objective attitude of behaviorism.

The early behaviorist's concern with operationalism, mechanistic viewpoints, determinism, prediction, and logical positivism is a function of the societal values at the turn of the century. Western culture was industrializing, growing, and success-oriented. Rugged individualism and pragmatism were prized (Buss, 1975). Analogously, industrial capitalism valued control, prediction, and mechanization. In this respect, Western culture became preoccupied with action and doing (i.e., behavior), not with reflection and experience. Science was advanced with religious fervor and at times a similar promise. Skinner (1971) typifies the behavioral attitude as he seeks to "operationalize" all behavior, even "covert behavior" (cognition). All is couched in the language of the physical sciences. It is possible, using this approach, to expose even "covert" occurrences to the objective rigors of the empirical method.

By this view, Skinner attempts to manage understanding by collapsing a myriad causes into operationalized contingencies. The implication is that if it is properly managed, one can gain some control over portions of one's life. Skinner reflects this optimism when he states, "In the behaviorist view, man can control his own destiny because he knows what must be done to have to do it" (Skinner, 1974, p. 240). Schafer (1976) sees this outlook as somewhat "comic" (in the traditional sense of the word) in its optimism. This view stands in contrast to the more "tragic" psychoanalytic perspective and to some extent to the family-systems perspective. In ideal circumstances, the therapist and client attempt to eliminate subjective influences from one's life and outlook. The emphasis shifts to values stressing *control, prediction*, and *effectiveness*.

Rychlak (1968) distinguishes two major approaches to how inference is formulated. These are "procedural evidence" and "validating evident". Procedural evidence holds that assumptions based on given plausibilities and reasoning are grounds for belief. In psychology, such evidence might be called clinical insight, theory construction, or hypothesis testing in clinical settings. Validating evidence is a relatively more rigorous sort derived from observable consequences of a prearranged succession of events designed to test a proposition. Rychlak sees behavioral approaches as more dominated by validating evidence. Arnold Lazarus has become so broad and varied in his techniques that many (including himself) no longer consider him a behavior therapist. Still his behavioral roots are reflected when he declares, "Empirical evidence is a higher form of validity" (Lazarus lecture, Rutgers University, February 1979). An appreciation for straightforward approaches then follows. Elsewhere, Lazarus states, "Don't look for troubles, don't look for complications. First take things at face value. . . . Is there any reason not to do the most obvious procedure. . . . Sometimes that will suffice" (Lazarus, 1979; also see Lazarus, 1989).

The ideal state of human functioning, according to behavior therapy, is intricately woven about the central values of behavioral effectiveness, control, and prediction of one's behavior, cognitions, and environment. These values seem to be descendants of the behaviorists and their ancestors among the British empiricists. Although behavior therapy is primarily a technical approach to human functioning, it implies certain theoretical features as well. It is characterized as objective, extraspective, realistic, optimistic, and normative. Those values that were involved in the procedures that helped found behaviorism are thereby subtly evident in today's behavioral approaches and can be found in what attracts behavior therapists to their work.

## Case History: A Committed Behaviorally Oriented Therapist

Dr. Q related his history in a willing, insightful, and intelligent manner. He adapted easily to the historical approach of the interview. Given Dr. Q's behavioral perspective on first impression this facility might appear to be a paradox. He did this with a slightly different viewpoint than that of the psychoanalyst who stressed the unconscious influences. Instead, Dr. Q described various events in his life as either pleasant or not, implying that some events produced a greater desire to experience or not experience such events and consequences again. Thus, even his historical perspective seemed to portray a behavioral perspective focusing primarily upon his conscious recollections.

Dr. Q sees himself as taking a very broad behavioral and technically eclectic approach to his work. He feels comfortable moving from cognitive approaches to narrow behavioral intervention, and when the situation deserves, focusing upon the affective realm.

Dr. Q was raised by both parents in an urban working-class home with two siblings 11 and 7 years his senior. His father is described as hardworking and generous, with a good sense of humor and an ability to "laugh at life." Although not highly educated, he is seen as intelligent and "street smart," having good common sense. Mother was more interested in socializing intimately and loved to "sit and talk." Nevertheless, she is viewed as rather anxious and often worried.

In reviewing his history, Dr. Q spent much time on the difficulties that arose when he was about 5 or 6 years old. At that time, his mother suffered a serious episode of depression and was hospitalized for months, producing a great deal of emotional and financial strain on the family. Later, when he was about 12 or 13, his sister suffered the first of many serious affective-disorder episodes. Although Dr. Q had never personally suffered mood disorders, his way of viewing and coping with these family circumstances left a major impression.

As the youngest member of the family, he learned to stand outside the turmoil. He recalled his mother's expensive and long-term psychoanalytically oriented therapy and the financial hardship that resulted. His brother and sister were highly intellectual, taking a serious approach to understanding life's dilemmas. He recalls hearing his siblings talk about their psychoanalytic treatment. Even as a young child, he saw their lives as overly involved and complicated by an intellectualized view of themselves and their problems. He stated,

> It seemed like a big intellectual mess. . . . I got very discouraged with all the intellectualization. I saw things a being so much simpler. . . . My raft out of this household was to see things simply. Following a plan, developing simple objec-

tives, sticking to a plan, and evaluating when I was done. . . . I associated intellectualizing as running in circles. . . . I saw it as confusing and overcomplicated and associated with a bad time.

Simultaneously, he was cast in the role of "helper." He recalls that his mother encouraged him to be friendly with a neighbor boy who had few friends and was lonely. In his teenage years, he discovered his brother's collection of psychology journals in the attic. He read them voraciously, especially those on hypnosis. At this very young age he learned to hypnotize his friends. Coming across a particularly hypnotizable friend, he brought him through visual suggestions and age regression!

His style of coping with early life stresses is evident in how he describes his clinical work today. At one point he said, "I'm a clinical chameleon," offering to provide what the client wants or needs. He sees his job as to help people. Dr. Q seems to have a great appreciation for tragedy and its influence, yet sees no reason to dwell unnecessarily upon it or to delve into any great detail. He stated,

> How do you work around it (tragedy), to avoid this, rise above it? But I don't see any value in explaining tragedy while you're in it. Once you're out of it, you can look back and learn about it.

Dr. W takes a thoughtful intellectual approach to his work but sees this as a double-edged sword; it can help or hinder problem solving. Perhaps some of his personal values are summed up in a statement about what he would like his children to learn from him.

> I want my kids to have a great sense of humor, to know when not to take life too seriously. They need to take responsibility and not depend on others for that . . . and appreciate people and relationships and value relationships.

Dr. Q's orientation as a behavioral therapist is apparently rooted in a successful mode of handling his family's problems. This has resulted in a rather optimistic attitude, a practical approach to problem solving, and a rather strong willingness and talent for helping others to transcend their problems.

## THE FAMILY-THERAPY PERSPECTIVE
### Theoretical Considerations

Defining the family-therapy approach poses particular problems. The approach encompasses several divergent perspectives, themselves proposing a rather eclectic approach. Some of these deserve separate study as independent theoretical frameworks. Here, I use the term in the broadest sense, pertaining to several schools of family therapy: the structural, systems, Bowenian, strategic, and related approaches. A precise definition is therefore not possible. I refer, however, to those therapies that usually prefer treatment of several family members simultaneously and a theoretical outlook that focuses upon the net effect of the interaction between its members and the history of that interaction. Treatment goals usually pertain to an ideal condition for the family as a whole, not just the individual.

The period after World War II found a greatly changed American culture. During the war, women took jobs that had traditionally been reserved for men, helping to establish women as family providers. As a victorious nation, America had an optimistic spirit. Traditional sex roles began to shift as family structure and values loosened. Divorce became more common and acceptable. Discontent within the family became a legitimate experience. Simultaneously, psychological treatment was increasingly available to those beyond the privileged and the seriously disturbed or psychotic. The widely used "traditional" psychoanalytic approaches, suited mainly for the verbal, educated, and affluent, could not apply easily to this more diverse population and their desire for more practical solutions. In burgeoning public clinics, children and members of minority cultures were frequently the identified patients. The type of services rendered had to adapt to the more immediate needs of this new patient population. Minuchin called his structural approach a "therapy of action" (Minuchin, 1974, p. 14).

Psychoanalytically oriented therapists began to experiment. Although men like Nathan Ackerman wrote about the family as early as 1938 (Ackerman, 1938), it was not until the 1950s that family therapy began to consolidate in a "founding decade" (Broderick & Schrader, 1981). Initially, these were extrapolations of psychodynamic approaches, such as Ackerman's, *The Psychodynamics of Family Life* (Ackerman, 1958). Meanwhile, in Palo Alto, Gregory Bateson (an anthropologist by training) put together an eclectic group. They sought to apply the ideas of Whitehead and Russell's notions of logical types and the resulting paradoxical statements. Jay Haley (originally a communications theorist) and John Weakland (originally a chemical engineer) studied Milton Erikson's controversial use of hypnosis, suggestion, and paradox. Needless to say, by the early 1970s, family therapy had become an established and unique blend of treatment approaches, with its own identity and spirit (Broderick & Schrader, 1981).

Family therapy has its origins in two diverse areas. First there are roots in traditional psychoanalytic treatment and the groundwork set by the interpersonal theorists Sullivan, Horney, and others. The second influence is communications and general-systems theory (Broderick & Schrader, 1981). Broadly speaking, this latter influence may be categorized as behavioral, especially in the sense that it seeks to address, predict, and then control the outward manifestations of interpersonal interaction. This is a unique blend, drawing heavily on theoretical notions that do not specifically originate in psychology. The first branch draws on the work of Ackerman, Bell,

Nagy, Satir, and Bowen, among others. The second force stems from the work of Bateson and the clinical applications of Haley, Weakland, M. Erickson, and Minuchin.

How can we best categorize the family-therapy approach? The most commonly used family-therapy approaches may be viewed as a specialized form of behavioral treatment. Minuchin states, "The tool of this therapy is to modify the present, not to explore and interpret the past" (Minuchin, 1974, p. 14). In this sense it is concerned with the overt behavior of the individual members of the family. Even in the intergenerational approaches where family therapy seems at first glance to focus intensively upon the intrapsychic, the true emphasis is actually on the interpersonal realm and the observable impact of familial effects. In accordance with behavioral therapy, family therapy shares an appreciation for observable clinical change as the goal of treatment. In this regard it is noteworthy that the *Handbook of Family Therapy* (Gurman & Kniskern, 1981) stresses measurable effectiveness by including a hefty final chapter that addresses the relevant outcome research. Elsewhere a contributor describes the most common approach of family therapy by saying that "this framework is used in selecting whatever variety of techniques and strategies appear most likely to resolve rapidly the presenting problems of the family" (Wynne in Gurman & Kniskern, 1981, p. ix).

To classify family therapy wholly as a branch of behavior therapy would be a serious injustice to the complexity of its therapeutic outlook. Certainly, like psychoanalytic therapy, family therapy holds an intense and central appreciation of interpersonal effects, the primary object of study. Family therapy generally focuses far less upon the individual psyche than psychodynamic treatment, primarily because it rapidly moves into a wider viewpoint and thereby does not limit itself to the individual subsystem. There is a significant trend toward applying psychoanalytic principles in family therapy, particularly object-relations theory. This suggests a thrust toward a more intensive focus and understanding of the interface between the intrapsychic and interpersonal. Parallel to behavioral approaches, family therapy seems to hold a rather optimistic view of problem solving as it seeks to control family interaction. Yet family therapy also maintains a distinct appreciation of the ironic and tragic as it recognizes and works with the reversing influences of generational styles and grapples with the twists and turns of paradox. With some origins in the field of logic (especially Whitehead and Russell), family therapy appreciates the complexities of semantic arguments. Recalling Rychlak's (1976) definitions of *procedural* and *validating* evidence, family therapy has many implicit values in common with behavioral outlooks, but its theory is often built on procedural evidence, lending it a more freewheeling technique.

Uniquely, a constructivist perspective seems to pervade and underlie a great deal of family-therapy theory (Efran, Lukens, & Lukens, 1988). In the

Kantian tradition, the constructivist views knowledge as the thinker's invention produced through interaction with the environment. That is, the constructivist recognizes that each person invents a reality. Efran, Lukens, and Lukens (1988, p. 28) explain this relative to the family therapist.

> For instance, techniques such as reframing and positive connotation, which constitute the lifeblood of many family therapy practices, have decidedly constructivist flavor. Moreover, the many family therapists already accustomed to thinking pragmatically in choosing clinical strategies may, unwittingly, be revealing their constructivist bias. Unlike the traditional Freudian analysts, who torture themselves over the *accuracy* of a given interpretation, such therapists are more apt to worry about whether a particular formulation will "sell well" to the family. "Utility," as opposed to "Truth," is high on the good constructivists list of priorities.

Similarly, these authors point out that the family therapist addresses the meaning of a statement according to the context in which it occurs. The family therapist, more than the psychoanalyst or the behavior therapist, "constructs" a view of the family dysfunction. If applied properly, this construction will help the family and the individuals within it to function in less self-defeating ways. At any given point, in an effort to produce such change or to join with a given member, the therapist may even propose a perspective that the therapist views (according to her own opinion) as false. This takes the utilitarian perspective of behavioral treatments one step further! It also stands in contrast to the nondirective psychoanalyst's focus on the "psychic reality" of the patient. Analysts may endeavor to understand this "reality," work with it, and even allow themselves to coexist within the transference paradigm, but are unlikely to engineer a given transference simply as a means to producing change more rapidly. In the name of rapid effectiveness in treatment, family therapy provides an enormous degree of freedom. At times, the family therapist not only seeks to understand the family system but deliberately becomes an active player in it, as an undercover double agent.

In accordance with its psychoanalytic ancestry, the constructivist elements within family therapy provide appreciation for illusion and the influence of tragic and ironic elements. The boy who hates his parents and is failing school may not be seen as having a block against schoolwork or simply displacing the anger he feels toward his mother and father. Instead, for the purpose of treatment, he may be viewed as showing his love for his parents and as willing to sacrifice his personal well-being to bring his parents together. The family therapist recognizes that what people say is often not what they mean or what they intend to mean. Within the context of the family system, as within the transference, any given statement takes on special circumstantial meaning. A person may be viewed as "bad" or "good" when she is "framed" as such. Events are understood almost totally as part of the context. Redefine the context, and the event is redefined as well.

Nevertheless, in clinical application, behavioral values once again seem to supersede the psychoanalytically oriented values. That is, there is a overarching appreciation for what is seen as the most effective way to proceed. The therapist may move about the family system, first adopting one perspective, then another, each calculated to produce a given reaction within the system. As with behavioral approaches, the family therapist may value control and effectiveness as the central criteria for including a therapeutic approach. She may choose to reframe a problem in a particular way, simply on the grounds that it works productively and quickly.

As a varied and loosely allied mode of treatment, family therapy leaves the therapist room for a tremendous range of potential values with which to resonate. In this respect, family therapy is philosophically a very eclectic form of treatment. Its root allegiance in clinical practice, nevertheless, appears to be to the behavioral values of effectiveness, control, and optimism. The pure family therapist's appreciation for the psychoanalytic values of understanding, interpersonal aspects, and inherent tragic and ironic elements helps to complement or widen the core values rooted in the behavioral outlook.

## Case History: The Committed Family Therapist

Dr. K describes herself as a multigenerational family therapist. Although her approach to family therapy is somewhat eclectic within this framework, she takes special interest in how the influence of past generations may have affected the relationship patterns that she sees in the consulting room. Dr. K's resonance with family therapy appears to demonstrate a dual perspective, with an emphasis on both the importance of "understanding"[1] and the relevance of taking behavioral action.

Naturally, Dr. K was very articulate about how interpersonal influence in family background helped her to become the person she is today. Raised in a midwestern middle-class home, she was exposed to a simple work ethic and to periods of financial hardship. An emphasis on the practical seemed to pervade her family history, her world view, and her professional work. She remembers being told that she was seriously ill and fragile as an infant and young child. Traditional medicine attempted to cure the problems but met with failure. Eventually, her treatment came under the care of a homeopathic physician. The advice was simply to expose her to plenty of fresh air. Long summer and weekend camping trips yielded positive results and lasting physical health.

During the interview Dr. K made a special point of indicating that within her family and generation, extensive education was viewed as highly unusual for a woman. Yet in some respects, her education was not surprising to either Dr. K or her family. She states, "For about six years (until her brother was born), I was viewed as the son of the family. That's why I got a Ph.D. It was a big deal to be a male in my culture." Dr. K mentioned that she was given the female version of her father's name, implying that her parents expected a male child. There is also an interesting interaction with another family myth. Dr. K was born with a "veil" (covered with the placental membrane). In her culture, this was seen as an sign of special abilities to soothsay, or the gift of parapsychic powers. She, of course, never took any stock in such an idea, seeing herself lacking in this regard and skeptical of the whole idea. Nevertheless, her chosen profession requires a certain intuition about how certain conditions influence a person.

Throughout the interview, Dr. K emphasized her interest in the practical. Originally a philosophy major, she was drawn to psychology because she felt it was a more likely way to make a living. Referring to bad economic times, Dr. K stated, "There is so much insecurity around you day after day that you really get to know what reality is. . . . We got that growing up."

When Dr. K first learned of family therapy as it surfaced in mainstream clinical practice, she was excited to come across a treatment approach that would "actually help" with her difficult cases. She criticized psychoanalysis as too lengthy and impractical. Dr. K stated that she could not muster the patience or interest to sit with a patient day after day, week after week, discussing the nuance of every emotion. Family therapy is viewed as a "let's-get-on-with-it point of view." Also, Dr. K stated that she liked the greater interpersonal distance that family therapy offered. "Psychoanalysts, they like the centrality of themselves with the patient. . . . Family therapy is somewhat interpersonally distant." Elsewhere she pointed out that in the practice of family therapy, "You have a relationship with the client. It isn't the focus. The focus is on their (the family's) relationship with each other."

In summary, Dr. K's resonance with family therapy demonstrates the dual perspective of family therapy; she stresses a rather optimistic, practical life perspective and, in keeping with more traditional approaches, the sense that reality is what we think it is. Thus we see major elements of behavioral outlook and to a lesser degree some aspects of the psychoanalytic approach.

## CONCLUDING REMARKS

What can be said about the relationship between therapists and their orientation? It is complex, and it is personal. Stereotypical personality descriptions of therapists from a given orientation would surely be inaccurate. The above discussion helps highlight the implicit outlook of each theoretical approach. However, the best we can do in precisely deciphering the connection between therapist and theory is to take it on a case-by-case basis. This chapter reveals some of the issues that are likely to form that connection. A rigid psychoanalyst may resonate to aspects of the theory that reflect her own rigidity. She may relate to theory as fixed and scientific. Similarly, an intuitive, free-wheeling psychoanalyst may relate more to the those elements of the theory that have their origins within the liberal arts. We may know behavioral therapists who are obsessively focused on how "effective" they are, as engineers might evaluate their work. Likewise, there are those whose personal style will resonate most with the theory's distinctly practical and optimistic view.

The opportunity to study a given approach to treatment certainly has an influence on what orientation people eventually espouse. We might expect that over time, therapists who are mismatched with their orientation will show a diminished interest in their outlook. The successfully matched therapist will undoubtedly demonstrate a deep personal connection to her theory. Person and theory interact, yielding a unique personalized form of treatment. If the mix fits the person and allows a healthy sublimation of major life themes, if the clinician feels that her therapeutic work is an expression of personal identity, then the approach is much more likely to work in the expected ways with the widest variety of clinical problems. The process of accommodation between therapist and theory is seen in senior clinicians. Informal observation suggests that many experienced therapists tend to take a less theorocentric approach and are more likely to practice in an idiosyncratic fashion.

I think it is accurate to say that it feels different to provide different forms of therapy. The therapist's focus and function vary tremendously. A successful analyst must appreciate the long periods of pensive introspection, the slow progress, and endure intense transference-countertransference experiences. The behavioral therapist must be ready to pursue vigorously irrational cognitions or coach a client through an exercise. The family therapist must thrive on the stimulation and complexity of sitting with several people simultaneously. Different philosophical perspectives underlie these approaches. Yet just as important, therapists of these orientations must have varying clinical dispositions. They must desire to do different things in the course of their clinical work.

Problems emerge when the fit is not a good one. If there are important opposing elements of the therapist's personality and value system, we might expect difficulties. Therapists in this circumstance may feel that their work is ineffective or inconsequential. In such procrustean circumstances the treatment may lack effectiveness or may be disabled by blind spots. The treatment might proceed according to a formula rather than as an individualized application. Some of these therapists may change clinical orientation in mid-career or even change careers.

Problems also occur if the fit between therapists and orientation is too good; that is, when the theories are adopted as a complete expression of their

world view. Therapists then relate to their clinical orientation more as someone might relate to a religion. The theory does not sit neatly within that person. Instead, theory and person blend. The theoretical approach may act to
reinforce elements of the therapist's personality that are countertherapeutic,
or allow the therapy itself to be an acting-out of unresolved spheres of conflict. Therapists may be unable to think critically about their approach, as an
outsider might. Narcissistic issues may operate unrestrained by a sense of
limitations. A rigid perspective about how treatment should proceed might
occur. For such therapists, the psychological theory and treatment represent
a complete perspective of how people function.

The "ideal" connection between therapist and theory is difficult to know.
The relationship between therapists and orientation may always involve
problems areas. Some patients, it might be argued, may do best during certain portions of their treatment with therapists who show different forms of
resonance. For example, patients with a loosely organized personality may
for a brief period do very well with therapists who relate to their theoretical
approach tightly. The structure may be rather helpful. Similarly, obsessive
patients may profit from treatment with clinicians who interpret their clinical
approach somewhat more loosely, as they might be more able to encourage
the patients to widen their viewpoint. Therefore, the "ideal" resonance between therapist and theory is a function of a particular patient's needs.

Nevertheless, some statements about the ideal connection between therapist and theory are possible. The resonance would probably be experienced
as comfortable to the therapist. More specifically, therapists who feel that
their therapeutic work acts as a major form of self-expression, but not their
only form of self-expression, are more likely to be helpful in a broad range of
treatment circumstances. The theory must take a place within the therapist's
world view, alongside a wider or more profound perspective of human functioning. The theoretical approach will then gain it's strength from the context
in which it is held. The clinical approach is available to become a creative outlook, drawing upon deeper, more essential, unspoken perspectives and sets
of values. In such an ideal situation, the theory becomes an artistic medium
through which the therapist is able to bring to bear the full involvement of
the whole self.

## ACKNOWLEDGMENT

Although Drs. George Atwood and Stanley Messer (Rutgers University,
Graduate School of Applied and Professional Psychology) were not actively
involved in my work on this chapter, their input and kind support is evident.
As chair and committee of my dissertation on a related topic, they helped to
form many of the ideas that are presented here.

## NOTE

1. I use the word *understanding* here in the special way that many family therapists use this term. This may not necessarily involve understanding the truth, reality, or the unique perspective of the client. Instead, it may just as well refer to the therapist's "reframing" of a circumstance as she attempts to construct a view of the problem that allows the family to work toward solutions. Dr. K stated that "family therapists know that they do not know what reality is."

## REFERENCES

Ackerman, N. W. (1938). The unity of the family. *Archives of Pediatrics, 55,* 51–62.

Ackerman, N. W. (1958). *The psychodynamics of family life.* New York: Basic Books.

Alexander, F. (1963). The dynamics of psychotherapy in the light of learning theory. *American Journal of Psychiatry, 120,* 440–448.

Atwood, G. E., & Stolorow, R. D. (1977). The life and work of Wilhelm Reich: A case study of the subjectivity of personality theory. *The Psychoanalytic Review, 64,* 5–20.

Atwood, G. E., & Stolorow, R. D. (1978). Metapsychology, reification and the representational world of C. G. Jung. *The International Review of Psychoanalysis, 41,* 197–214.

Broderick. C. B., & Schrader, S. S. (1981). The history of professional marriage and family therapy. In A. S. Gurman & D. P. Kniskern (Eds.), *Handbook of family therapy.* New York: Brunner/Mazel.

Buss, A. R. (1975). The emerging field of the sociology of psychological knowledge. *American Psychologist, 30,* 988–1002.

Chaust, J. (1978). Personality and opportunity in psychotherapist's choice of theoretical orientation of practice. *Psychotherapy: Theory, Research and Practice, 15*(4), 375–381.

Creelan, P. G. (1974). Watsonian behaviorism and the Calvinist conscience. *Journal of the History of the Behavioral Sciences, 10,* 95–118.

Cummings, N. A., & Lucchesc, G. (1978). Adoption of psychological orientation: The role of the inadvertent. *Psychotherapy: Theory, Research and Practice, 15*(4), 323–328.

Efran, J. S., Lukens, R. J., & Lukens, M. D. (1988). Constructivism: What's in it for you? *The Family Therapy Networker, 12*(5), 26–35.

Gurman, A. S., & Kniskern, D. P. (1981). *Handbook of family therapy.* New York: Brunner/Mazel.

Franks, C. M., & Wilson G. T. (1974). *Annual review of behavior therapy, I and II.* New York: Brunner/Mazel.

Henry, W. E., Sims, J. H., & Spray, E. L. (1975). *Public and private lives of psychotherapists.* San Francisco: Jossey-Bass.

Herron, W. G. (1978). The therapist's choice of a theory of psychotherapy. *Psychotherapy: Theory, Research and Practice, 15*(4), 396–401.

Holt, R. R. (1972). Freud's mechanistic and humanistic images of man. In R. R. Holt and E. Peterfreund (Eds.), *Psychoanalysis and contemporary science* (Vol. 1). New York: Macmillan.

Lazarus, A. A. (1989). *The Practice of multi-modal therapy*. Baltimore: Johns Hopkins University Press.

Lazarus, A. (February, 1979). Lecture, Rutgers University.

Mark, C. B. (1981). A case study exploration of the relationship between the values of psychotherapists and their theoretical orientations. *Dissertation Abstracts International, 41.*

Mosse, G. I. (1974). *The culture of western Europe*. Chicago: Rand McNally.

Minuchin, S. (1974). *Families and family therapy*. Cambridge, MA: Harvard University Press.

Napier, A. Y., & Whitaker, C. A. (1978). *The family crucible*. New York: Harper & Row.

Reiff, P. (1964). *Freud: Mind of the moralist*. New York: Holt, Reinhart and Winston.

Rychlak, J. F. (1968). *A philosophy of science for personality theory*. Boston: Houghton Mifflin.

Schafer, R. (1976). *A new language for psychoanalysis*. New Haven: Yale University Press.

Skinner, B. F. (1971). *Beyond freedom and dignity*. New York: Bantam/Vantage.

Skinner, B. F. (1974). *About behaviorism*. New York: Alfred A. Knopf.

Steiner, G. L. (1978). A survey to identify factors in therapist's selection of a therapeutic orientation. *Psychotherapy: Theory, Research and Practice, 15*(4), 371–374.

Stolorow, R. D., & Atwood, G. E. (1976). An egopsychological analysis of the work and life of Otto Rank in the light of modern conceptions of narcissism. *The International Review of Psychoanalysis, 3,* 441–459.

Stolorow, R. D., & Atwood, G. E. (1978). A defensive restitutive function of Freud's theory of psychological development. *Psychoanalytic Review, 65,* 217–238.

Stolorow, R. D., & Atwood, G. E. (1979). *Faces in a cloud, subjectivity in personality theory*. New York: Jason Aronson.

Stolorow, R. D., & Lachman, F. (1980). *Psychoanalysis of developmental arrests*. New York: International Universities Press.

Walton, D. E. (1978). An exploratory study: Personality factors and theoretical orientation of therapists. *Psychotherapy: Theory, Research and Practice, 15,* 390–395.

Wynne, L. C. (1981). Forward. In A. S. Gurman & D. P. Kniskern (Eds.), *Handbook of family therapy*. New York: Brunner/Mazel.

Yates, A. J. (1975). *Theory and practice in behavior therapy*. New York: John Wiley and Sons.

# II

## WOMEN TREATING WOMEN

# 4

# The Case

## Karen Zager

## REFERRAL

Mary was referred to me in 1981 by the director of a counseling center at a local university. She had been seen for counseling there for 2 years, but since she was about to graduate, she was no longer eligible for those services. She was thought to be in need of continuing therapy. The following information was sent to me shortly after the phone referral was made:

> Mary is a dependent, almost infantile personality with a profound need for nurturance. She has a very poor self-concept and needs a great deal of support. Her relationship with her mother has been conflicted, with the struggle for autonomy succumbing in her dependency needs. Mary was seen for two years and at times was seen twice a week. The thrust of the work was to develop a sense of self-worth, independence from others (particularly her mother), and support her desire for autonomy and maturity. Further therapy is needed to establish this sense for Mary. Her prognosis in therapy is good, but her tendency to establish a dependent relationship with the therapist has to be monitored.

## FIRST SESSION—PRESENTING PROBLEM

Mary appeared for her first session with me half an hour late, having underestimated the time it would take to get to my office by bus. From the start, she was very emotional, anxious, animated, and talkative. She described herself as "trying too hard to please others and be supportive of them," and said that she "wasn't her own person." She viewed herself as warm and friendly but feared that she acted that way for selfish reasons, so that others would like her. She didn't feel that she really knew who she was, presenting a facade to others that was not genuinely felt. Mary stated that her primary problems were her insecurity and her conflicted relationship with her mother. She wanted to break loose from her mother's influence but couldn't, and she couldn't live up to her mother's expectations either. She was a "good girl" and followed her mother's teachings and values: no smoking, no drinking, no drugs, no sex. Even so, she was constantly criticized by her mother. Although she knew that her mother's criticisms were unjustified, she couldn't help but incorporate them into her self-image, feeling bad, unworthy, stupid, fat, unsociable, just as her mother told her she was. And most recently Mary had failed her mother by not graduating from college as she was supposed to have done. She had failed two courses in her last semester and would have to go to summer school. She was ashamed to tell her friends and afraid to tell her family. She knew her mother's reaction would be to criticize, embarrass, and humiliate her. She knew, too, that her own reaction would be a typical one: lie to her friends to save face; avoid telling her family for as long as possible. Once her family *had* to know, she would tell the truth, let them criticize her, then finally react by arguing bitterly with her mother, becoming a "rebellious" daughter, being nasty and mean to her mother because she "couldn't take it anymore."

## BACKGROUND INFORMATION

Over the next few months of therapy, the following background information began to unfold: Mary was the 21-year-old daughter of Italian immigrant parents. When the parents had been married in Italy, they barely knew each other since the union had been prearranged. They had come to the States a few years before Mary was born, bringing with them Mary's three older brothers, each of whom was now in his mid to late thirties. The family lived in an Italian neighborhood in lower Manhattan, clinging to traditional values and a strictly Italian Catholic upbringing.

The parents owned and managed the small apartment building in which they lived, and they rarely had to venture beyond the borders of their Italian neighborhood. In fact, after almost 25 years of living in a major metropolitan area, the mother spoke only a few words of English. The oldest brother had become a priest, leaving home against the mother's wishes, and he had a parish located about 2 hours outside the city. The second brother lived at home and worked as a salesman for a large corporation; the third brother also lived at home and was employed in a large department store in a management-training position. The parents hoped that Mary would graduate from college, get a job to help support the household, and remain single, staying at home to care for her aging parents. The parents' marriage was very unhappy, the father spending almost all of his time in the basement of the building, doing maintenance work. The parents rarely spoke to one another, communicating only when necessary. Mary's contact with her father was infrequent; she typically saw him only when she brought his dinner down to the basement each evening or when there was a family argument over some major issue.

## COURSE OF TREATMENT

Mary was seen twice a week for 2½ years, then once weekly for the next 2 years. She quickly became attached to and very dependent on the therapist, upon whom she relied for a great deal of support and comfort. Nevertheless, she was frequently late (by 20–25 minutes) for her sessions. On many occasions, Mary wanted to terminate therapy because she was becoming too dependent on the therapist, a feeling that disturbed her enormously. If her goal was to become independent of her family, she certainly did not want to feel dependent on her therapist instead. She felt that dependency was to be avoided at all costs. Yet she relied heavily on the therapist to allow her to "be herself" and not have to live up to someone else's expectations. She often asked for the therapist's opinion or for direct guidance when in sticky or conflictual situations. She wanted the therapist to tell her that it was OK to rebel against her mother, that it was OK to feel angry, that it was OK to have a boyfriend. She did not want to discuss her lateness, other than to find excuses for it. She did not want *ever* to feel a shred of anger toward the therapist, and she wanted the therapist to love her and think about her all the time.

Her ambivalence in other areas of her life was clear as well. She wanted to graduate, but managed to fail the same two courses three times until she finally switched her major, returned for one full semes-

ter to take the few courses needed for a new major, and was then able to
graduate. She wanted to be independent of her family but never made
any attempt to move away from home. She wanted to be a self-support-
ing, assertive career woman but managed to give such a poor impression on each job interview that she remained unemployed for almost a
year after graduation.

A few typical vignettes will serve to illustrate the major themes and issues as they surfaced in therapy.

During the first year of therapy, Mary was invited to go sailing for a
weekend with some friends. Although she had never been away from
home before and was a bit afraid of what might happen during the
weekend, she was sure that she wanted to go. She was able to realize
that this would be an important developmental step for her to take, that
at age 22 she should be able to handle the freedom and responsibility of
2 days with friends. However, deciding to go on the weekend trip
meant openly defying her parents, who adamantly refused to allow her
to leave the house on such a dangerous excursion. Mary sought help
from the therapist. She wanted the therapist to tell her it was OK to go,
that she *should* rebel against her parents. She did go on the sailing trip,
enjoying it fully. But the repercussions lasted for months. She returned
home from the trip to a furious, critical, hostile family scene. Even the
older brother, the priest who knew what was best for Mary, was called
back home to have a talk with her, to make her feel guilty, irresponsible,
and bad about her decision. The parents were unyieldingly accusatory
about everything she did for weeks after her trip. After several months
of this pressure, Mary too began to feel that she had made the wrong
decision, that her mother's high blood pressure and other medical conditions had become worse as a result of the aggravation and that Mary's
selfish enjoyment just hadn't been worth the price.

During the second year of therapy, Mary began to date a man (one of
the first relationships she had) whom she described as romantic, exciting, emotional, and free-spirited. He was not Italian, not Catholic, and
of course her family hated him. They tried to forbid her to see him, but
by this time, Mary had enough strength to stand up for what she
wanted. She dated him for about 6 months. For the first 2 or 3 months,
the relationship went relatively well. Mary was in love, had her first sexual experience, and was thrilled to have a boyfriend. None of her
friends liked him though. They found him arrogant and abusive, self-
centered and emotionally volatile. She stopped seeing her friends because she couldn't deal with their criticisms of him or their comments
about her poor judgment in seeing him. When Mary finally ended the
relationship because his criticism of her was overwhelming, she became
depressed and withdrawn for some time. She knew she had made a

mistake, she knew her family had been right, and she did not want to admit defeat. She was unable to forgive herself for choosing a man who was so much like her mother, and she did not date again for almost 1 year.

During the third year of therapy, Mary had a succession of job interviews, each ending in failure. (During the first year of treatment, she was taking courses to graduate; during the second year, she was unemployed.) She was rarely called back for a second interview, and she was rejected for job after job. She felt unwanted and incompetent. When she did get a job as a customer service representative with a large corporation, she was terminated from the training program because she could not grasp the content. Next, she obtained a similar job with a smaller retail store and was terminated after a few months because she was not accurate in her record keeping. She blamed the therapist for giving her a false sense of hope about her capabilities. She became depressed and spent her days sleeping and watching TV. Being at home most of the time was especially conducive to major conflicts with her mother, and "war" broke out at home. She was told that she was the black sheep of the family. The brother was once more called back from his parish to intercede and "straighten Mary out." The family finally became so unbearable that Mary became angry at them (even at the long-worshiped brother). She stood up for herself, demanded that they stop ridiculing her, and mobilized to find a job.

As can be seen from the above vignettes, dependency, ambivalence about growing up, conflicts with the family, and anger were themes that surfaced repeatedly during the 4 years of therapy. During the last year of treatment, Mary had become a more assertive, self-assured woman who was able to deal with her family in a less destructive manner. However, she was still living at home and had not found a steady job. She did socialize much more and had recently met a friend of the family at a social gathering. This young man lived in Italy and was visiting this country for the first time. They dated a few times prior to his return to Italy and corresponded for several months. Mary then decided to make a trip to Italy to visit him. They become seriously involved, and eventually she moved to Italy to marry him and live close to his family and job. She was very happy in this relationship, for the first time. Mary felt that she had not only found a man who adored her, was kind to her, and respected her but had also inherited a happy family life. Treatment ended when she left for Italy.

## EPILOGUE

One year after Mary left for Italy, she returned to the United States and contacted the therapist. She had returned to arrange her wedding and wanted to see the therapist again for a few sessions. She was getting married in a few months, was happy in the relationship with the man with whom she had spent the past year, but had some gnawing conflicts that she felt ought to be discussed.

Mary saw the therapist for three follow-up visits. She briefly updated the therapist. Mary and her boyfriend had been living with his parents in Italy. By living with his family, Mary felt that she had exchanged one family for another, but at least the new family was less problematic and more loving and accepting of her. After the wedding, Mary and her husband would return to Italy but would be living on their own. She felt strongly that she loved her boyfriend, but she was surprised by the intensity of her jealousy and possessiveness toward him. She wanted in particular to resolve those feelings prior to her wedding. Since her return, she had been doing some office work through a temporary agency and was so liked and respected by her employer that she had been asked to stay on permanently. This was a boost to her shaky self-esteem. During these few sessions, some successful and unsuccessful aspects of her therapy were highlighted. She had chosen a man who was loving and respectful toward her. She did not feel criticized or unwanted. On the negative side, she felt she was still "in the fold," not yet fully independent but taken care of by his family. She had made decisions and plans about work and marriage, and was following through on them without unconsciously sabotaging those plans. Yet, on the negative side, she was still looking to the therapist for permission and approval, for the answers to her problems, and was not confident enough to live fully on her own. Mary was able to see that she still relied on others for approval and was even able to laugh at her shortcomings. Her passive-aggressive, angry, and self-defeating behaviors had largely been overcome, and she was able to maintain a more moderate stance without swinging between being a good little girl and a rebellious naughty daughter.

# 5

## An Analyst Views
## the Case

### Judith L. Alpert

### INTRODUCTION

I have been asked to (1) formulate a theoretical analysis of the case and (2) discuss the expected course of treatment with particular focus on aspects of the therapist-client relationship. Further, I have been asked to do this from a psychoanalytic perspective. Two questions arise from this: the first concerns the case material, the second the psychoanalytic perspective.

Can I analyze psychoanalytically when the case material was not derived from a psychoanalytic treatment? Psychoanalysis would lead to material that is not presented here. For example, there is no information on free association, dreams, or countertransference. Clearly, the material would be of a qualitatively different nature with respect to the questions asked and the information derived if the therapist were a psychoanalyst or a psychoanalytically oriented psychotherapist. Obviously, I will work with the material Dr. Zager has given us. However, sometimes I may be making suppositions as I move from the case material to the analysis of the case.

Can I present a psychoanalytic perspective when there are many psychoanalytic perspectives? Actually, there should be at least four analytic chapters in response to each case, each chapter representing a different theoretical perspective within psychoanalysis. Even writing a chapter for one of four analytic orientations would be controversial as there are multiple views within each theoretical perspective.

For purposes of the present chapter I will briefly review theory, specifically drive theory, ego psychology, object-relations theory, and self psychology. Next I will indicate how these theoretical stances are used in clinical work. I will conclude the section by pointing to some limitations inherent to this chapter. The case will be discussed in the final section.

In my chapter on women treating men, there is elaboration of theory dealing with gender issues. Specifically, I consider such issues as (1) the coexistence of psychoanalysis and feminism; (2) the contributions of feminist psychoanalytic thinking to our understanding of men and women; and (3) treatment differences as a function of the analyst's gender. Thus, while the theoretical consideration in this chapter is broad, in the chapter on women treating men it is focused on gender issues.

## THEORY

There are many books about each theory, and I cannot possibly do justice to several theories within a section of a chapter. This brief review will serve to introduce the reader to the richness, depth, and complexity of psychoanalytic theory. The reader is referred to Alpert (1989), Eagle (1984), Greenberg and Mitchell (1983), and Guntrip (1971) for a consideration of contemporary psychoanalytic theory and a discussion of salient contributions and significant themes.

### Drive Theory

Psychoanalytic theory represents a family of personality theories that are derived from and related to the works of Sigmund Freud. His theory is sometimes referred to as drive theory, instinct theory, structural theory, classical theory, and conflict theory. The theory focuses on instinctual drives, especially the sex drive and its expression in infancy. According to drive theorists, asocial impulses conflict with socially enlightened defenses against those impulses. It is this conflict that constitutes mental life. Thus, according to drive theory, the sources of our unconscious wishes and feelings are instinctual or biological drives in the form of sexual and aggressive impulses. When such instincts are incompatible with civilized living, the guilt-inducing superego and the controlling ego assume a regulatory function.

Freud identified the structural aspects of the mind; they focus on the instincts and the controlling function of the ego. According to Freud, the human psyche is divided into three parts: (1) the id, composed of instinctual energy that is present at birth; (2) the ego, which develops out of the id over time, operates in relation to the id and has no independent functions, and serves to limit action to what is socially acceptable; and (3) the superego, which emerges later and is the internalized voice of the parents, and through the parents, culture.

Also related to the structural component of his theory is the topographical model. Freud proposed that one's level of awareness could be (1) preconscious, where there is access to awareness with effort only (2) conscious; and (3) unconscious, where there can be no voluntary access to awareness.

While the structural component of his theory is well developed, the personal component is not. The personal component basically concerns the way the child's personality is formed and the way one relates with others. According to Freud, personality is formed through interactions and identification with parents. However, individuals seek others to achieve tension reduction or derive gratification. They do not seek others as an end in itself.

## Ego Psychology

Psychoanalytic theory is no longer the same as classical Freudian theory. There are three major revisions: (1) ego psychology, which is associated with the writings of Mahler (1974), Jacobson (1964), and Hartmann (1964); (2) object-relations theory, which is associated with the writings of Fairbairn (1952), Klein (1964), Balint (1965), Guntrip (1971), and Winnicott (1965); and (3) self psychology, which is associated with the writings of Kohut (1971, 1977) and Goldberg (1984). Ego psychologists attempted to maintain the basic id-ego structural model and the basic assumptions of traditional theory. They did, however, reconsider the structural components. While Freudians focus on the development of defensive ego abilities, ego psychologists focus on the development of adaptive ego abilities, such as the ability to engage with others. Hartmann clearly stated, for example, that the ego has some functions that do not emanate from the id and are not in conflict with the id. Ego psychologists, then, were the first to question Freud's concept that instincts lead to all behavior and psychic functions. The ego-psychological stance recognizes that human behavior can be rational and logical

## Object-Relations Theory

Object-relations theory, the British version of psychoanalytic theory, along with self psychology, is presently the focus of attention from the psychoanalytic community. Object-relations theory calls into question the preeminence of instincts and emphasizes human interactions. Within this theoretical orientation, individuals are perceived as seeking contact with others as an end in itself rather than as a means to release tension as Freud postulated. Object-relations theory is conceptualized as a fulfillment model rather than a conflict model. While some object-relation theorists (e.g., Fairbairn, 1952; Sullivan, 1962, 1964) have abandoned the drive model completely, others (e.g., Kernberg, 1980) adapt classical-drive theory in a way that enables recognition of the importance of object relations. *Person* is referred to as "object" in psychoanalytic terminology.

What is important for object-relational theorists is (1) the primacy of object relatedness and (2) the view of mental life that is organized around self and object (or other) representations and their relations and repetitions. Thus, while drive theorists say that instinctual needs are major determinants of personality, the object-relational theorists generally point to the child's earliest interpersonal experiences. The object-relational theorists hold that social relations motivate human behavior. They place primary emphasis on the ways the child's very first affectional bond with the primary caretaker affects all later relationships. As the primary caretaker is usually the mother, I will refer to "mother" throughout. According to this theory, the infant's developing awareness of self takes place within the context of relationship to mother. It is during this stage that the infant comes to understand and emotionally experience separation, the attainment of a sense of separateness from the mother, and individuation, a sense of wholeness as an independent being.

The infant experiences both satisfaction and deprivation. The reason the infant experiences deprivation is that his or her needs are not met, as it is impossible constantly to meet all the infant's needs. What does the infant do with these satisfying and depriving experiences? The infant internalizes the early object-relational experiences. This means that he or she transforms these experiences or, alternatively, eliminates them from consciousness.

Let me state it differently. According to object-relations theory, the infant is intent on viewing the mother as "the good mother." Only in this way, given the infant's cognitive and emotional immaturity, can the infant feel totally loved. Actually, however, the infant experiences two mothers: a good one, who satisfies, and a bad one, who deprives. The infant has to find a way to deal with the bad depriving mother in order to preserve the image of "the good mother." The infant represses the bad depriving mother. However, more than just the bad depriving mother is repressed. Also repressed is the bad unlovable part of the self, which is, of course, a part of the relationship with the "bad mother." There is internalization of negative object relations by means of the unconscious splitting of mother into good object and bad object. These internalized objects will influence perceptions of self and of others. They may account, for example, for an individual feeling unworthy when faced with objective worthiness. Thus, we see the neurotic ways individuals deal with the unconscious feelings about the "bad mother" and the "bad self" who was "unworthy" of having all his or her needs met.

## Self Psychology

Self psychology is the most recent revision of classical theory, one which is receiving a good deal of contemporary attention. While Kohut initially conceptualized self psychology to complement classical theory, he later rejected drive theory. In Kohut's 1977 writings, he indicates that the basic issues in both development and pathology do not emphasize conflict among the instinctual wishes. Rather, the basic issues concern the development of an intact and cohesive self, characterized by clarity of identity; ability to express one's talents, ambitions, aspirations, interests, values, ideals, and goals; and capacity to relate to others. Thus, Kohut views as basic the strivings of people to become and remain cohesive and to fulfill a creative and productive potential. According to self psychology, mental health is not related to drive gratification but to expression of talents and skills in one's basic ambitions and ideals. Also, psychopathology is not related to inner conflict but to self-cohesion.

A firm and cohesive self is believed to develop from early relationships with others in which empathic mirroring and the opportunity to idealize parental figures is experienced. Without these, narcissistic disorders and self defects result.

Object-relations theory and self psychology are presently the focus of attention within the psychoanalytic community. Several analysts (e.g., Eagle, 1984) have suggested that these theories may better "fit" the problems facing contemporary patients. Problems patients bring to us today differ from the problems individuals faced in Victorian times. Freud's patients presented neurotic problems related to oedipal issues and experienced inhibitions that made it difficult for them to do what they wanted to do and to be who they thought they were. In contrast, many patients of today could be labeled narcissistic, borderline, or schizoid. They present problems concerning inability to relate to or to commit to others; problems with self, other differentiation, and self-cohesiveness; conflicts of identity; and conflicts around autonomy and self-esteem. They complain of feelings of emptiness, depression, unre-latedness, and lack of sustaining interests, goals, ideals, and values. These contemporary problems are also the subject of contemporary films, plays, and novels.

## Analytic Theory in Clinical Work

Each theoretical perspective favors different ways of interpreting. Clearly, theory shapes technique. For example, while empathy and un-derstanding is important in the work of all analysts, it is particularly im-portant for self psychologists. The role of theory in technique is clearly indicated in Reed's (1987) article, in which she compares interpretations from the perspectives of drive theory and self psychology. It is also evi-dent in Pulver's (1987) special issue of a journal, in which a case is pre-sented and considered from many psychoanalytic perspectives.

Some analysts hold tightly to one theoretical orientation. They theo-rize and interpret within that orientation only. Other theorists identify with one theoretical orientation but are able and willing to pull from other theoretical orientations when helpful. Other analysts consider their theoretical orientation eclectic and comfortably move from one stance to another.

While there are attempts to integrate the psychoanalytical develop-mental theories referred to by our concepts of drive, ego, internalized object, and self, the attempted integration is not occurring at a theoreti-cal level (Pine, 1985, 1989). Rather, it is attempted by some analysts in their clinical activity. Pine (1985) points out that within the course of analysis, formative experiences are considered and that these experi-ences are relevant to all four phenomena. They are relevant to drives, in that we all have urges. The ego is relevant as well, in that achievement, coping, and mastery are issues for us all. Object relations or internal-ized objects are important, as we have relationships and form connec-tions with others. Lastly, self psychology has relevance, in that issues of boundaries, continuity, cohesion, and self-esteem are important to us all. The point made by Pine (1985) is that issues relevant to the four per-spectives are raised in an analysis.

In my analytic work, I try to keep the four phenomena in mind, and I utilize different theoretical perspectives as indicated. With some pa-tients, one perspective seems more appropriate than others. At this point, the reader may be wondering what my theoretical perspective is within analysis. I am reminded of Roy Schafer's (1987) comment to this question, which I paraphrase here. He said that his theoretical orientation was "broadly Freudian," and then he defined that as interpersonal, self psychological, Kleinian, and object relational.

## Limitations

Given space limitations, I cannot possibly review all the theoretical perspectives relevant to the case, nor can I consider all the theory within one perspective relevant to Mary. Stated simply, I cannot do a just analysis of this case, given space limitations and limitations posed by the nonanalytic material presented. Therefore, I will focus only on broad issues with respect to two theoretical perspectives. I select drive theory because feminists have been most critical of this theory. I will show how the theory can help a feminist psychoanalyst conceptualize the case. I select object-relations theory because this is the theory that feminists are most excited about. Further, I will consider aspects of the two theories that are most relevant to Mary's case. Also, while I may agree with the views of the case presented by the other contributors (the "feminist," the "family therapist," and the "behaviorist"), I will focus on what is dissimilar as a means of clarifying the unique contribution of psychoanalysis.

## CASE DISCUSSION
### Drive Theory

Four concepts important to drive theory and most relevant to Mary are the concepts of (1) instinctual drives and urges; (2) conflicts between the instincts and the defenses against them; (3) resulting anxiety, guilt, shame, and symptom formation, and (4) structural aspects of the psyche—the id, ego, and superego. Mary's aggressive drives and her defenses against them, as well as her unrelenting superego, would be a focus of analytic work. Mary is unable to accept her aggressive thoughts and urges. She is angry at her mother's controlling behavior and angry at her dependence on her mother. Since her mother seems to be the only predictably available parent, Mary feels excessive guilt about her anger toward her mother.

We see that anger is not directly and consistently expressed in this family. In general, family members do what they are supposed to do and therefore do not directly express anger. Although Mary's priest-brother left home against his mother's wishes, he still belongs to mother; that is, he is available on call, as we see from the case material, and he supposedly remains celibate. Family members also try to hide anger. Mary's father generally keeps his anger locked up with him in the basement. While family members try to keep their anger under control, sometimes it cannot be contained. Family arguments come in "bursts." When the anger can't be contained anymore, it bursts out, just as steam escapes from a pot when the lid is removed. One important analytic effort would be to help Mary become aware of her aggression and the defenses that hold it in check.

To consider how Mary deals with her aggression, we look at her defenses. My effort would be to get the energy that is bound up in the defense structure to join again to the personality. Mary has not found her active aggression. She is passive-aggressive. She learned passive-aggression from her parents, who do not communicate well with each other. She fights her mother passive-aggressively. She is compulsively defiant in a passive-aggressive way. For example, she "defeats" her mother passive-aggressively by failing in college. Obviously, graduating from college is an accomplishment I assume her mother wants her to achieve. By not graduating, she "gets back" at her mother. Obviously, too, this defense is not serving Mary in a good way. We saw Mary's passive-aggressive behavior, at the beginning of treatment, toward the analyst as well. This was evident with her late arrival.

Mary uses the defenses of reaction formation also. Another way Mary holds her original aggressive drive in check is doing the opposite of what she really wants to do, while the opposing attitude still exists in the unconscious. The point is that Mary cannot let out or own up to her aggressiveness. For example, Mary tries to please people. This was clearly illustrated by the second vignette, in which Mary could not maintain her boyfriend and her friends who did not like her boyfriend. She felt that everyone had to be pleased, and it was an impossible task. In order to please the people around her, she felt she had to leave the relationship or her friends. Only then would she experience no dissatisfaction from them. Another example of the reaction formation is when she "makes nice" to the therapist.

A third defense mechanism used by Mary is reversal. With the therapist, Mary plays the role that her mother plays with her. That is, she is tough with the therapist in the same way that Mary's mother is "tough" with Mary. In the course of treatment, the analyst would refuse to play the victim role. This would enable Mary to have a relearning emotional experience and allow Mary to be a nonvictim. Or, stated differently, her treatment would show her another way of being, other than that of victim.

Mary does not have a benign permissive conscience. Rather, she has an unrelenting superego. She sees herself as her mother sees her: bad, unworthy, fat, stupid, and unsociable. In drive-theory language, she has incorporated the "introject" of her mother. Stated differently, her mother's superego is incorporated in her. Because she sees herself as her mother sees her, she does not "sponsor" herself. We see this again and again. We see it in her initial choice of a man; she chooses a man who is not good to her. One could also conceptualize her "failing behaviors" (failing college, failing on jobs, and poor impressions on job interviews) as evidence of not sponsoring herself.

## Object-Relations Theory

Object-relations theory is relevant to Mary. While the case material does not focus on the first two or three years of life, I believe that many of Mary's problems stem from this preverbal, preoedipal period. It is during this period that one forms a core orientation and inner representation toward others, a core orientation toward one's own impulses and affects, and a core boundary formation and feeling about self. As I consider Mary and object-relations theory, I will focus on (1) separation-individuation, (2) object representations, and (3) self-representations.

### *Separation-Individuation*

There is a difference between pathology of the relation to the *differentiated other* and pathology of the relation to the *undifferentiated other*. Mary is aware of separateness. Mary is aware of self-other differentiation. Clearly her language implies a sense of self-feeling. For example, Dr. Zager states, "*She* didn't feel that she really knew who *she* was." We know that Mary is aware of self-other differentiation as she indicates what she thinks her problems are. Mary tells Dr. Zager that she wants to be *herself*. She tells her that she wants to break loose from her mother. And she talks of her *self-image*. In addition, she seems related and somewhat articulate; she does not sound like someone who is "not there."

While Mary is aware of her separateness, she is not individuated. Mary's problem lies in the area of individuation. Mary is a "self as nobody." Mary's mother expects her to be a nobody, a nonself, and Mary has become a nobody for her mother. Mary has found a way of keeping her mother; this way involves Mary's giving up her own feelings. "What should I do?" she asks her mother. And her mother responds. It seems that Mary's mother does not treat Mary as a separate other. Rather, Mary's mother treats Mary as an extension of herself.

Engagement with fathers is important in the separation and individuation process. Unfortunately, Mary's contact with her father in infrequent. We are told that Mary typically sees him only when she takes his dinner down to the basement each evening or when there is a family argument over some major issue. In many ways he is an absent father. If he were more available, perhaps Mary could experience in relation to him a sense of individuated selfhood that her close and demanding relationship with her mother does not allow. That is, the father is an *other*. He is the differentiated parent. In relation to her father, Mary could experience separateness and differentness. At the same time she turns to her father, she would not have to give up mother in the process. With her father, however, it is possible that Mary could resolve issues of individuation.

## Object Representations

According to object-relations theory, the first relationship—the relationship we knew as infants in relation to mother—is repeated in adult relationships. That is, there is a tendency to reenact the primary way of being and relating. We see that Mary repeats her relationship with her mother, in that her relationships have qualities that are reminiscent of her first relationship. She repeats aspects of this early relationship in her relationships with men, girlfriends, and her therapist. For example, Mary experiences a lot of criticism in her adult relationships. Her first boyfriend was abusive and critical. Her friends are critical. And her performances at her job and in school lead to criticism. Possibly she "pulled" for criticism from her therapist as well by arriving late to some sessions. Clearly, Mary selects friends and engages in behaviors that will lead to a reenactment of her early relationship with mother.

In addition, Mary structures relationships in a way that results in intense attachment and dependence. With her therapist, for example, she asked for opinions and guidance. We also see this in her attempt to be the "good little girl." She tries to do what she thinks her therapist wants her to do, at least in some ways. She tries to please her friends as well. When her friends are displeased with her boyfriend, for example, she drops her friends.

## Self-Representations

We know that she has incorporated her mother's criticism and that she sees herself as bad, unworthy, stupid, fat, and unsociable. We understand that this is related to her having internalized the bad object (the bad mother) and along with it the infantile parts of the ego that interacted with these objects. The point is that her internal psychological reality or inner object world affects her emotional state and her perception of external reality.

## Expected Course of Treatment

In summary, drive theory helps us to see that Mary is unable to accept her thoughts and urges, and in this chapter I spoke of Mary's aggression. Mary is angry at her mother's controlling behavior and at her dependence on mother. She also feels guilty about her anger. Mary deals with her aggression by passive-aggressive behavior and by reaction formation. The former is exemplified by her failing college and "failing" job interviews and jobs. The latter is exemplified by her "make nice" behavior. These behaviors, in general, do not serve her well. Drive theory also helps us to see her unrelenting superego. Mary sees herself as her mother sees her, and she has incorporated the introject of her mother.

When we consider object-relations theory, we can see that Mary is aware of her separateness and that her problem lies in individuation. Basically, Mary keeps mother by giving up her own feelings, and mother expects Mary to be a nonself. Also, we see that Mary is reenacting in her adult relationships something from the past. We see an early mode of being and relating played out in the present. Mary is actively creating and searching for situations in which she experiences criticisms from others that she received from her mother. She searches out and creates relationships in which she is attached and dependent.

Mary was described by the referral source at the onset of treatment as needy, dependent (especially on her mother), and with poor self-concept. Dr. Zager indicates that treatment ended when Mary left for Italy. It appears that Dr. Zager may have felt that (1) treatment terminated prematurely; (2) Mary found a new family (her husband's) on which to be dependent; and (3) Mary's intrapsychic problems remain. Dr. Zager does indicate, however, that at the end of their work, Mary was more assertive and self-assured and was able to settle into what is described as a happy relationship. Dr. Zager has obviously helped Mary in some important ways. I will describe how Mary and I may have worked together in order to achieve a desired change.

Interpretation can occur in the context of abstinence or support. Abstinence involves, for example,, nongratification of the patient's wishes, neutrality, objectivity, and impersonality. An example of abstinence would be my abstaining from answering the question "Should I rebel against my mother?" Rather than answer this question, I would focus on why Mary wanted me to tell her whether she should rebel against her mother, why she felt she could not decide herself, and what it would mean to Mary to rebel or not to rebel against her mother. Support involves a way of speaking or relating that helps the patient to deal with interpretations. Development occurs under conditions of optimal abstinence and support. Both abstinence and support lead to growth. Thus, I would attempt to balance frustration and support.

Analysis of transference is an important part of analytic work. It is part of interpretation, and it involves moving issues from Mary and her mother, for example, to Mary and the analyst. In analysis of transference, the focus of interpretation is to help the patient recognize herself as an active agent. We saw in the course of treatment that Mary was angry that she was dependent on her therapist. We know that she was angry that she was dependent on her mother. Mary dealt with her anger at the therapist, at least initially, as she usually does—by passive-aggressive behavior. I would analyze this passive-aggressive late behavior. I would analyze it, reanalyze it, and analyze it again. In this way, I would give her a corrective experience, and she would learn a new way to express anger.

There would be an analysis of defenses as well. I assume Mary would become angrier and angrier at me as she became more and more dependent on me. I assume that she would next begin to "fail" in therapy as she failed in college. "Failing" would be her passive-aggressive way to express her anger, and of course this would be interpreted.

Internalized object and self relations would also be dealt with through the analysis of transference. There would be a repetition in the analysis of the internalized objects, and I, as the analyst, would interpret them. The aim, of course, would be to enable Mary to approach future relationships in a fresh way, without the baggage from her earliest object relations. For example, Mary would probably think I saw her in a negative way, just as she felt her mother did. This would be interpreted. I might say something like "The fact that your mother said you were fat and stupid leads you to expect me to say and think that also."

What else might I do as I worked with Mary? Clearly I would be empathic. I would feel with her, and over time, she would experience my caring. There would be a matter-of-fact acceptance of her impulse life as well. Mary needs to express her anger, and she needs to experience acceptance of this anger. It is important that her anger not be followed by rejection or retaliation. In time, Mary would begin to accept herself and her urges as I accepted them. Mary's superego and the way Mary views herself would also alter. Mary would gradually feel better about herself. She would come to realize that she was valued as I listened, as I saw what Mary had previously thought was unacceptable, and as I accepted Mary.

In some ways, the relationship between the therapist and Mary is similar to a parent-child relationship. Obviously there are differences, and Mary is not a child. However, Mary would use the therapist as a child uses a parent. She would use the analyst as someone to identify with, to learn from, and to be supported and affirmed by. In the course of treatment, Mary would grow and develop.

What would happen to Mary in an analysis or psychoanalytically oriented psychotherapy? Mary would become better able to cope with the internal problems of living. In time, she would see herself as the navigator of her life rather than a passive victim. She would assume responsibility for her life and her actions. She would learn that to a great extent, she can create her life and is responsible for both the negative and positive patterns that emerge in interpersonal relationships.

Finally, how might Mary's treatment have differed if she were in treatment with a male therapist? Theoretically, in the course of a complete analysis, both maternal and paternal transferences are established and worked through. In practice, however, all analyses are not complete. Countertransferential issues may differ, based on the analyst's gender. Countertransferentially, some female analysts may be more comfortable with preoedipal transferences than with erotic or aggressive oedipal transferences. Also, it is difficult for some male analysts to acknowledge that they are perceived and responded to as if they were women. Some male analysts may be more comfortable with oedipal transferences than preoedipal, given concerns about passivity and/or castration fear, and concern about merger with a powerful mother. There are believed to be differences in *treatment process* based on the analyst's gender. Usually the initial transference is consistent with the analyst's gender, and that transference (maternal or paternal) is experienced more intensely and is inescapable.

Mary needed to work on the preoedipal issues of separation-individuation. In this light, it was particularly beneficial that Mary was in treatment with a woman. The closeness with a female analyst seems to pull for preoedipal maternal transferences early, more intensely, and inescapably. It appears that the presence of a woman therapist enabled Mary to deal with such classical transferences as separation-individuation issues, dependency issues, and defiance-compliance with the preoedipal mother. In time, she would probably present paternal transferences and particularly an erotic oedipal father transference.

Thus, in a complete analysis, the treatment *process* would differ, depending on whether Mary saw a male or female analyst. Theoretically, treatment outcome is comparable in a complete analysis. Although what would have transpired in Mary's treatment with a male analyst is qualitatively different from what would transpire with a female analyst, a successful resolution of problematic issues could be achieved in a *complete* analysis with either a male or a female analyst.

# REFERENCES

Alpert, J. L. (1989). Contemporary psychoanalytic developmental theory. In H. Tierney (Ed.), *Women's studies encyclopedia*. Westport, CT: Greenwood Press.

Balint, M. (1965). *Primary love and psycho-analytic technique*. New York: Liveright.

Eagle, M. (1984). *Recent developments in psychoanalysis: A critical evaluation*. New York: McGraw-Hill.

Fairbairn, W. R. D. (1952). *An object relations theory of the personality*. New York: Basic Books.

Goldberg, A. (Ed.). (1984). *How does analysis cure? Heinz Kohut*. Chicago: University of Chicago Press.

Greenberg, J. R., & Mitchell, S. A. (1983). *Object relations in psychoanalytic theory*. Cambridge, MA: Harvard University Press.

Guntrip, H. (1971). *Psychoanalytic theory, therapy, and the self: A basic guide to the human personality in Freud, Erikson, Klein, Sullivan, Fairbairs, Hartmann, Jacobson, & Winnicott*. New York: Basic Books.

Hartmann, H. (1964). *Essays on ego psychology*. New York: International Universities Press.

Jacobson, E. (1964). *The self and the object world*. New York: International Universities Press.

Kernberg, D. (1980). *Internal world and external reality*. New York: Jason Aronson.

Klein, M. (1964). *Contributions to psychoanalysis, 1921–1945*. New York: McGraw-Hill.

Kohut, H. (1971). *The analysis of the self*. New York: International Universities Press.

Kohut, H. (1977). *The restoration of the self*. New York: International Universities Press.

Mahler, M. (1974). Symbiosis and individuation: The psychological birth of the human infant. In *The selected papers of Margaret Mahler* (Vol. 2). New York: Jacob Aronson.

Mitchell, S. (1984). Object relations and the developmental tilt. *Contemporary Psychoanalysis, 20*(4), 473–499.

Pine, F. (1985). *Developmental theory and clinical process*. New Haven, CT: Yale University Press.

Pine, F. (1989). Motivation, personality organization, and the four psychologies of psychoanalysis. *Journal of the American Psychoanalytic Association, 37*, 27–60.

Pulver, S. E. (Ed.). (1987). How theory shapes technique: Perspectives on a clinical study. *Psychoanalytic Inquiry, 7*(2), 141–299.

Reed, G. S. (1987). Rules of clinical understanding in classical psychoanalysis and in self psychology: A comparison. *Journal of the American Psychoanalytic Association, 35*(2), 421–446.

Schafer, R. (1987, August). Discussant. In R. V. Frankiel (Chair), *Preparation for analysis in the face of massive resistance*. Symposium conducted at the meeting of the American Psychological Association, New York.

Sullivan, H. S. (1962). *Schizophrenia as a human process*. New York: Norton.

Sullivan, H. S. (1964). *The fusion of psychiatry and social science*. New York: Norton.

Winnicott, D. W. (1965). *The maturational process and the facilitating environment*. New York: International Universities Press.

# 6

# A Feminist Therapist
# Views the Case

## Lenore E. A. Walker

## AN OVERVIEW OF PRINCIPLES OF
## FEMINIST THERAPY

The principles of feminist therapy grew out of the women's movement that began in the late 1960s. Feminists, highly critical of traditional psychotherapy theories, claimed that psychotherapy served to keep women oppressed and "in their place." Assisting women to adapt to unhappy home lives was in opposition to the goals of the feminist movement, among which were to empower women, celebrate in their strength and uniqueness, and reduce barriers toward achieving equality between women and men in every area of life. In addition to criticisms of the therapist's behavior, the theories underlying psychotherapy systems were attacked for accepting and perpetuating sex-role stereotyped behavior.

Although there have been many critiques of all existing psychotherapy theories (see Dutton-Douglas & Walker, 1988), it is fair to say that psychoanalysis initially was the main target of the feminists. Freud and his erroneous views of "little girls' fantasies of sex with their fathers" placed an undue emphasis on adaptation to sex-role socialization as a way for women to achieve happiness. In this schema, all women developed incompletely because they envied men the penis they could never have. Freudian theory suggests that one way they could feel like a "whole" person was by giving birth to a boy who had the coveted penis. Marriage and the inevitable role of women serving their husbands and children was seen as the height of women's lives; anything less than that would be indicative of serious mental illness. For example, the term *hysteria*, a form of mental illness that was frequently diagnosed in women, had its origin in the belief that a woman's uterus (that is barren, of course) is wandering and needs to be brought back to its proper place to allow the woman to fulfill her natural role as mother and, it is implied, homemaker (see Lerman, 1986, for a more complete discussion of feminist critiques of psychoanalysis).

In addition to critiques of all psychotherapy theories as gender-biased, the feminist movement also examined the issue of mental-health standards for men and women. Chesler (1972), in her now classic study of women's mental health, found that women were often labeled mentally ill for political rather than objective reasons. Being branded with a diagnosis of mental illness that sometimes leads to involuntary hospitalization was (and still is) a punishment for women not adhering to the expected sex-role standards. Although it is now taken for granted that certain diagnostic categories occur in high frequency for women (Russo, 1984), those revelations were just beginning to be publicly acknowledged in the early 1970s. Psychotherapists were found to hold different standards for mental health for women and men in another classic study (Broverman, Broverman, Clarkson, Rosencrantz, & Vogel, 1970). They asked therapists to list characteristics necessary for one to be considered a "normal" male, female, and person. Interestingly, they found that the "normal" male and "normal" person were ascribed the same characteristics—intellectual, rational, aggressive, and others usually thought to be necessary to be successful in today's society, while those ascribed to women were more passive, nurturing, and emotional. Women were not considered to have the requisite characteristics to be mentally healthy persons. Of course, this resulted in a double bind for women. If they had the characteristics of normally healthy women, they were not considered normally mentally healthy people! Most therapists ignored the double bind inherent in such sexist theory and simply directed their female clients toward becoming normally healthy women. No wonder they were accused of perpetuating the sex-role stereotypes rampant in society! Unfortunately, despite a greater awareness of gender issues, therapists have not changed their attitudes much in the past 20 years (Rosencrantz, DeLorey, & Broverman, 1985).

Unlike other psychotherapy theories, feminist therapy does not have one specific leader, as it grew out of the grass-roots movement that encompassed feminist ideas. Feminist women therapists throughout the United States and the rest of the world began to apply feminist tenets to a new therapy philosophy that encouraged women not to adapt to the limiting social and cultural stereotypes but to move toward equality. Dutton-Douglas and Walker (1988), Rosewater and Walker (1985), and Walker (1984) provide historical as well as explanatory material documenting the development of feminist therapy. Dutton-Douglas and Walker (1988) suggest that there are three phases in the development of feminist-therapy theory. The first phase, which has just been discussed, began in the early 1970s and lasted about 10 years. It developed an activist approach and borrowed techniques from other therapies that fit within feminist philosophy. The goal of early feminist psychotherapy was to empower all women by strengthening individual women. This goal is reflected in one of the feminist tenets, "the personal is political," meaning that what affects one woman affects all women.

The second phase, which began shortly after the earlier development of feminist therapy itself, is the mainstreaming of feminism into other therapy theories. After the application of a political gender analysis to mainstream therapy theories, particularly those that are reported in this book, feminists began to try to eliminate the more sexist parts of the theory while keeping those sections that made theoretical sense. Jean Baker Miller and her colleagues at the Stone Center, Wellesley College, have been looking at the notion of women's development of a relational self rather than the theories of autonomy that have dominated the psychodynamic theories (Kaplan & Surrey, 1984). Some feminist-therapy theorists believe that salvaging psychoanalytic theory is an impossible process and have concentrated on developing a new theory (Brown, 1988; Cammaert & Larsen, 1988; Lerman, 1986; Rosewater, 1988), although many of the modified theories and techniques are integrated within the new feminist theory too.

The third phase is ongoing and concerns the development of a complete theory together with developmental explanations for the common experiences of women who grow up in societies that do not value them for their full range of individual capabilities. The theory holds that there are situational factors for women who live in a male-oriented world that devalue women separate and apart from individual factors arising out of women's personal backgrounds that combine and impact on an individual woman's mental health. Integrated within feminist developmental theory are the ethnic, racial, and cultural conditions that women of color experience as well as other oppressing situational factors such as bias against class and age (Brown & Root, in press). This theory questions the notion that certain behaviors are a product of an individual's distortion and asserts that they are coping skills developed as a way to survive in an oppressive world. A feminist theory of women's development, separate and different from men's, has been presented by Conarton and Silverman (1989).

The tenets of feminist-therapy theory were clearly articulated by the various therapists who were developing the new therapy in different parts of the world, even though they had little communication with one another. These tenets have grown out of the feminist philosophy and include

- *Egalitarian* relationships between therapist and client as a model for women to take personal responsibility to develop egalitarian relationships with others instead of the more traditional passive, dependent female role. The therapist and the client are not considered equal in their skills; obviously the therapist is usually better trained in psychology, but the client knows herself better, and that knowledge is as critical as the therapist's skills to make the therapy relationship succeed.
- *Power* in relationships and independence for women. Women are taught to look at ways of gaining and using power and control in relationships, and the consequences. For example, while early feminist therapists found it important to teach assertiveness to women—that is, to train women to identify their own rights and then learn how to be assertive in asking for what they want—it also became apparent that there were prices to pay for acting assertively in many business and social situations (Fodor, 1985). However, although tempering the encouragement of taking power by discussing the realities of many situations, feminist therapy celebrates the strength of women.
- *Enhancement of women's strengths* rather than remediation of their weaknesses. Learning to look at one's own strengths and to admire them is a new experience for many women who are busy supporting others' strengths and ignoring their own. A model of the selfless nurturer who spends her whole life as a caregiver often encourages the examination of the individual's faults rather than looking at her positive qualities. Acceptance of the other's blame and subsequent personal scrutiny is encouraged in the recipient of her nurturance, who becomes concerned when she isn't meeting expectations that stress attention to this person's needs. When it is a man who makes the complaints, such as accusing the woman of

not performing the wifely duties that he believes he is entitled to, it is even more likely that the self-blame will become part of her personal guilt and needs to be reframed or cognitively restructured into less biased generalizations.

- *Nonpathology-oriented and non-victim-blaming*, rejecting the medical model commonly used in other therapies such as psychodynamic theories. Women's problems are seen as a combination of situational factors, genetic components (some call it a level of hardiness), and intrapsychic personality characteristics. Behavior is observed and analyzed for its coping or adaptation qualities rather than labeling it pathology. One particular area of concern for many feminist therapists is the proliferation of personality-disorder diagnoses that are gender-biased and easily confused with the characteristics of a woman who exhibits traditional socialization features. Victims of men's violence are not considered mentally unhealthy; rather, their behaviors are understood as part of the coping process necessary to survive that violence.

- *Education*, as a way to change some of the cognitions that are detrimental to enhancement of women's strengths. Sex-role socialization patterns can be understood and relearned, especially when women bond together and give one another support. The movement's slogan, Sisterhood is Powerful, is applied in group therapy that may even result in some kind of collective activism. Women are encouraged to learn more about the condition of women, and *bibliotherapy* is frequently an adjunct to psychotherapy. The therapist is more a teacher and facilitator than an authoritarian doctor who tells her patients how to live. Although a healing model is advocated, it is an educational rather than ameliorative and reparative model.

- *Acceptance and validation of feelings*. Feminist therapists are more self-disclosing than other therapists, and removal of the we-they barrier between women therapists and their clients is a feminist goal that is thought to enhance the relationship (Brown & Walker, 1990). This permits more empathic connections around issues brought up in therapy.

Feminist-therapy theory also has selected several issues that need to be raised during therapy because of their frequency in interfering with women's mental health. These include the identification and expression of *angry feelings; women's sexuality; self-nurturance; relationships with parents, spouse, children, and friends;* and *victimization experiences.* The emphasis on sociocultural influence on mental health also dictates the need to spend time on understanding its impact on an individual woman. A special sensitivity is expected towards those women who have experienced other aspects of society known to be oppressive to individuals who are members of such targeted groups, such as those experiencing racial discrimination, ethnic bias, and discrimination against age, able-bodiedness, sexual orientation, class or financial means.

Feminist therapy also calls for a particular knowledge base for those therapists treating women (see APA-Division 17's *Guidelines for Counseling and Psychotherapy with Women*, 1981, that has been adopted by many other APA divisions). Developmental issues are attended to, and special stages where resolution of conflict is known to be difficult for many women is attended to by feminist therapists. For example, it is expected that a woman will have greater difficulty in separating from a family where ethnic and cultural ties are strong than from one in which they have less importance, so a feminist therapist would be less likely to diagnose and treat such a client with separation issues as having a major disorder.

Finally, feminist therapy has a good track record with certain disorders that have been more resistant to other types of therapy. This is particularly true in cases of women who have been battered by their partners and/or experienced incest and other forms of childhood and adult sexual abuse such as acquaintance or stranger rape, sexual exploitation by a previous therapist or other trusted professional. Many of these clients have developed anxiety and avoidance reactions often expressed as a posttraumatic stress disorder or more traditional disorders such as phobias, panic attacks, other severe-anxiety reactions and eating disorders. The feelings of betrayal associated with victimization by someone who demonstrates both cruel and loving behavior toward a woman make subsequent treatment difficult since the ability to establish a trusting relationship is impaired. The earlier-described rules that govern feminist therapist-client relationships make it a comfortable therapy process for those who have been damaged by significant relationships.

Feminist therapy has begun to be applied to men (Ganley, 1988), children (Walker & Bolkovatz, 1988), racial minorities (Mays & Comas-Dias, 1988; Brown & Root, in press), and the elderly (Midlarsky, 1988), populations that have typically not been well served previously. Its philosophy has affected every other major therapy system, as will be evidenced in the other presentations in this book. Its philosophy is consistent with natural, holistic methods of healing that make its practice exciting for those therapists and clients engaged in it.

## FEMINIST THERAPY WITH MARY

Mary is a feminist therapist's ideal client; her presenting problems are commonly seen in clients that select a feminist therapist for treatment. Mary's problems tend to cluster in several main areas: difficulty in accepting her family's power and control over her life, ambivalence in accepting the cultural and sex-role socialization patterns standard for a first-generation Italian Catholic girl, lack of confidence in her intellectual competency, inability to decide on a career or even get a job, and poor social skills resulting in destructive romantic relationships.

## Feminist Analysis of Presenting Problems

It is obvious that the presenting information was not gathered by a feminist therapist; the data concentrates on all of the problem areas in Mary's life, and little information is given about her strengths. A feminist-therapy treatment plan builds on the client's strengths initially. In Mary's case, it would be important to know what she perceives as her past successes. Although there is plenty of information provided about Mary's conflicts between independence and dependence, autonomy and family relatedness, competency and skill deficits, to do a proper feminist analysis we would need more information so that the therapist could understand what the client had learned from her unique family and life experiences that affect her current functioning and what she has internalized from being a woman in a sexist society that does not value women.

It shall be assumed, for the purposes of this analysis, that the messages she reports receiving as a 22-year-old woman are similar to those she heard when she was younger. For Mary, this includes the powerful message that the world is an unsafe place for a girl/woman who is unprotected by males or the watchful eye of her mother. Given the experiences of most girls and women in our sexist society, this message can be expected to have been continuously reinforced. The developmentally age-appropriate ambivalence between independence and dependence, then, takes on additional anxiety that being independent is dangerous for a first-generation Italian Catholic woman and will need to be approached from a variety of perspectives in a successful therapy encounter.

In looking for Mary's strengths, important for a feminist therapist, there are a number of indications from which they can be inferred. One strength that stands out is the fact that she does have the ability to complete a college curriculum (despite her emotional difficulties) and perhaps fears that graduation will force her out into the unsafe world or back into her protected but intolerable home situation. In fact, her ability to perceive college as a safe extension of her home environment suggests that her anxieties around safety issues can be reduced enough to permit her to participate in some independent situations calling for intellectual and social competence. Therapy should help Mary identify other such safe situations to begin with and create new ones as it progresses.

I have made the assumption that getting an education is also considered a safe activity by Mary's mother, whose own anxieties could be the
source of those learned by Mary. In fact, the relationship between Mary
and her mother is one of the more important areas that successful feminist therapy will focus upon at some time during the therapy process.
Although the therapist will raise the issue whenever appropriate, it is
expected that it will be dealt with slowly, as Mary is ready. This is important because Mary seems to have the ability to negate her own
strengths in order to avoid growing up and accepting the inevitable separation from her mother. It is also possible that not conforming to her
mother's demands will precipitate the loss of any relationship with
Mary's mother, at least temporarily.

Developmentally, young women in their early twenties sometimes
perceive greater safety in remaining a child under the domination of an
anxious and nonnurturing mother, rather than tolerate the anxiety of
being independent, guilt at having been disobedient, and permanent
loss of any maternal approval and affection. If Mary perceived her
mother's intrusive and hostile behavior toward her as coming from the
mother's need to assert her critical, judgmental attitude because she
must control what she fears might be Mary's potentially unsafe behavior, then rejecting it raises the possibility that when Mary experiences
the normal difficulties in life, she will attribute them to her mother's rejection of her. This attitude, of course, gives Mary's mother an enormous control and power over Mary's life, and Mary needs to learn how
to take responsibility for using her own power and control.

It is common for mothers who have been harmed by men's abusive
behavior to pass down their fears to their daughters. Although we do
not have such information about Mary's mother, Mary's comments
about her mother suggest commonalities often found among other battered women. A feminist therapist would try to get more information
from Mary about the possibility that her mother was battered and
whether Mary witnessed the abuse. It is assumed that a combination of
sex-role stereotypes; socialization experiences; strong religious, cultural,
and ethnic factors; and individual anxieties and fears have also helped
shape Mary's mother's world view.

Certainly, being taken to America by a man she hardly knew, far from her
family in Italy, must have been a traumatic experience for this woman. Her
inability and unwillingness to learn English or venture much beyond the
borders of her Italian neighborhood could only have reinforced her fears for
her children, who have more ability to move out further in the world. She
may have adopted her critical and harsh style of relating as a means of controlling her own anxiety when her children stray from the "safe" path rather
than being unloving or nonaccepting of Mary. It is important to know about

Mary's mother's world view as Mary seems to have learned much it, yet is struggling with its inevitable behavioral consequences.

It is interesting that the mother's message of danger in the larger world has been passed on to her sons as well as Mary. The father's withdrawal to the basement of their building may also be a result of her fears or an acceptable expression of his own fears as an Italian immigrant. We are told that Mary's oldest brother became a priest (which may be considered a protected occupation) and lives in a parish within driving distance. The second-oldest brother is living at home and works as a salesman. As there is no mention of intimate relationships for either son, it can be assumed that socializing was discouraged for them too. It can also be inferred that each of the sons has struggled with independence-dependence issues similar to Mary's. However, it is Mary who has been singled out to spend her life being her parents' caretaker, thus creating even more of a dilemma for her.

Mary, like her brothers, has been struggling with following the strict moral values of the family while also wanting to become a part of her friends' world. She likes the label of being a "good girl" and does not seem to be struggling about no-smoking, no-drinking, no-drugs, and no-sex values. Her sailing trip is an example of how difficult were the choices that she was being forced to make. Simply going off on an adventure with friends was viewed as a rejection of the family and their values by all the members. It provides a clue to the narrow margin of independent behavior Mary will be allowed to engage in without full-force confrontation with the family. The hostile, critical, unyieldingly accusatory treatment from her family after she went on the sailing trip without their approval was simply too much for Mary to handle, and she retreated from trying to become her own person, apparently even giving up her friends. This information provides another clue to Mary's current tolerance of disapproval by her family.

Reversal of Mary's inability to feel powerful as an independent person without the complete approval from her mother (or other family members or therapist) would be a major goal of feminist therapy. Attainment of this goal would be measured by changes in how Mary felt about herself, evidence of greater self-confidence, Mary's interaction with other significant people in her life (including her mother), her career choices, and her relationship with the therapist.

## Feminist Treatment Approach

### Setting the Stage

One of the first issues that needs to be raised in feminist therapy concerns the relationship between Mary and the therapist. The attention paid to *power dynamics* between therapist and client will help establish the *egalitarian nature of the relationship* and provide a model from which Mary can learn to take control of her life. It is predictable that it will be difficult for Mary to share the power of the therapy relationship with the therapist, as her background of having been raised to submit to authority figures and her dependence upon their approval before she takes any action would make it easier for her to submit to the therapist's authority. However, feminist therapy is uniquely qualified to help set up structures for Mary to assume more and more of her own power as she becomes ready by jointly building the structure initially.

One way to accomplish this task is for the therapist to develop a *mutual goal-attainment plan* with Mary at the conclusion of the session in which they agree to begin therapy together. If I were Mary's therapist, based on the information she presents at the first session, I would tell her that it is my impression that she wants to become more independent but doesn't know how to do that and still have a relationship with her mother. Also, I would suggest that she wants to feel better about herself and find a comfortable role in life. I would assure her that these are issues people deal with in therapy.

I would stop at this point and check whether she thinks I have accurately pinpointed her major concerns. If she does not agree, I would listen to her explanation, ask her further explanatory questions, and incorporate the details in a revised statement. For example, if Mary says she knows that she cannot have a relationship with her mother if she pursues independent actions, I would modify the statement to reflect her more positive opinion. Thus, I might say, "Mary, it seems that you want to be independent but you think you cannot still have a relationship with your mother if you go ahead with your wishes, so you aren't sure which you want—to follow your own way or follow your mother's plans for you. Whatever you choose doesn't seem to feel good for you."

*Reframing* the statement by incorporating Mary's comments and adding an affirmative but matter-of-fact statement of her feelings accomplishes several purposes. First, it tells Mary that you are listening closely to what she says. Second, it validates her statements and helps her value her own thoughts and feelings. Third, it helps Mary see herself as a partner in therapy. Fourth, it decreases the need to view the therapist as the all-knowing authoritarian source of what is right for Mary.

Once she agrees, or seems to have contributed at least something to the formation of the statement, I would proceed to develop an *informal contract* that explains how therapy can try to help Mary find out whether her assumption is accurate. That is, will she have to give up a relationship with her mother if she pursues her own independence, and how can she monitor her own feelings as she goes about her therapy journey? I would then describe how we could proceed, including discussing the need for me to get to know her better so that I could help her look at many options from which she can choose.

Each step in this process needs to be approved by Mary in order not to raise her guilt level so high that she will continue to be stuck at the no-decision point. It is expected that Mary will be frightened about becoming too dependent upon the therapist as therapy progresses.

One way to deal with her fears is for the therapist to become a real person rather than permit her to project her own image of a therapist. *Self-disclosure* is a tool used by feminist therapists to assist in this demystification process. Of course, only selective information about the therapist is disclosed, according to the client's needs. In Mary's case it might be important for her to know that her therapist has worked with other young women who have had a similar problem, believes that some of the problem is natural for a woman her age to be struggling with, is or is not a mother herself (this would be disclosed only if it seems appropriate; e.g., if Mary is insistent that she is ungrateful and selfish for not treating her mother better), and has experienced some double binds herself because it is difficult for women to be independent without feeling guilty, fearful, and unrewarded. This establishes that the therapist does not view Mary as hopeless or crazy, gives her hope that she can resolve her problems, and underscores the fact that they are both women in a world that sometimes treats women unkindly just because they are female.

## Therapy Sessions

The emphasis in the beginning of feminist therapy would be to continue gathering information about Mary, using an open-ended question-and-narrative-answer approach. I typically suggest to a new client that she tell me about experiences that she liked best. This places the interaction on a positive note and underscores the message that she is not a complete failure and does indeed like some things about herself that work fairly well. Mary would be encouraged to describe things in a narrative mode, and I would ask questions if she slows down or is unable to give me certain details, so that I could understand her experience.

Initially, I try to ask fewer questions if she is talking freely. This reinforces her need to believe I will listen to what she has to say nonjudgmentally. I make mental notes about her style of recounting episodes, looking for consistencies and inconsistencies, meanings of relationships, areas in which she puts herself down, feelings she expresses or omits, and natural reinforcers. I would be particularly interested in episodes that are pleasant for her with and without connection to her mother or family.

Usually, in each session, I try to pick out one or two areas where she may get stuck *with negative self-images* and try to use *cognitive restructuring techniques* to help her look at the situations in a different way. For example, with Mary it can be assumed that she might describe her older brother's behavior in an almost reverent way that highlights his role as enforcer of her mother's fears. I would suggest alternative images of him—perhaps that her brother may also have been placed in the double-bind she is now in and chose to go into the priesthood and help enforce her mother's wishes as a way of reducing his own anxiety at trying to be somewhat independent. She is free to accept, modify, or reject this hypothesis. We may even be able to go one step further and discuss what impact being the oldest male might have had on her brother's relationship with her. If she is willing to pursue this avenue of inquiry, a next step would be to ask her to *describe the sex-role patterns* in her family as well as in other first-generation Italian Catholic families. In fact, each one of these groups might be broken down individually before they are put together. Thus, stereotyped expectations for those children born to immigrants (Italian boys and girls) and Catholics would be discussed first. If Mary is unaware of the stereotypes, she might be given a homework assignment to find them out, using observations, interviews, and reference materials.

The above exercise might be continued over more than one therapy session, and Mary would be asked to describe her mother's expectations for herself, both here in America and in Italy. Once those are described, Mary would be asked if she could divide them up into role categories; for example, which expectations come from being a woman, a wife, a mother, a daughter, a member of the Italian-American community, a Catholic. It is expected that Mary might not know many of these expectations in any other way than viewing them as unreasonable demands on her.

This exercise would help her learn to view her mother as a person with connections to other ideals, people, and places besides Mary and the family. If she has to go out and dig for the information, it may even provide her with a different perspective on her mother. Hopefully, it will help her see her mother as a person and reduce some of the powerful hold her mother has on her. Perhaps, she may even be able to ask her mother questions about her history that can provide a more equal way to relate to each other. I sometimes find having a daughter ask her mother to see pictures or describe stories of her life at a similar age helps realign the balance of power in their relationship. Obviously, these techniques might take place over a number of therapy sessions and might even have to be repeated more than once, depending on Mary's readiness.

In helping Mary try *to make informed choices about what she wants to do with the rest of her life,* feminist therapy would concentrate on the realities of the economic situation and the client's strengths, interests, and ability to make decisions for herself. The history suggests that Mary is about to complete college, but we do not know what her major has been, nor do we know her career options. Since therapy is taking place during the time she makes her decision to return for an additional year of school to change her major so that she doesn't have to retake for a fourth time the course that she keeps failing, in feminist therapy all of her options would have been described, and her decision-making process would have been monitored. It is expected that she will discuss some of the course work in at least one of the vignettes she gives when describing things she has enjoyed. Perhaps a graduate-school program, so that she can gain further skills in an areas she enjoys and is competent in, would be an option for Mary when she is having difficulty in getting a job. At some point, it will be necessary to concentrate on Mary's feelings when she is successful in an independent task. It seems clear that she has attached some of the emotional anxiety and guilty feelings to tasks in which she feels competent, making it difficult for her to become *economically independent*. Helping her identify the conflicting feelings she experiences when engaging in a competent or independent activity will be necessary for her to learn how to separate the positive feelings of success from the negative ones expected from home.

## Dealing with Feelings

Since *anger* is a feeling Mary has not allowed herself to acknowledge, it will be important for her to discuss her associations with the emotion cognitively until she can allow herself to experience angry feelings. An *educational approach* may be used here to help Mary get in touch with the variety of emotions most people feel, acknowledge, and perhaps even express. Discussion of the punishment most women experience when they express anger may also be helpful in getting Mary to recognize what she does with her own legitimate feelings of injustice, upset, and anger. This is an area that most feminist therapists deal with routinely, especially since "good girls" are taught not to display angry feelings.

If Mary had experienced any *abuse as a child* or witnessed her *father abuse her mother*, her reluctance to deal with anger would need additional work. The destruction caused by witnessing or experiencing domestic violence can be overwhelming, particularly the fear that any anger expressed could erupt into terrifying violence. It is not unusual for girls to blame their mothers more than their fathers for the violence. Their anger is often from their perception that their abused mother either had the power to stop the father's abuse and didn't use it (one common example is the daughter who can't forgive her mother for always being verbally abusive toward her father) or should have had the power to protect the child but didn't (sometimes the daughter understands her mother's helplessness but still blames her for not meeting the expectation that a mother can always protect her child if she wants to). In either situation, giving up the anger or even rage toward their mother is seen as an acknowledgment of their own powerlessness as a woman.

In Mary's case, her fear of expressing her anger at her mother (and perhaps her father, too, for being absent and permitting her mother so much control) may well be related to her fear that doing anything to cause her mother's disapproval will result in a severed relationship. However, successful treatment will result in Mary's coming to grips with her buried feelings of anger, and unless dealt with in therapy, her initial expression of these feelings could be as destructive as she fears.

This fear would be expected to transfer to the therapist also, so dealing with angry feelings toward the therapist could not be expected to be an appropriate learning technique, at least initially. Sometimes it is helpful to practice feeling angry and use *behavioral rehearsal* to learn how to express it nondestructively around less significant items, as is often done with *assertiveness-training exercises*. Perhaps Mary can learn how to accept her feelings and express them appropriately around a natural problem, as when a new pair of shoes breaks or some other unexpected problem. If Mary continues to be stuck in this area, a *book* detailing exercises on being assertive might be used as an adjunct to the therapy sessions.

I often help women get in touch with unexpressed feelings of anger by using mirrors and videotaped recordings of the woman in a variety of situations, including sitting and listening to something that is annoying. Often the resting facial expression gives away the existence of buried angry feelings, even when the woman does not perceive them herself. Paying attention to nonverbal cues of actors during scenes when angry feelings would be appropriate, whether or not expressed, is another task that helps women get in touch with their own feelings. When preparing a woman to testify as a witness in a legal proceeding, I help her pay attention to her body cues of how she is feeling at a particular time. This technique may be particularly well suited for Mary, who is obviously performing poorly in job interviews.

One exercise that works well is to ask the woman to look in the mirror and make her face look pleasant. Then help her note the feeling of the muscles in her mouth, jaw, cheeks, forehead, and so on. Have her try to re-create the position of those muscles without looking in the mirror until she is finished. Thus, she is trying to re-create the look she liked just by feeling the position of the muscles. When she thinks she has done it, she can look in the mirror and see if she still has the pleasant look she liked earlier. If not, then she needs to re-create it visually, then try again to duplicate it by feeling the muscles. This exercise calls her attention to her ability to control the nonverbal image she gives to others. It makes her more sensitive to the messages about her feelings she gives, even when she blocks those feelings from her own awareness. She also can use it to learn how to recognize messages other people give by their nonverbal cues. For women like Mary who need more *training in social skills*, this exercise can be utilized in a variety of other situations.

## Competency Issues

Feminist-therapy principles include a belief that women need to make *informed choices about their life roles*, including options for economic independence. Mary's economic independence seems to be tied to her emotional independence. It also seems apparent that Mary's inability to function at her own level of competency has something to do with her mother's expectation that her major adult role in life is to be her parents' caretaker. As long as she is viewed as stupid and incompetent, she will not have to succumb to that role. These emotional binds pose an interesting dilemma for the therapist because each step toward independence will be viewed as a step away from her mother and family values. Thus, it will be necessary to find ways for Mary to perform competently without having to make a choice between the two values—traditional family or modern college woman.

It is clear that Mary's failed attempts at getting a job reinforced her feelings of being unwanted and incompetent. It is possible that her poor performance was due to a lack of concentration, probably due to her high levels of anxiety. Yet, she was able to keep the second job several months longer than the first one. Her retreat back into her home is typical of the precursors to development of phobic responses, particularly agoraphobia. The family's unbearable hostility may have been just what Mary needed to force her to begin to get out of the home. Here, the ultimate situation occurred. Mary was at home all of the time, and her mother still didn't like it. This obviously gave her the strength to stand up for herself and get a job, although she was still unable to move out of the house or separate from her mother.

## Friendship Patterns

Mary obviously had a friendship network, perhaps made up of child-hood friends or those made in college. It is apparent that her friends represent the more modern world and have nothing in common with the traditional lifestyle her family adheres to. However, they remained friends throughout some difficult periods in Mary's life, suggesting that they accepted and liked her a great deal. This is a strength that indicates that Mary has some appropriate social skills. The friends also may pro-vide a cushion for Mary in case she is totally rejected by her family. Yet Mary is able to keep these friendship patterns without having to give up her traditional values, indicating that there are some important areas of her life where she does not succumb to the either-or split that occurs around economic independence.

However, Mary does seem to reject both her family and her friendship support network during the 6 months she dated a totally inappropriate man, who was as critical as her mother. Here a feminist therapist would provide support for Mary as she tried out new behaviors such as dating, sex, and independence, as well as the new feelings associated with be-ing in love, and then the disillusionment that one's choice wasn't all she thought he was. The fact that she retreated back to the notion that she had to give up the others in her life who were critical of her choice of a boyfriend indicated a return to her use of either-or splits when she was confronted with too much controversy.

However, her ability to end the relationship when she perceived it as too hurtful to her is an indication of some real emotional strength. In this case, the therapist's support may have been the constant to help Mary make her own decisions. Once she terminated the relationship, however, it is appropriate to discuss what parts of her life are negotiable in a relationship and what aspects are not. Also important are identify-ing clues to a man's abusive nature, so that Mary can feel more confi-dent in her choice of a man in the future. The role of feedback from friends and family also needs to be put in some perspective for Mary to learn how to handle their comments without feeling she has to reject or succumb to them.

Mary's next choice of a man is a family friend met at a social gather-ing. He is of the same background, Italian and Catholic, but lives with his family in Italy. Obviously, he is safe, and dating him meets with the approval of her family. Mary decides to visit him in Italy, spends 6 months getting attached to his family, and then marries him and moves to Italy.

At this time, therapy ended, prematurely for feminist therapy. The goal of feminist therapy is the *empowerment of the woman*, and entering a marriage without working out the other issues is not seen as taking control of her life. This is an interesting ending in that it does help Mary resolve her conflict with her mother by moving back to the country where her mother was happy and finding another family to substitute for her more dysfunctional one. However, once again, she must give up her friends, any expression of her intellectual competence, and her pursuit of economic independence for her relationship with a man. As a feminist therapist, I would predict that her happiness will be short-lived and that sometime in the future she will return to therapy to continue her journey to find herself.

# REFERENCES

Broverman, I. K., Broverman, D. M., Clarkson, R., Rosencrantz, P., & Vogel, S. (1970). Sex role stereotypes and clinical judgements of mental health. *Journal of Consulting and Clinical Psychology*, 34(1), 1–7.
Brown, L. S. (1988). *Feminist therapy perspectives on psychodiagnosis: Beyond the DSM and ICD*. Keynote address presented at the International Congress on Mental Health Care for Women. Amsterdam, the Netherlands.
Brown, L. S., & Root, M. P. P. (in press). *Diversity and complexitites in feminist therapy*. New York: Haworth Press.
Brown, L. S., & Walker, L. E. A. (1990). Feminist perspectives on self disclosure. In G. Striker & M. Fisher (Eds.), *Self disclosure in the therapeutic relationship* (pp. 135–154). New York: Plenum Press.
Cammaert, L. P., & Larsen,C. C. (1988). Feminist frameworks of psychotherapy. In M. A. Dutton-Douglas & L. E. A. Walker (Eds.), *Feminist psychotherapies: Integration of therapeutic and feminist systems* (pp. 12–36). Norwood, NJ: Ablex.
Chesler, P. (1972). *Women and madness*. New York: Doubleday.
Conarton, S., & Silverman, L. K. (1988). Feminine development through the life cycle. In M. A. Dutton-Douglas & L. E. A. Walker (Eds.), *Feminist psychotherapies: Integration of therapeutic and feminist systems* (pp. 37–67). Norwood, NJ: Ablex.
Dutton-Douglas, M. A., & Walker, L. E. A. (Eds.). (1988). *Feminist psychotherapies: Integration of therapeutic and feminist systems*. Norwood, NJ: Ablex.
Fodor, I. G. (1985). Assertiveness training for the eighties: Moving beyond the personal. In L. B. Rosewater & L. E. A. Walker (Eds.), *Handbook of feminist therapy: Women's issues in psychotherapy* (pp. 91–117). New York: Springer Publishing Co.
Ganley, A. (1988). Feminist therapy with male clients. In M. A. Dutton-Douglas & L. E. A. Walker (Eds.), *Feminist psychotherapies: Integration of therapeutic and feminist systems* (pp. 186–205). Norwood, NJ: Ablex.
Kaplan. A., & Surrey, J. (1984). The relational self in women: Developmental theory and public policy. In L. E. Walker (Ed.), *Women and mental health policy* (pp. 79–94). Beverly Hills, CA: Sage.

Lerman, H. (1986). *A mote in Freud's eye*. New York: Springer Publishing Co.

Mays, V. M., & Comas-Dias, L. (1988). Feminist therapy with ethnic minority populations: A closer look at Blacks and Hispanics. In M. A. Dutton-Douglas & L. E. A. Walker (Eds.), *Feminist psychotherapies: Integration of therapeutic and feminist systems* (pp. 228–251). Norwood, NJ: Ablex.

Midlarsky, E. (1988). Feminist therapies with the elderly. In M. A. Dutton-Douglas & L. E. A. Walker (Eds.), *Feminist psychotherapies: Integration of therapeutic and feminist systems* (pp. 252–275). Norwood, NJ: Ablex.

Rosencrantz, P. S., DeLorey, C., & Broverman, I. K. (1985, August). *One half a generation later: Sex role stereotypes revisited*. Paper presented at the annual convention of the American Psychological Association, Los Angeles.

Rosewater, L. B. (1988). Feminist therapies with women. In M. A. Dutton-Douglas & L. E. A. Walker (Eds.), *Feminist psychotherapies: Integration of therapeutic and feminist systems* (pp. 137–155). Norwood, NJ: Ablex.

Rosewater, L. B., & Walker, L. E. A. (Eds.). (1985). *Handbook on feminist therapy: Psychotherapy issues with women*. New York: Springer Publishing Co.

Russo, N. F. (1984). Women in the mental health delivery system: Implications for research and public policy. In L. E. A. Walker (Ed.), *Women's mental health policy* (pp. 21–41). Beverly Hills, CA: Sage.

Walker, L. E. A. (Ed.), (1984). *Women and mental health policy*. Beverly Hills, CA: Sage.

Walker, L. E. A., & Bolkovatz, M. A. (1988). Play therapy with sexually abused children. In L. E. A. Walker (Ed.), *Handbook on sexual abuse of children: Assessment and treatment issues* (pp. 249–269). New York: Springer Publishing Co.

# 7

# A Family Therapist Views the Case

## Sandra B. Coleman

## THEORETICAL BACKGROUND

Twenty-five years ago a brief overview of basic principles underlying family therapy would have encompassed a few pages of explanation. Today the same task would require many volumes. Clearly such an undertaking exceeds the needs of this chapter; thus the information that follows must be understood as merely a skeletal model of the major theoretical constructs that influenced my hypothetical treatment of the presented case.

### Systems Theory

Family treatment as we know it today is rooted in the biological concepts of von Bertalannfy's (1968) general systems theory, which is based on the view that living organisms are more than the sum of their parts. Von Bertalannfy saw the family as an organized whole, open to the exchange of energies and information from the outside environment by which it dynamically maintains itself, grows, and develops. Since the family system functions as a whole, it is important to understand that change in one part of the system (i.e., one family member, affects the rest of the system, the other family members). This "feedback" function can be growth-enhancing and constructive to all the members or, unfortunately, may have a deleterious or negative effect. The latter is what family therapists are most often asked to help change when the family presents its "problem" for treatment. When a family therapist examines a presenting problem, often expressed by an individual member's symptomatic behavior, she must translate that problem into a systems framework. Thus the major treatment requirement that pervades the entire range of family-therapy models is to "think systems." This is in marked contrast to individual-therapy models, which generally rely on unidimensional or integrated theories relative to an *individual* pattern of development or behavior. Although the family therapist also subscribes to individual developmental theories, these concepts are organized within the context of systems.

The concept of "feedback" or "feedback loops" derives from the field of cybernetics (Weiner, 1954) and augments the model proposed by general systems theory. Many family therapists prefer a cybernetics model because the very nature of looking at a family in terms of feedback loops places the focus on the *circularity* of interactions rather than on the cause-effect model of understanding human behavior, thus lessening the sense of blame that families so often fear when asked to participate in the "patient's" treatment. For example, in my own research on drug-addict families (Coleman, Kaplan, & Downing, 1986; Coleman, Kaplan, Gallagher, Downing, & Caine, 1982), I studied intergenerational familial patterns of loss and separation as well as the role of religion or spirituality in the context of a family. In this model, drug use is viewed as a means of coping with the extensive multiple loss issues throughout the life cycle—a circular pattern developed over many years. A contrasting *linear* model, on the other hand, might view drug use as a direct result of an earlier traumatic event. For example, the death of a father early in childhood leads to drug abuse in later life (the implication being a *causal* relationship). A linear model would not necessarily take into account the extent to which other factors surrounding that death influence the long-range outcome. In contrast, the *circular model* always looks at the context of the event. It is not merely an early death that is examined but also the family transactions surrounding it that are significantly associated with future behavior.

## Family Functioning

It is important to understand that when a family therapist refers to her "client," she is really talking about a "family." As Nichols and Everett (1986) point out, "thinking family" is as necessary as "thinking systems." Nichols and Everett underscore the importance of viewing the family as an integrative system. Their operational definition of "family" is that of "a multigenerational system characterized by several internally functioning subsystems and influenced by a variety of external, adjunctive systems." The authors emphasize that family systems are composed of people. Thus, the integrative nature of family must be recognized "because of its developmental role in the formation and functioning of persons both while they live within the nuclear family and long after they have left their family of origin." "The family is integrative because of the family processes that work over several generations and that continue to operate long after one has physically left home." More specifically, Nichols and Everett explore the family's function with regard to personality formation and the corresponding aspect of role determination.

In addition to examining the importance of the family's integrative function, Nichols and Everett also underscore the *interactive* nature of the family. The authors state that the interactive aspect of the family has to do with "what a system looks like and how it behaves. It is the interactive nature of the system that comes the closest to disclosing its 'living' characteristics and the power of its collective components and subsystems. The interactive aspect of a system is that part that is in a continual and reciprocal interrelationship with the external environment and that processes informational feedback. It is the interactive nature of a system that conveys its organization" (p. 117).

## The Family Life Cycle

Most family therapists consider family life as taking place within a developmental or life-cycle framework. Similar to the classical developmental stage-concepts of child psychology theorist Erik Erikson (1950), families are viewed as having normal "passages" over time, with each stage presenting a major task to be accomplished. If a family is unable to accomplish a particular stage-related task successfully, the family as a system becomes "stuck." The symptom or problem presented by one member, the "identified patient," at the time the family enters therapy is viewed as an indicator of the way a particular family is expressing its inability to transcend the stage of life it is currently facing, or to describe it in other terms, the family cannot accomplish the necessary task in order to progress.

All families have repetitive circular patterns of interacting. Some are developmentally constructive and growth-enhancing, while others are dysfunctional and growth-inhibiting. The latter are representative of the behaviors and emotional disorders that we see in clinical practice. Problems that become unmanageable and resistant push families to seek professional help.

## A Multigenerational-Feminist Family-Therapy Approach

Therapeutic approaches to families vary, as do those of individual or group therapies. Within the overall umbrella of general systems theory, families may be treated vis-à-vis models based on communications theory, intergenerational theory, psychodynamics, behavior therapy, structural and/or strategic therapy, experiential therapy, and several others. My own system of practicing family psychology is firmly anchored on one end by general systems theory and cybernetics, and on the other end by individual-developmental theories, feminist theories, and those of the family life cycle. Between these two pillars I incorporate tenets from structural and strategic family therapy. A brief overview of the major components of my treatment model provides a framework for understanding the clinical case that will be presented.

### Intergenerational Family Therapy

In order fully to understand the family system and the presenting symptoms confronting the family therapist, one must view that system from the perspective of several generations. Clearly the problems that we see in treatment are not isolated, are a function of many aspects of life, not the least of which are often associated with intergenerational patterns of relating. Bowen (1960, 1978) was one of the early pioneers whose work with schizophrenic families places him among the founding fathers of family therapy. As early as the mid-1950s, Bowen was working with family groups, based upon his firm belief that family networks are highly significant therapeutic resources. Although he did not often see entire families in his practice, he developed a system of sending people for therapeutic visits with extended-family members.

Bowen also developed a method of mapping the family, known as the *genogram*, which has since become an integral part of many family-therapy approaches. The genogram is a graphic representation of the extended family and generally includes information concerning the names and ages of all family members, their dates of birth, marriages, separations, divorces, deaths and the cause of the deaths, and any other significant life events. Additional data regarding occupation, geographical locations, illnesses and so on are included. Symbolic representations (heavy double lines connoting conflict or disconnected lines of relational "cutoffs," etc.) describe the degree to which particular family members are overinvolved or disconnected, providing evidence of the emotional intensity of one member's relationship to another.

Recently, McGoldrick and Gerson (1985) have expanded Bowen's earlier work on the genogram, giving it a wider range of application. The construction of a genogram is an interesting process for families to develop together. In addition to the time and effort it takes to recall all the significant people and their accompanying data, the experience of making a genogram creates an arena for members to share information and feelings, some of which were previously couched in secrecy.

In summary, the intergenerational model of the family provides the therapist with a comprehensive understanding of the long-term patterns, connections, and overall background for what she observes in the treatment room. When we can grasp the significance of a particular presenting problem relative to its ancestral ties, we have a greater opportunity for a more successful resolution. Thus, the time we spend on developing our hypotheses within a historical context is a worthwhile investment for both therapist and family.

## Feminist Family Therapy

It cannot be denied that we live in a patriarchal society, with greater advantages in general given to men. As a result of the women's movement that began in the late 1960s, considerable attention has been directed to the inferior role of women in both society and the family. Feminist family therapy acknowledges the realities that surround women and distinguish them from men. Much of what has been presented here in terms of the systems model is in general accepted by major feminist therapists, who also state that a feminist approach is somewhat like a nonsexist approach in that it promotes equality between men and women, particularly with regard to issues of power (Wheeler, Avis, Miller, & Chaney, 1989). Wheeler et al. add, however, that feminist family therapy goes further in looking at "the unique problems women face as a result of their socialization, as well as to making changes that will benefit women (Gilbert, 1980). Additionally, most feminist perspectives on therapy emphasize the sharing of power in the therapeutic relationship rather than the usual therapist-client hierarchy." Also significant is the fact that "feminist family therapy is distinguished from other forms of feminist therapy by its particular focus on changing family structure and its involvement of the family system in this process."

Women involved in the Women's Project in Family Therapy (Walters, Carter, Papp, & Silverstein, 1989) delineate nine guidelines for doing feminist family therapy:

1. Identification of the gender message and social constructs that condition behavior and sex roles.
2. Recognition of the real limitation of female access to social and economic resources.
3. An awareness of sexist thinking that constricts the options of women to direct their own lives.
4. Acknowledgment that women have been socialized to assume primary responsibility for family relationships.
5. Recognition of the dilemmas and conflicts of childbearing and childrearing in our society.
6. An awareness of patterns that split the women in families as they seek to acquire power through relationships with men.
7. Affirmation of values and behaviors characteristic of women, such as connectedness, nurturing, and emotionality.
8. Recognition of and support for possibilities for women outside of marriage and the family.
9. Recognition of the basic principle that no intervention is gender-free and that every intervention will have a different and special meaning for each sex.

A more elaborate review of the literature on feminist family therapy goes beyond the purposes of this chapter; however, the discussion presented here includes the significant belief systems associated with the feminist-therapy leaders.

The efforts of women family therapists to include feminist thinking in our work has not always met with agreement by feminist therapists who are *not* family therapists. Despite the justifiable criticisms and negative attitudes some feminist therapists have toward the failure of systemic concepts adequately to support the rights of women (Bograd, 1984; Goldner, 1985; James & McIntyre, 1983; Lerner, 1987), I am able to integrate feminist theory and concepts with those of family systems. Perhaps one of the reasons I do not feel as theoretically restricted is that my own nontraditional life experiences have created a context within which I am able to look at a family's gender issues with a wide-angled lens (Coleman, 1990). I also feel comfortable confronting a family's beliefs, practices, or power plays that demean or blame women for the dysfunctional situation. In addition, I am always aware of how other social systems intervene and influence family life. Thus, my approach as a family psychologist is often akin to that of my feminist-therapy sisters and to my own built-in mechanism that "thinks systems," "thinks families." Also, in the words of Walters, Carter, Papp, and Silverstein (1989), I "think gender."

## Structural Therapy

Structural family therapy is based upon the work of Minuchin (1967, 1974). It is one of the most widely used therapies and one of the best organized. Its major constructs provide a model for clear understanding of a family through observing its structural components, including its boundaries, subsystems, and major source of power. Minuchin's work provides a concise means of mapping a family to understand how it functions. Particularly important is identifying the degree to which families are either "enmeshed" or overinvolved so that individual boundaries are permeable and diffuse or "disengaged" (a state of rigidified, impermeable boundaries). Often child-presenting families are controlled by the symptomatic member so that the base of power lies within a very young person. One parent is frequently overinvolved with the child, creating what is known as a cross-generational alliance. A major task of the structural family therapist is to reorganize the family to keep each generation within its own boundaries and to help parents become better "executives," more in charge of their children. The restructuring of the family is felt to be the major intervention that alleviates the symptomatic behavior and creates the needed family change.

An important principle within the structural-therapy framework is that of *joining*, the term used to describe the therapist's means of entering the family system enough to induce the necessary change. Unless the therapist has truly "joined" the family by understanding each member and his relationship to every other member, little real progress can be made. Thus, within this model, the early relational processes between therapist and family are extraordinarily important. Clearly, without solid joining, no important therapy can ensue. I routinely apply structural-therapy principles to each family I see, for without an understanding of the way families are organized, it is not possible to generate meaningful change.

## Strategic Therapy

Strategic therapy derives from a communications model; its techniques are described by Haley (1973) as those in which the therapist assumes the responsibility for directly influencing what happens in therapy to effect positive change. Strategic therapists see symptoms as attempts at communication, which occurs within a relational context (i.e., the family). These symptoms regulate family transactions, and although they appear within one "chosen" family member, they cannot be alleviated unless the entire system changes. Because most people in emotional conflict have a tendency to do more of the same despite disappointing results, strategic therapists use this repetitive behavior as a means of developing tactical interventions that are more likely to promote change.

An example from my own strategic therapy casebook (Coleman, 1983) provides a glimpse into how strategies may be used. The case involved a family who presented with a 13-year-old son who was a behavioral problem in the classroom. Although neither the parents nor the child acknowledged that the acting-out was a problem, the school was persistent in its view that it was indeed quite troublesome. After more than a year of unsuccessful family therapy with another therapist, the school referred the family to me, with the condition that the boy would be accepted back into the classroom only if he and his family were in regular weekly therapy. I was hesitant to take this case after learning the identity of the former therapist, who, in my opinion, was quite experienced and competent in treating such youngsters. Also, I could "feel" the family's resistance to seeking more treatment.

Thus I reached for an innovative means of inducing change and designed a strategy in which the prescription for therapy was in fact *not* therapy. In brief, this consisted of a traditional evaluation of the family for a few sessions, followed by a plan in which the symptomatic boy called me on the telephone once a week at a specified time and, while one of his parents listened on an extension phone, reported to me about his school behavior. If he did not get into trouble and there were no "pink slips" sent home to his parents, there was no therapy session that week. On the other hand, therapy sessions were held immediately if there was any acting out and/or any member of the family requested a session. Because the child preferred to play ball with his friends instead of losing an evening to therapy, there were very few times that we met, and when we did, the impetus for therapy was due to the parents' need for marital help.

Here, I was able to integrate the system's (family's) view that the problem was really not a "big deal" and the adolescent's desire to spend his time with friends (rather than with a therapist) with an innovative therapeutic plan that really placed the responsibility to change on the family. I knew that direct confrontation of the issues would only create a no-win power struggle. Thus, I decided to accept their stance and use it to accomplish the school's goal of more compliant behavior in the identified patient. In the end, I even achieved my goal of moving the children *out* of center stage and putting the marital pair *in* (I perceived the pair to be the more critical unit for treatment). This case demonstrates the use of strategic therapy to achieve a goal that was not likely to occur with more traditional family-therapy methods.

The previously described concepts might easily lead one to regard "family" as a highly intellectualized construct. Such a notion unfortunately would serve almost to eliminate the flesh-and-bones nature of the folks that actually make a constellation of relatives a "family." Therefore, it must be remembered that these constructs are presented as a means of describing how a family therapist organizes a treatment model and not how she relates to families on a humanistic level. For no matter what theories or methods of treatment we choose to identify as our own, the ultimate outcome regarding the effectiveness of therapy is often the quality of the therapist-client relationship. While this has been well established, it is perhaps nowhere more influential than in the treatment of families.

The following case study is "hypothetically treated," and as such may not demonstrate all of the theoretical issues just discussed. It is important, however, to note that the presented concepts are the foundation for the way I believe these people would have been treated if they had been referred to me.

## THE CASE OF MARY

When Mary was referred to me, I would first have agreed to a consultation consisting of one to four sessions, the purpose of which would be to explore Mary's circumstances and assess her goals and therapy requirements. Unlike individual therapists, family therapists need to examine the entire system's relationship to the presenting problem. If Mary had never been seen at the college counseling center, I would treat the case as I do all other referrals. For example, when someone calls to make an appointment at my center, a standardized telephone intake is conducted, and the referring family member is asked to bring her spouse, family, or significant others to the initial session. A brief explanation is given ("Your husband is going to be affected by what we do in your session. We find it helpful to meet with him initially so that he does not feel excluded. He may or may not attend sessions regularly; this we will all determine at the conclusion of our consultation period"). This immediately allows the client to know that she will have a major decision-making role in therapy. It reinforces the view that the therapist perceives her clients as competent human beings, and only rarely does this explanation meet with objection. This approach is an important aspect of feminist family therapy in that it serves to eliminate the therapeutic hierarchy, making the therapist less authoritarian (Hare-Mustin, 1978) and less intimidating.

Many years ago, a request to see the whole family would frequently have met with opposition. Today, people are more accepting of family therapy as an important means of resolving family problems; thus, asking a person to bring other members to a session is not considered particularly unique, especially in our large urban communities on the East Coast.

Because Mary had spent two years in counseling at the university's counseling center, she deserved the consideration of at least a few individual sessions so that she could acquaint me with her previous therapy, her current level of functioning, and her present goals. I would also want to determine whether she had sufficiently resolved the loss of her former therapist at the counseling center and whether Mary was emotionally ready to establish a relationship with me. Most importantly, I would use the consultation period to gather family-background information, which could include having Mary make a genogram of her family. Hopefully this process would elicit significant therapeutic material previously undiscussed. These initial steps would facilitate the transition from an individually oriented therapy model to that of family systems.

## Family-Background Information and Case Hypotheses

### Separation Issues

Mary's presenting symptoms are embedded in both the individual and family life-cycle tasks of breaking loose and letting go. Specifically, this is the phase of life during which one must separate from adolescence and move toward autonomous adulthood. Successful separation results in an emptying of the family nest. For all families this is a critical phase, and the many-faceted contingencies associated with it are a major resource for a family psychologist's case load.

### The Loyalty Dilemma

In Mary's family, the problem of separating was consistently conflictual for Mary was the fourth child to express a similar dilemma. Evidence of this lies in the fact that Mary's eldest brother, in a sense, merely traded one family for another. He substituted for parents and siblings the church's holy "foster" family and stayed within its nest; thus in a particular kind of paradox, he left home but didn't leave home. Because the details of his decision to become a priest are unknown, we cannot draw any unfair conclusions; however, we do know that his mother did not want him to move away.

Mary's other brothers never left home. Although they worked for large corporations during the day, they returned to eat and sleep with their biological family. The corporations could be perceived as transitional or "day-care families," so that like their elder brother, they too left home but didn't. For each brother, a large highly structured organization became the alternate form of family life. None of the sons was able to move beyond a certain level of developmental autonomy. Mary's imposed legacy was that she too, after college graduation, would leave home only during the day and would remain single and care for her parents when they became elderly.

Mary's struggle with college completion, represented by repeatedly failing a course during her last semester, was her way of demonstrating the conflict she had about conforming to the family pattern. If she graduated from college, she was expected to return home to fulfill her assigned caretaking role. If she did not graduate, she could create another conflict, which in a sense protected her from dealing with the family's expectations of her future obligation to them.

The rigidity of the dilemma regarding one's loyalty to oneself versus one's loyalty to the family of origin is reinforced by the family's inability to allow anyone to leave. Although the parents physically departed from their native Italy, they remained loyal emotionally to their homeland, re-creating it by remaining in an ethnic Italian neighborhood they seldom left. That English was rarely spoken had to create considerable confusion for the children about ethnic alliances. This preservation of the Italian language in the home reinforced cultural expectations of the kids' obligation to their parents and ran counter to the American tradition of getting out and breaking free of parental bonds.

Also, it is logical to assume that Mary's parents never left their families of origin either. Evidence that they were married only in a legal sense derives from the fact that they were unhappy together, lived in separate parts of the house sharing little. "The parents rarely spoke to one another, communicating only when necessary." A subset of this behavior is represented by the fact that Mary didn't talk to her father (as dictated by mother and apparently accepted by father, in view of the lack of evidence that he ever challenged it)! There did not appear to be much of a sibling bond; Mary's brother, the priest, treated her like a child and acted in the role of reprimanding parent, which further served to keep the family problem in stasis.

## Conflicts of Sex and Gender

Akin to the loyalty and separation problems are the conflicts of sex and gender. Mary could not learn healthy attitudes toward the expression of mature sexuality from the estranged relationship of her parents. Neither of her brothers married or demonstrated any affinity for a relationship with the opposite sex. Her elder brother's vow of celibacy is a strong statement to this effect. Mary's mother communicated both covertly and overtly that sex, dating, and adult peer relationships between men and women are dangerous and should be avoided. Clearly, Mary's mother had considerable ambivalence and confusion regarding her own sexual identification, and Mary's father's peripheral role, along with his passive acceptance of his wife's "teachings," further suggests that he too was uncomfortable and bewildered about gender issues.

Although Mary claimed to want independence and a successful career, she had no model to encourage such goals. The only other woman in her family was sharply critical of any attempt Mary made to attain autonomy and conveyed her own sense of insecurity and dependency by holding on to the expectancy that her daughter would return to take care of her.

Lack of confidence and a sense of impotence in both sexes were major characteristics in this family. These were accompanied by an extreme degree of family enmeshment, making it unlikely that either Mary or her brothers could achieve adequate levels of adult sexual functioning.

## Marital Conflicts

It is clear that Mary's parents have a lengthy history of marital difficulties, some of which are embedded in the previously presented issues related to sex and gender. Their relationship would require extensive exploration; although their rationale for remaining together needs clarification, one can assume it is likely to be a function of Old World customs and religious values. There is, of course, a strong connection between the struggle to keep the "children" home and their inability to relate to each other in a mutually fulfilling way. The marital component of the systematic problem is undoubtedly a major contributing force in the adult children's inability to extricate themselves from their "homebound" training program. For if the children were truly to grow up and leave, the parents would be alone with each other. Thus, by staying at home, Mary and her brothers ensure that the marriage will never have to endure an honest confrontation.

## Summary

Within the confines of the limited family-background information, it appears that the case of Mary is a function of a three-generational repetitive family pattern. One might readily hypothesize that Mary's parents left their homes as a consequence of a prearranged marriage and were never able to make a serious emotional commitment toward mature couplehood. If one assumes that they also lacked adequate guidance in becoming sexually mature and independent adults, how could they transmit such experiences to their offspring? What then could they possibly teach their children, except that to stay home with one's family of origin is the sacred way. Because the marital relationship was unsatisfactory, the childrens' departure from home posed a serious threat to the intactness of the marriage.

Unfortunately, Mary suffered from an inherited deficiency that led her to therapy. Despite her immaturity, however, she was still strong enough to become the "patient" with the potential to lead the whole family, as well as her parent's marriage, across the bridge to freedom from the repetitive transactions that bound them to past tradition, no longer viable.

Certainly if my initial consultation with Mary yielded such information, I would view her symptoms as the family's attempt at change. It would be only through direct systemic intervention with the entire family, however, that I could expect to succeed in helping Mary.

## Family-Therapy Treatment Approach

At the conclusion of our consultation period, I would ask Mary if she wanted to enter therapy with me. If her response was positive, I would next encourage her to gather the family together to engage them in our treatment plan. In an effort to avoid the anticipated anxiety surrounding this request, I would make two suggestions designed to facilitate therapy. First, I would offer to provide an Italian-speaking family cotherapist to eliminate the inevitable barrier that Mary's family would erect with regard to our cultural differences and their probable fear that I would influence Mary to rid herself of her ethnic connections. Although I would certainly respect and want Mary to honor her Italian heritage, I would encourage her to hold on to her American roots. The use of an Italian cotherapist would allow for bicultural team modeling, which is essential for this particular family. Second, I would suggest that to lessen her family's anxiety, Mary should impress upon them that they were being invited in to help *her*. This would minimize the tendency for people unfamiliar with family therapy to assume that they were being called in to be "blamed." By viewing the presenting problem as a systemic symptom, family therapists, perhaps more than any others, tend to distribute responsibility for problems rather evenly among family members. Feminist thinking also serves to eliminate the long-standing attitude of blaming a parent, which more often than not translated into the "mother's fault."

Initially, my cotherapist would facilitate much of the joining of the family members. Although I would be quite social and interested in getting to know them, I would want the major role of making connections to be that of the Italian team member. The importance of acknowledging and supporting ethnicity and its related norms and values must be underscored. McGoldrick, Pearce, and Giordano (1982) emphasize that without understanding a family's specific ethnic values, the therapist is unprepared to join them.

Once we felt that we had at least a beginning alignment with the family, we would ask each one to identify the "problem" from his perspective. It is readily predictable that the family would want to focus on Mary, her "bad" school performance, lack of compliance with parental expectations, and so on. I would accept their point of view, but over the next several sessions, I would gently urge them to let me know them better by understanding each of them—their individual and family histories, their interests. Through careful questioning, I would move them to the origins of their past struggles, paying particular attention to their painful losses and separations. I would have Mary show them her genogram and have them add their knowledge of the family to it. This would not only help me to understand their genetic background and legacies but also allow the family to recognize, vis-à-vis the graphic representation, its own repetitive patterns.

Because a major hypothesis about Mary's problems centers around the issue of "leaving home," therapy would concentrate on issues surrounding her parents' decision to leave their native land, the associated family of origin; vicissitudes regarding their exodus; and whatever historically significant factors affected their move from Italy to the United States. Particularly important would be the difficulties that arose when Mary's grandparents were her age. Undoubtedly, at that time young people remained at home until they married, frequently living with parents and extended family long after marriage. Despite these customs, however, other loyalty conflicts may have prevailed, making growing up very painful.

As the family continued their sessions, I would learn whether my initial hypotheses were substantiated. Only after a very careful study and reconstruction of the family history could I then move into more direct interventions. However, if my understanding of the prevailing issues was correct, therapy would most likely involve creating some family rituals around the theme of loyalty conflicts, loss and separation. More effective grieving of lost loved ones and abandoned lifestyles would have to occur. Family albums of significant people and their homes could be an important catalyst for successful bereavement. Also, the sharing of significant materials such as letters from home when Mary's parents first arrived in the United States could play an important role. Perhaps a few intercontinental family phone calls during therapy sessions to family still living in Italy could be part of the healing process.

The family as a group might be encouraged to take a trip to Italy and visit relatives. Cemetery visits to deceased family members are another consideration, as are letters written in Italian to long-lost relatives or the deceased. They all could be a part of the completion of any unfinished business that might help to release the family "logjam."

Once the family appeared ready to move beyond the grief work, my next goal might be to develop a better understanding of each individual in the family. I would possibly explore each person's dreams or fantasies by asking, "What would you wish for if you could change or have anything you want in life?" Although this is interesting to do with the entire family present, I might very well conduct the same "wish" investigation in subgroup sessions with the parents alone and in a session with just Mary and her brothers.

Later I would want to work on the marriage as the major treatment goal. Once I separated the parents' therapy from that of Mary and her brothers, I could then suggest that Mary join a women's group. At the same time, her brothers might also be ready for a referral to either group or individual therapy, and a male therapist at this point could become a particular asset.

The major goal here shifts toward helping each of the siblings to differentiate from the family as well as from one another. Thus, the sex of the therapist could become highly significant. In this particular family, gender issues would be expected to become more important as the family progressed. Because of their inhibited sex-role development, earlier phases of family therapy would be more dependent on the theoretical posture of the therapist than her gender.

Only later would therapist gender be a serious consideration. At this time, as a woman, my role modeling would have a special effect. My comfortable self-assured behavior and independence combined with my nurturing would demonstrate to Mary how a women can be strong without giving up her soft edges. Mary's mother would also benefit from my letting her know how I can love my own adult children without placing unfair demands or imposing my personal needs on them. My ability to share the person I am could help Mary's mother to acquire contemporary American culture.

From his growing relationship with me, Mary's father might learn that he needn't retreat from women. Also, I could help him to feel safe in expressing his emotions with me, which could transfer back to his wife and Mary, markedly changing their unhealthy triangulation. I, like many family therapists, believe that our gender-related treatment differences depend more on whether we uphold a feminist ideal by being sensitive to family issues associated with sex-role problems than whether the therapist is male or female. Being a "feminist" is a political point of view about power and hierarchy in the family. Without understanding this basic tenet, therapist gender is hardly sufficient. Obviously it is extremely difficult to project specific interventions from this "meta" position accurately; however, from my experience with similar cases, these general approaches to helping Mary's family overcome their problems appear worthwhile.

## Case Comment

Based upon my theoretical position as a family psychologist, this case as it actually evolved (vis-à-vis the *real* therapist) has a marvelous ending in that Mary's real-life solution clearly honors the family's transgenerational themes: You can *leave* home (in America) if and only if you return home to Italy! By marrying a native Italian and returning to Italy near his job and family, Mary upheld and fulfilled the family's systemic intractable legacy. Thus she ensured that her children and grandchildren would probably never dare to transgress the family tradition. In other words, what goes around comes around.

## REFERENCES

Bograd, M. (1984). Family systems approaches to wife battering: A feminist critique. *American Journal of Orthopsychiatry, 54,* 558–568.

Bowen, M. (1960). A family concept of schizophrenia. In D. D. Jackson (Ed.), *The etiology of schizophrenia.* New York: Basic Books.

Bowen, M. (1978). *Family therapy in clinical practice.* New York: Jason Aronson.

Coleman, S. B. (1983). A case of non-treatment treatment of a non-problem problem. *Journal of Strategic and Systemic Therapies, 2*(3), 62–66.

Coleman, S. B. (1990). Zen and the science and art of being a family psychologist. In F. W. Kaslow (Ed.), *Voices in family psychology.*

Coleman, S. B., Kaplan, J. D., & Downing, R. W. (1986). Life cycle and loss— The spiritual vacuum of heroin addiction. *Family Process, 25*(1), 5–23.

Coleman, S. B., Kaplan, J. D., Gallagher, P. R., Downing, R. W., and Caine, C. (1982). *Heroin—A family coping strategy for death and loss: Final report 1979–1981.* National Institute on Drug Abuse, Grant No. R01-D-02332-02, Achievement Through Counseling and Treatment, Washington, DC.

Erikson, E. (1950). *Society and childhood.* New York: Norton.

Gilbert, L. G. (1980). Feminist therapy. In A. M. Bradsky & R. Hare-Mustin (Eds.), *Women and psychotherapy: An assessment of research and practice.* New York: Guilford Press.

Goldner, V. (1985). Feminism and family therapy. *Family Process, 24,* 21–47.

Haley, J. (1973). *Uncommon therapy: The psychiatric techniques of Milton H. Erickson.* New York: Norton.

Hare-Mustin, R. T. (1978). A feminist approach to family therapy. *Family Process*, *17*, 181–194.

James, K., & McIntrye, D. (1983). The reproduction of families: The social role of family therapy. *Journal of Marital and Family Therapy*, *9*, 119–129.

Lerner, H. G. (1987). Is family systems therapy really systemic? A feminist communication. *Journal of Psychotherapy & the Family*, *3*(4), 41–56.

McGoldrick, M., & Gerson, R. (1985). *Genograms in family assessment*. New York: Norton.

McGoldrick, M., Pearce, J. K., & Giordano, J. (Eds.). (1982). *Ethnicity and family therapy*. New York: Guilford Press.

Minuchin, S. (1974). *Families and family therapy*. Cambridge, MA: Harvard University Press.

Minuchin, S., Montalvo, B., Guerney, B., Rosman, B., & Schumer, E. (1967). *Families of the slums: An exploration of their structure and treatment*. New York: Basic Books.

Nichols, W. C., & Everett, C. A. (1986). *Systemic family therapy*. New York: Guilford Press.

von Bertalannfy, L. (1968). *General systems theory*. New York: George Braziller.

Walters, M., Carter, E., Papp, P., & Silverstein, O. (1989). *The invisible web*. New York: Guilford Press.

Weiner, N. (1954). *The human use of human beings: Cybernetics and society*. New York: Doubleday.

Wheeler, D., Avis, J. M., Miller, L., & Chaney, S. (1989). Rethinking family therapy training and supervision: A feminist model. *Journal of Psychotherapy and the Family*, *1*, 53–71.

# 8

# A Cognitive Behaviorist Views the Case

## Ellen Tobey Klass and Joann Paley Galst

## THEORETICAL PERSPECTIVE

A basic premise of cognitive-behavior therapy is that learning processes play an important role in the acquisition, maintenance, and change of thoughts, feelings, and actions. (The term *cognitive-behavior therapy* conveys the view that cognitive as well as overt behavioral processes are legitimate targets and methods of change for psychological difficulties.) Although environmental constraints are recognized, there is considerable optimism about the possibilities for change in that the therapist provides direct environmental input, and as the individual changes, he or she may elicit different responses from or react differently to the environment. Cognitive-behavior therapy also emphasizes specificity in construing problems, causes, and change techniques. Psychotherapy is seen as a process of applying particular techniques to alter particular difficulties. Based on its intellectual heritage in academic behaviorism, cognitive-behavior therapy strongly values operationalizing constructs and evaluating outcome. In this section, we present central features of cognitive-behavioral views on the causes of psychopathology and the process of therapy,[1] including pertinent gender issues.

The causal model in cognitive-behavior therapy seeks the origins of current psychopathology in past learning and current maintaining conditions, although the possible role of innate and biological factors is acknowledged. Learning is viewed as a continual process, so that in naturally occurring situations, the contributions of intentional teaching and learning are relatively minor. Three specific types of learning are seen as sources of both adaptive and maladaptive responses: respondent conditioning, operant conditioning, and observational learning. *Respondent conditioning* (classical conditioning) is learning by association. The paradigm involves the pairing of an unconditioned stimulus (an environmental input that already elicits an "unconditioned response") with a previously neutral "conditioned" stimulus. After enough pairings, the previously neutral stimulus brings out a similar "conditioned response" to that initially given to the unconditioned stimulus. For example, John's parents consistently insult him (unconditioned stimulus), eliciting feelings of anxiety and shame (unconditioned response), for behaviors they call weak (conditioned stimulus). Over time, John comes to feel anxious and ashamed (conditioned response) about these behaviors, whether or not he is overtly criticized for them. Through stimulus generalization, stimuli that resemble the original conditioned stimulus come to elicit similar conditioned reactions.

*Operant conditioning* involves the effects of consequences (or reinforcement) on behavior. Operant researchers have described four categories of reinforcement: (a) *positive* reinforcement, in which the presence of a stimulus increases the likelihood of a behavior; (b) *aversive* reinforcement (punishment), in which the presence of a stimulus decreases the likelihood of behavior; (c) *extinction*, in which the absence of a stimulus decreases the likelihood of behavior; and (d) *negative* reinforcement (avoidance), in which the absence of a stimulus increases the likelihood of behavior. For example, Jane is praised (positive reinforcement) when she complies with her parents' wishes, and her rudimentary efforts to stand up for herself have no impact (extinction). Over time, she becomes highly compliant and does not know how to assert herself. As individuals become more socialized, approval and disapproval from others (social reinforcement) play a larger role relative to tangible, or material, reinforcers. Operant researchers have studied schedules, or patterns, of reinforcement, and established that intermittent schedules, in which a consequence only sometimes follows a behavior, lead to greater difficulty with unlearning if reinforcement conditions change. Behaviors may persist for long periods of time in the face of apparently unrewarding circumstances because of the original reinforcement schedule.

*Observational learning* involves the effect of a model (behavior demonstrated by another person) on the individual's behavior through direct observation or through "symbolic modeling" representations, as in the mass media or stories. Observational learning affects cognitive processes like expectancies and self-evaluative standards as well as overt actions (Bandura, 1978). For instance, Dana's father continually criticized her mother for being "too fat." In adulthood, Dana was extremely self-conscious about her body despite her ordinary weight and shape. Observational learning can occur although it is not immediately manifested. For instance, Bandura (1965) found that after observing an aggressive model, girls were less likely than boys to demonstrate similar aggressive behavior. However, when offered incentives to demonstrate the modeled behaviors, girls showed as much aggression as boys, suggesting that some sex differences reflect perceptions of expected consequences for particular behaviors rather than lack of knowledge of the behaviors.

In considering learning origins, cognitive behaviorists view most complex adult behaviors as stemming from combinations of respondent, operant, and observational learning. The term *social-learning history* is used for originating factors because so many important learning experiences of human beings involve interpersonal rather than tangible stimuli. Although the principles of learning are universal, the content of learning is specific to cultures and the vagaries of individual experience. Psychopathology is defined by a poor fit to the current situation rather than by reference to absolute standards of mental health, and problematic behaviors are termed *maladaptive* or *dysfunctional* rather than *abnormal*. Intrinsic differences in male and female personality development and psychopathology are not posited (although cognitive behaviorists would be open to empirical evidence on this point). Men and women could, however, differ substantially in personality and psychopathology, depending on systematic differences in the environmental contingencies that they encounter in socialization and later life. Moreover, in a culturally diverse society like ours, individuals can acquire skills, values, and reactions that are not internally consistent or adaptive for current situations. As environmentalists, cognitive behaviorists have been social critics. For instance, they have suggested that our society's rigid standards for female physical attractiveness contribute to the etiology of eating disorders. Explicit challenges to these sex-stereotyped standards are an element in cognitive-behavioral treatment of anorexia nervosa (e.g., Garner & Bemis, 1982) and bulimia nervosa (e.g., Weiss, Katzman, & Wolchik, 1985).

Cognitive-behavioral treatment is designed to provide opportunities for new learning, including the acquisition of more behavioral and cognitive patterns and the unlearning of maladaptive ones. Assessment is considered essential before intervention. The aim is to make a *functional analysis* of the controlling conditions that affect the client's difficulties to guide the focus and methods of therapy. Cognitive behaviorists thus see themselves as addressing the causes of clients' difficulties in current situational, cognitive, affective, and behavioral processes. In treatment, cognitive behaviorists emphasize *proximal* causes, which are more immediately related to outcomes, rather than *distal*, more removed causes (e.g., historical origins).

The salient variables for assessment are summarized with the S-O-R-C mnemonic (Goldfried & Sprafkin, 1974) for stimuli, organismic variables, response variables, and consequences. Stimuli are the immediate environmental antecedents or cues for problematic behavior. Organismic variables mediate between *stimulus* and *response* variables. They include: (a) background variables such as social-learning history of specific problems; (b) biological factors such as general health; and (c) cognitive variables, including specific readily accessible thoughts and images (*self-statements*) that precede and accompany problems, standards for self-reinforcement, anticipated consequences of change and failure to change, and expectancies of therapy. Response variables involve the client's pertinent overt behaviors; consequence variables involve the impact of target behavior on the individual and other people and thus reflect possible operant factors.

Several methods are used to gather assessment data. Cognitive-behavioral interviews aim to pinpoint information on the S-O-R-C variables, treating the client as a generally credible though possibly inaccurate source of information. In addition to taking a participant-observer stance toward the client's interactions with the therapist, cognitive behaviorists try to observe specific problematic experiences. Since observation outside the office is usually impractical, the therapist often devises activities to bring pertinent behavior into the therapy session (e.g., role-playing; using a "think-aloud" procedure in which the client imagines a pertinent situation and narrates his or her thoughts and feelings). Self-monitoring assignments are also frequently used. The client is asked to note and record the occurrence of specified behaviors outside the session, along with possible controlling conditions such as situational context, antecedent thoughts, and reactions of others (Bornstein, Hamilton, & Bornstein, 1986). Questionnaires that directly assess salient variables are often used; for example, the Beck Depression Inventory (Beck, Ward, Mendelson, Mock, & Erbaugh, 1961) and the

Agoraphobic Cognitions Questionnaire (Chambless, Caputo, Bright, & Gallagher, 1984).

Based on the functional analysis, cognitive-behavior therapists select from an array of technical interventions and make treatment recommendations to the client. The therapist generally explains the treatment in light of the functional analysis and thus gives the client a cognitive and social-learning explanation of his or her difficulties that closely resembles the therapist's formulation. Cognitive-behavior therapists tend to view talk alone as a weak method to accomplish clinically significant change (cf. Bandura, 1977). They often use enactive methods of change, in which the client is guided to respond differently, usually in a hierarchical fashion of gradually increasing difficulty. In-session time is frequently used for practice of pertinent responses, such as more constructive self-talk or relaxation. Change is generally seen as a gradual linear process.

Cognitive-behavior therapy thus uses a skills-learning model in which the client's difficulties are seen as correctable by new learning through technical interventions. A set of core techniques, such as cognitive restructuring, systematic desensitization, and assertion training, are adapted to the particulars of the client's problems (cf. Dobson, 1988; Goldfried & Davison, 1976; and Masters, Burish, Hollon, & Rimm, 1987, for manuals of core techniques). Recently, well-specified "treatment packages" including various techniques have been developed for clients in specific diagnostic categories (cf. Barlow, 1985, for examples) as well as for people with specific problems (e.g., role strain in adult daughters who care for their elderly mothers, Scharlach, 1987). Many of these treatment packages have received empirical evaluation.

In cognitive-behavior therapy, the therapeutic relationship is generally viewed as a means to the end of implementing technical interventions. It can also provide specific new learning, such as social reinforcement and observation of particular patterns, in contrast to the global learning conveyed by constructs like corrective emotional experience (Alexander & French, 1946) and unconditional positive regard (Rogers, 1959). The client's life outside the therapy sessions is usually the focus of therapy. Cognitive behaviorists take an active, directive, and educative stance toward the client. The client is generally viewed as a collaborator who is competent to judge his or her goals, arrive at mutually agreeable treatment plans, and carry them out with the therapist's guidance.

In addition to the standard cognitive-behavioral model that we have portrayed, some cognitive-behavior therapists (including ourselves) have recently broadened their conceptualizations and practice. The notion of self-schemas—implicit organizing principles that summarize experience and guide perceptions of external events (Fiske & Linville, 1980)—has gained currency as a cognitive process that is not available to conscious self-report and can impede change. There is greater attention to possible conflicting emotional investments that may alter the expected linear-change process (e.g., Klass, 1990). There is more emphasis on exploring and experiencing affect (e.g., Safran & Segal, 1990) and on helping the client develop an understanding of historical sources of his or her difficulties (e.g., Klass, 1990). Nonetheless, these newer developments remain cognitive-behavioral in that they are used to provide an awareness of controlling variables and are generally followed by direct change efforts.

As empiricists, we emphasize that abstract discussions like this one may not match the richness or the realities of clinical practice. The portrayals of cognitive-behavioral therapy in action that follow may allow readers to come to their own conclusions about the characteristics of women as cognitive-behavior therapists.

## INTRODUCTION TO THE CASE

The presentation of a case study with the advantage of hindsight might be thought of as a clinician's dream. After all, at this point we are fully aware of the problems that have surfaced for Mary over the course of her therapy. Keeping this advantage in mind, we hope to present the major points of departure in how a cognitive-behavioral therapist would conceptualize the case and work with Mary.

Mary presents a complex case for cognitive-behavior therapy, with problems of conflicted motivation frequently encountered in clinical practice but rarely discussed in the cognitive behavioral literature (Turkat & Maisto, 1985). Her dysfunctional behavior, nevertheless, is seen as resulting from the way she has learned to cope with living, based on the antecedent and consequent conditions to which she has been exposed. Since her dysfunctional behavior has been learned, it can be treated directly through the application of learning principles.

## ASSESSMENT

The first component of cognitive-behavior therapy involves a thorough and specific assessment of the client's presenting problems. Emphasis would be placed on how Mary behaves, thinks, and feels in specific life situations and on the consequences of these responses. Since much of the specific information required for cognitive-behavioral assessment is missing in Mary's case presentation, I will create details needed to give an accurate portrayal of cognitive-behavior therapy.[2]

The goals of the initial interviews are to obtain information relevant to the presenting problems so that they can be defined in operational terms and to establish the rapport necessary to implement a therapeutic program. I would begin with a rather general discussion of the problems as Mary presents them and would move to elicit the specifics of her meaning (e.g., "In what ways is your relationship with your mother conflicted?"). While initial signs of dependency were present (e.g., requests for reassurance in session), indicators of a more conflicted behavioral style were manifested early (e.g., lateness to sessions, not completing initial self-monitoring assignment to record information about conflicts with her mother with the claim that she "forgot"). Based on these indicators, along with Mary's report that she had not graduated from college as she was "supposed to," I would be considering the diagnosis of passive-aggressive personality disorder and would begin to ask quite specific questions to investigate this. With the *Diagnostic and Statistical Manual of Mental Disorders* (*DSM III-R*, American Psychiatric Association, 1987) criteria in mind, I would explore indirect resistance to other people's expectations of her. So as not to create defensiveness on Mary's part, I would ask questions such as: What happens when someone expects her to do something that is very difficult for her? What happens when she gets angry or is unjustly treated? Does she do a better job than other people think she does? I would probe for specific examples and would use empathic reflections as we discuss Mary's responses to these questions. While I would expect Mary to have considerable passive-aggressive tendencies, she probably would not meet the full diagnostic criteria for this disorder. Thus I shall henceforth refer to her dysfunctional behavior as an indirect defiant-compliant pattern.

To begin to assess the antecedent, organismic, and consequent variables leading to the development and maintenance of this indirect behavioral pattern, I would inquire into her general functioning in family, educational, social, and occupational settings. I would also obtain a developmental history; inquire about drug, alcohol, and medication usage; and ask about her perceived areas of strength. As Mary is at present unaware of her contribution to her conflicts with others, I would attempt to abstract a functional analysis of her indirect defiant-compliant behavior pattern through in-session observation and examination of her history of interactions around differences between what she and others wanted. Following the S-O-R-C model of assessment, I would seek to answer the following questions:

1. Antecedent variables. How did the problematic behavior develop? What familial variables were associated with its development? At

present, what particular aspects of a situation trigger the arousal of the indirect defiant-compliant pattern?

2. Organismic variables. What are Mary's expectations and appraisals of herself and her parents? For instance, what are her criteria for being a "good" daughter? How do these relate to her view of Italian cultural expectations for daughters? I would consider ways that self-statements express dependent and anger-instigative qualities and would also assess affective variables. For instance, is Mary tense or agitated? Is she capable of seeing the less serious side of life? How sensitive is she to the feelings of others?

3. Response variables. What are the dimensions of the indirect defiant-compliant behavior pattern (e.g., its frequency, intensity, duration, typical mode(s) of expression, effect on performance, effect on relationships)? These parameters would be examined with respect to the various behavioral settings Mary functions in and the persons in these settings she interacts with. What is the stability of the dysfunctional pattern over time, (i.e., does its severity or mode of expression fluctuate, and what events are associated with these fluctuations)? For example, when Mary becomes upset with her mother's unreasonable demands or criticisms, she often argues bitterly. But how does she respond to the expectations of her college professors or friends? How capable is Mary of communicating her feelings to others? Can Mary express herself *assertively* (defined as standing up for one's rights and expressing one's beliefs, thoughts, and feelings in a direct, honest way without violating the rights of others; Lange & Jakubowski, 1976)? With whom? Under what circumstances? A brief assertion inventory (e.g., Alberti & Emmons, 1970; Rathus, 1973) might be administered to investigate this more efficiently. How does Mary go about attempting to resolve problems for herself? Information on Mary's past attempts to cope with problems is important in helping her develop effective approaches.

4. Consequent variables. How do others react to Mary's indirect defiant-compliant behavior and efforts to be assertive? How does Mary's indirect behavior pattern affect her feelings? What are the short- and long-term advantages and disadvantages of this behavior pattern for Mary?

From assessment thus far, I find that Mary's parents, while saying that they want her to be independent, often actively discourage it. For instance, they have not allowed her to open a checking or savings account of her own, her mother still does her laundry and cooks for her, and her parents continue to have veto power over Mary's decisions. Mary's indirect defiant-compliant behavioral pattern takes the following form. When an external demand that Mary perceives as unjustified is made, she often responds defiantly, although indirectly. She receives intense and bitter family criticism and eventually admits she was wrong out of fear of losing the meager familial support that she otherwise receives. With her compliance, the parental criticism subsides (a pattern of negative reinforcement). This pattern is most frequently activated by Mary's mother. With her college professors, she does not argue or find fault but procrastinates and hands in assignments late. She has a few friends with whom this pattern manifests itself far less frequently. Feelings of anxiety, while usually present, are most intense when Mary is in the throes of a dependence-independence conflict. She feels guilty about disappointing her mother and arguing with her, but is also angry at her for her frequent criticisms and unrealistic standards. Mary describes herself as unattractive, incompetent, stupid, testy, and unable to make decisions, and she doesn't believe she has any special talents or skills.

## CASE CONCEPTUALIZATION

Following the basic S-O-R-C model of assessment, Mary's pattern of vacillation between indirect defiance and compliance is understood as resulting from the repetitive environmental influences to which she has been exposed. Looking first at historical antecedents, there are several contributing factors. From an operant perspective, Mary experienced inconsistent and intermittent reinforcement for dependency and independence. Sometimes she was reinforced for complying with parental wishes that she remain dependent, and at other times she was criticized for her lack of independence. Mary was also exposed to intrafamilial communications that transmitted conflicting and incompatible messages. The contradictions in these parental messages were subtle and cloaked the hostility behind them. For example, Mary's parents hoped she would graduate from college and get a job, becoming independent, but also hoped she would remain single, help support the household, and stay at home to care for them, thus remaining dependent on her parents for establishing her role in life. Through exposure to these inconsistencies, Mary was frequently forced into approach-avoidance conflicts, situations in which a single goal has both desirable and undesirable attributes and the individual is both attracted and repelled by it. Mary was never sure what her parents really wanted of her, and no matter what action she took, she was often criticized. For instance, when she took an independent action such as going away for a weekend with friends, she was accused of being irresponsible and bad for making this decision. Moreover, the consequences of pointing out these parental contradictions were severe and generally included weeks of criticism of her every behavior.

Mary's behavioral vacillations, indecisiveness, and resistance to external demands become understandable when one realizes that because of the parental inconsistency, she was never able to discern a clear pattern of consequences for behavior, to predict which course of action would be instrumentally more effective, or to extricate herself from irreconcilable demands. Thus, she has not been able to anticipate the effects of her actions or develop a consistent and reliable strategy to achieve the reinforcers (e.g., security) that she seeks. Experimental research has demonstrated that behavioral oscillating characterizes individuals caught in approach-avoidance conflicts (Miller, 1959). Mary's behavioral vacillations reflect such contradictory motivations, suggesting a constant state of insecurity (e.g., asking for frequent advice and reassurance) and anxiety. The frustration and confusion she feels turn readily into anger and resentment. Guilt subsequently emerges and frequently serves to curtail her anger. Moreover, experimental research indicates that intermittent reinforcement strengthens behaviors, making them more persistent under conditions of extinction, the absence of positive reinforcement (Ferster & Skinner, 1957).

Observational learning also contributes to Mary's dysfunctional behavior. Mary has had few, if any, models of independently functioning, straightforward, and assertive adults. Her parents continue to be manifestly in conflict with each other, and most of their interactions with each other express this discord. Mary thus fears family dissolution and dreads that the few family supports she receives will be lost. In addition, she was slotted to serve as a mediator to moderate the tensions that her parents generate (e.g., she took dinner down to the basement to her father each evening). She was not free to be herself with either parent, as she was expected to switch sides and divide her loyalties to satisfy the antagonistic parental expectations. Mary has not only become confused and anxious because of her inconsistent reinforcement contingencies, but has also learned to have similarly erratic contradictory actions and attitudes. Mary was also taught to adhere to a strongly moralistic prohibitive code of conduct. Her mother frequently pointed out how much Mary's behavior hurt her. Thus, guilt was an additional punishment for self-expression, and the avoidance of guilt became another motivation. Because of the inconsistencies, and since decisions have been made for Mary by her family most of her life, she has skills deficits in problem solving and assertion that have also contributed to her inability to have a positive impact on the world around her.

As a result of this social-learning history, Mary has developed a self-schema composed of contradictory appraisals replete with dichotomous thinking (i.e., seeing things in extreme, all-or-nothing terms, Burns, 1980). She doesn't know whether to think of herself as competent or incompetent, weak or strong, good or bad, loving or hating those upon whom she feels dependent. Instead, she alternates between seeing herself in these opposing ways.

Mary currently remains stuck in an approach-avoidance conflict. When she acquiesces to the wishes of her parents, she feels resentful and angry for giving up her independence and allowing herself to be weak. When she behaves in an aggressive and defiant manner to express her independence, she becomes anxious for having endangered her tenuous dependent security and anticipates feeling guilty for hurting her mother. While the disadvantages of Mary's indirect defiant-compliant behavioral style are apparent (e.g., high levels of anxiety, fear of abandonment, indecisiveness, alienating people), there are also hidden benefits. The behavioral chain usually begins when Mary feels that too much has been expected of her. After reacting to this in a defiant, albeit surreptitious, manner, she usually expresses guilt and then self-condemnation. She then solicits forgiveness and reassurance from others, which also serves to keep them from making other demands on her for the time being. Thus, she gains the attention and support she craves while also subtly venting anger and resentments without incurring her most feared consequences. In addition to ongoing reinforcement experiences in her family, these hidden benefits and the sense of covert power they engender are current maintainers of Mary's maladaptive behavior.

Some cognitive-behavior therapists might choose to work with this entire family because of the many dysfunctional reinforcement contingencies that they present to Mary. I choose to work individually with Mary, however, to help her become solidly independent and disengaged from the destructive behavioral style of her family. I believe there is a greater likelihood for Mary to change and access new, consistent supportive networks than for this whole family to be modified.

In summary, Mary is experiencing a conflict between her desire for autonomy and her need to lean on others. We can think of her indirect defiant-compliant behavior as a coping skill that she has learned to deal with her fears of abandonment while allowing her to express anger about the conflicting incentives that have been presented to her by her family. Perhaps the most proximal controlling condition for the indirect behavioral style is the sense of power that Mary experiences when she thwarts others' attempts to make her do things she does not want to do. While such conflict is not typically addressed by cognitive-behavior therapists, it is well within the constructs of the experimental learning and motivation literature upon which cognitive-behavior therapy was built.

## GOALS

Stemming from this conceptualization, I would begin to formulate treatment goals:

1. Reduction of Mary's anxiety level.
2. Recognition of the character of her approach-avoidance conflict and her indirect defiant-compliant behavior pattern.
3. Greater awareness of her needs and wishes and more effective ways to gratify them.
4. Development of greater consistency in social behaviors and greater control over her erratic and volatile emotions.
5. Reduction of her dependence on others and increase in her self-reliance through the acquisition of skills for competent and independent functioning.
6. A more positive, integrated, and consistent self-schema.
7. Recognition of the sources of her indirect defiant-compliant behavior pattern in the familial environment as a means to increase her sense of control over this response style.

While cognitive behaviorists tend to work to accomplish specific goals from the outset of therapy, it is important for both therapist and client to recognize that Mary is likely to need long-term treatment. In addition, when a client presents so many issues of conflicting motivation, it is unrealistic to expect a straightforward linear therapeutic approach to be successful. Nevertheless, cognitive-behavior therapy does offer much to a client with these difficulties in that it presents many techniques that can help Mary develop skills she can use to function more effectively in the world.

## INTERPERSONAL ASPECTS OF THERAPY

The interpersonal aspects of therapy with a client who vacillates between dependent compliance and indirect defiant resistance to external demands are of utmost importance. The use of collaboration and guided discovery, in which the therapist uses Socratic dialogue, helps counteract the client's tendency on the one hand to transfer her dependence to another person, and on the other hand to become enraged at what she experiences as externally imposed demands and attempts to undermine her independence. Consistency and limit setting in therapy are crucial. The therapist needs to be aware of attempts at manipulation within therapy (e.g., forgetting to do homework assignments, requesting reassurance about decisions) and, without punishing these attempts, to make sure they are not inadvertently reinforced. At the same time, the therapist needs to attend to more adaptive attempts to define and meet genuine needs and, without putting undue pressure on the client to continue to succeed, to reinforce these efforts. The therapist needs to show empathy and sympathy for the difficulty that the client experiences in attempting to extricate herself from her approach-avoidance conflict.

In cognitive-behavior therapy, the therapist purposefully uses the reinforcing capacity that is developed through the establishment of rapport to encourage the client to make desired changes. The therapist encourages self-reinforcement (e.g., "How did you feel when you did x?) and gradually reduces her use of explicit positive reinforcement as the client obtains environmental reinforcers and becomes able to reinforce herself for changes. In addition, through the use of judicious self-disclosure, the therapist can provide the client with a coping model of an independently functioning adult (i.e., one who shares problems she has had in the areas discussed and the ways she has learned to deal with them).

I would expect that Mary would assume dependent and indirectly defiant roles during sessions. One tactic I would use to deal with Mary's indirect expression of anger would be to predict how she is likely to react to therapist communications. I would also suggest, rather than require or prescribe tasks. I would expect that these tactics would lessen the extent to which Mary experiences a direct conflict between my wants and her wants. To help further the development of Mary's independence, I would utilize a role-switching procedure. For example, when she asks, "How should I handle this situation?", I would switch roles with her, become the individual with the problem in decision making, and prompt Mary to provide the solution to her query. I would expect and hope that after numerous such experiences, the signal to switch roles might become our private therapeutic joke and, through a cuing process, trigger Mary's independent problem solving. Ultimately, I would hope, Mary would catch herself in the middle of asking for help and provide her own answers.

From a cognitive-behavioral perspective, Mary's noncompliance with interventions could indicate any number of problems. These would include the need for additional training in a technique, redefining goals, breaking a task down into more manageable subunits, adding cues in the environment as triggers, or finding a more appropriate incentive system. In Mary's case, noncompliance will sometimes also be a behavioral sample of her indirect defiance or reflect the conflicting incentives in her environment. I would be sure to analyze instances of noncompliance carefully to address the pertinent controlling conditions.

## THERAPEUTIC INTERVENTIONS

While cognitive-behavior therapy is goal-oriented in its approach, in actual clinical practice, therapists tend to work on goals in an interrelated manner rather than one at a time. Cognitive-behavior therapy is also known by its techniques, however; thus, for clarity in presentation, my therapeutic analysis has been organized primarily by technique.

### Anxiety Management and Problem Solving

The learning theory underlying cognitive-behavior therapy provides little guidance on where to begin therapeutically. Some authors suggest beginning with the goal most meaningful to the client, while others focus on the importance of early success in treatment (Goldfried & Davison, 1976). I would choose to address Mary's high level of anxiety first, as this is an area in which I would expect to be able to have some initial impact. Learning to modulate her anxiety level can serve a second purpose for Mary. She can, in a small but important way, come to experience a greater sense of control over her affective intensity.

I might begin by suggesting that Mary track when her anxiety level goes up during a session. I would expect this would be difficult for Mary, and we would follow up on this by discussing how she can discriminate when she is anxious and when she is not. I would suggest that she begin to notice physical and physiological cues that indicate her anxiety (e.g., tightness in her shoulders or jaw, increased rate of respiration). This is the first step toward increasing her awareness that she may be confronting a conflictual situation. I would suggest that it might be interesting to continue to self-monitor her high levels of anxiety and the situational contexts during the week.

Next, I would teach Mary to monitor her anxiety level in a more finely differentiated manner (e.g., rate it on a scale from 0 to 100) and help her discern the source of the anxiety. Once Mary is more cognizant of her generally high anxiety level, the following rationale would be shared: "Mary, it's no wonder you feel so anxious so much of the time with the inconsistent reinforcement history you grew up with, sometimes being rewarded for a behavior and at other times being punished for the same behavior. But it seems that your high anxiety level is currently functioning like static on a radio. When there's too much static, you can't hear the message. Also, you tend to want to walk away from that radio because it's so distracting. We need to find ways to turn down this static, so that you can begin to hear your inner guide directing you to what you want in a situation."

I would begin to incorporate the use of problem solving at this time to help us find appropriate anxiety reduction techniques. Problem solving involves four basic steps: problem definition, generation of alternatives (brainstorming), decision making (after predicting consequences of each course of action and determining how effective each course of action is likely to be), and taking action (D'Zurilla & Goldfried, 1971). Through the use of this approach, Mary can be helped to recognize her alternatives in problem situations and to make conscious choices. I would initially model this procedure and generate ideas to try to reduce her high level of anxiety. She would then be taught some techniques to reduce the intensity of her anxious feelings (e.g., diaphragmatic breathing, Smith, 1985; progressive muscle relaxation, Bernstein & Borkovec, 1973). I would make a change in standard progressive muscle relaxation training at this time. I would suggest through imagery that Mary explore with herself and find her own inner guide or supportive inner observer (Wilson, 1986). This supportive inner observer can help her to determine her wants and needs, assist in making decisions, and provide support for these decisions. Thus, we would already be setting up some initial groundwork for self-reliance.

I would make it clear that Mary need not use any of the above techniques, only be aware of their existence. I might ask her to consider practicing the breathing and muscle relaxation exercises as well as continuing to monitor her anxiety level between sessions, and we both might predict her reluctance to do these assignments. A problem-solving approach would be woven into the therapy as deemed appropriate without making any demands on Mary actually to incorporate its use.

## Assertion Issues

### Recognition of Indirect Style

As Mary gains some degree of control over the intensity of her anxiety level, I would begin the process of helping her become more cognizant of her indirect behavior style. I might attempt to bring her indirect anger into focus by tracking affective changes during the session and probing how she feels when she complies with me.

The first goal would be to help Mary admit her anger and that she is expressing it in indirect ways. It would be suggested that she self-monitor when she feels "bad" during the week and note when she has given in to the demands of others. From this I would hope to discover a correlation between negative feelings and compliance, and I might try to track backward to find any evidence of indirect defiance. From Mary's self-monitoring records and much discussion, we would learn that a typical episode would progress as follows: Mary's mother criticizes her for doing something (e.g., coming home late one night). This would be followed by subvocal cursing on Mary's part, progressive tensing of her body (with particularly high tension levels in her neck, shoulders, brow, and jaw), and verbal abuse between mother and daughter lasting for days. Mary would behave in an indirectly defiant manner during this period (staying out late many nights), and finally the cycle would end with Mary subjugating her independence needs, apologizing, being given a stern lecture by her mother, and feeling defeated. Normal communication between mother and daughter would then resume. A sequence such as this would occur twice a month, on the average.

After Mary begins to be somewhat more comfortable about recognizing her indirect defiance, I might suggest the following to explain how this pattern developed: "There have been many things you have wanted in your life. For example, you have desires for closeness and being taken care of as well as to be independent and assertive. Many of these desires have been dealt with in harsh and inconsistent ways; for example, when your mother told you to stay home and keep her company on Saturday, which you did, then accused you of being cold and uncaring when you made plans to see a movie with your friend that evening. Your direct assertion has been punished severely. For example, when you told your mother that you felt uncomfortable about her doing your laundry and that you wanted to learn how to do it yourself, she called you an ingrate and stopped speaking to you. Despite these negative environmental consequences, you still have the desires, so you've learned to gratify them indirectly. You know, you don't have to have a confrontation with your family whenever your wishes for you differ from their wishes for you, but maybe you don't have to give up on what you want, either." I would also try to validate Mary's angry feelings. For example, in response to her telling me how she overslept for one of her college exams, I might say, "Lots of people might feel angry when others keep telling them to get a college degree and they feel scared to death that they won't be able to handle getting and keeping a job after graduation."

At this point, I would probably begin to address Mary's lateness to sessions as an example of this indirect behavioral style. I would try to help Mary to express her true feelings (e.g., "Well, people have mixed feelings a lot of the time when things happen") and to own the fact that she is expressing her ambivalence about coming to therapy in an indirect manner. We might use the problem-solving approach again to generate ideas about how she might be able to get to her session on time. Together we would predict that she is likely to be even later to her session next week, in response to what she may experience as an external unrealistic demand. Perhaps this discussion will (paradoxically) serve to short-circuit her tendency to feel victimized, and to rebel and resist.

As Mary's recognition of her indirect defiance increased, we would begin to look at the hidden benefits of this indirect style (e.g., covert power to express anger at demands of her parents without threatening her needs to depend on them). Alternative direct approaches to obtain the same goal might be generated, while recognizing that this might not be possible with her parents. In reviewing Mary's self-monitoring assignments, I would suggest the alternative of reframing Mary's valid needs (Bandler & Grinder, 1979) in situations where she finds herself acting in an indirectly defiant manner. I would suggest that she ask herself, "What is the valid need I am trying to meet in this situation, and how can I meet this valid need in ways that are less destructive to me than undermining myself and feeling so guilty afterward?" Standard problem-solving techniques introduced earlier in therapy can be used to generate alternative possibilities, and role-playing would take place.

## Emotional Recognition

With an indirectly defiant client such as Mary, the process of assertion training would require different tactics than the typical teaching of skills for direct communication of wishes, beliefs, and opinions. First, assertion is punished at home. Second, such an independent stance is too threatening to Mary's need to maintain family support, no matter how hostile and contradictory that support is. Thus, work on Mary's assertion deficits would be woven into the general therapeutic approach, addressing emotional recognition, assertion, and adaptive methods of anger management together, as well as recognizing the tremendous difficulty that Mary will have implementing these skills in her family. Recognition of Mary's conflicts every step of the way would differentiate this therapy from a more standard cognitive-behavioral approach.

I would work toward increasing Mary's emotional recognition by first establishing that she often does not seem to know what she wants. Already we would have looked at physical symptoms of stress or tension as clues that Mary is experiencing discomfort, possibly due to a conflict situation. The first step in "getting in touch" with her feelings is to be able to recognize and accurately label her emotions and desires. We could begin with situations she has brought into session for her anxiety self-monitoring assignments. I might use periodic probes during the sessions, asking her how she is feeling at that moment. A useful assignment at this time would be *Yes's* and *No's* (Barbach, 1975), in which Mary would be asked first to observe herself in interpersonal situations and notice on three occasions when she says yes but wants to say no, and on three occasions when she says no but wants to say yes. A follow-up discussion of this assignment could segue into an exploration of what is preventing Mary from expressing her desires and emotions openly. This would lead to a discussion of how Mary's parents have punished her attempts to stand up for herself and how she has become fearful of losing their love (e.g., "You haven't ever learned what you want because someone has always been telling you what you should do, criticizing you, or yelling at you"). Thus an early goal in this domain would be to help Mary give herself permission for her feelings.

Giving Mary permission to have her feelings and her needs, especially her healthy need for independence, may eliminate one of the reasons her anger was forced underground. Of course, the environmental contingencies at home for overtly expressed assertion or anger may channel them back into a mode of indirect expression. This is a real therapeutic bind, for how can one expect to change a pattern that continues to be so highly reinforcing? Indirect anger and aggression may appear to be the only ways Mary can express her resentment of an intolerable situation. For this reason, self-reinforcement for gradual approximations to the desired goals would be absolutely vital. In addition, I would encourage Mary to join a carefully chosen therapy group addressing general interpersonal issues at the same time that I introduced assertion skills in her individual therapy. I believe the group format can reinforce assertive behavior and help Mary acquire more consistency in social situations. Building in the reinforcers for more direct expression of her feelings would be important. Therapy is unlikely to be effective if Mary continues interacting with people primarily within her dysfunctional family since the maladaptive style will be reinforced and healthier patterns of direct expression of feelings punished.

## Assertion Training

After Mary and I defined assertion together and generated reasons for her to consider expressing herself assertively, we would begin to discuss the differences between assertive, unassertive, aggressive, and indirectly defiant responses. The discussion would include characteristics of the behaviors, feelings when engaging in the behaviors, and other people's feelings when you engage in the behavior. Abstracting from material Mary has brought into session, we would begin to articulate her rights and responsibilities as an adult (e.g., the right to ask for what she wants, make mistakes, and make decisions for herself, Alberti & Em-

mons, 1970). This would begin to lay the foundation for Mary to develop an assertive belief system (Lange & Jakubowski, 1976).

After this introduction to assertion, I would start to focus more on the
interaction between us during sessions. We would discuss Mary's antici-
pation of other people's reactions to her behavior (e.g., "How do you
expect I will react when you want to reschedule an appointment next
week? What about when you call fifteen minutes before the session to
reschedule? How does each expectation make you feel?"). Mary has
learned to behave in a manner that indirectly expresses her feelings because she anticipates, based on the reinforcement contingencies to
which she has been exposed within her family, that people will react
negatively to her direct expression of independence needs (e.g., "Of
course you expect I'll be upset with you for assertively expressing a
need. That's happened to you so often at home. I wonder how this expectation makes you feel? I wonder if it affects your behavior?"). Discussion about the extent to which these expectations fit here and now
would ensue.

Our approach to the enactment of assertive behavior would obviously
need to be very cautious in light of the punishing responses that Mary
is likely to encounter from her family. Based on Mary's social-learning
history, I would sympathetically recognize with Mary how difficult putting this new skill into practice will be. I would suggest that Mary needs
to proceed in ways that feel safe and that it makes sense to choose not
to assert oneself in a situation that feels unsafe. I would encourage her
to start using assertive behavior with people more likely to respond positively than her parents. I would also emphasize defining goals in any
assertive exercise in terms of her own behaviors, cognitions, and affective responses, so that they do not depend on the other person's response. Thus, Mary could separate her sense of accomplishment from
the specific environmental consequences. I would emphasize self-reinforcement as well as ways for Mary to maintain assertion in the face of
others' aggression (e.g., escalating assertion, confrontive assertion, and
repeating assertions while responding to legitimate points made by the
other person, Jakubowski & Lange, 1978, pp. 233–260).

Being fully aware of the empirical literature that indicates that women
are often negatively evaluated by others for their assertive expression
(Kelly, Kern, Kirkley, Patterson, & Keane, 1980; Romano & Bellack,
1980), I would discuss these findings with Mary. I would help prepare
her for this, and together we would review her ideas as to why assertion
can be a useful skill. To help Mary handle potential rejections effectively, we would role-play potential rejections, and I would introduce
the concept of empathic assertion (Lange & Jakubowski, 1976). Research
has shown that women's empathic assertive responses (i.e., an asser-

tion with extra consideration for the other person's feelings) are received more positively by others than more direct and straightforward assertion (Romano & Bellack, 1980; Woolfolk & Dever, 1979). It is often inappropriately assumed that women's and men's assertion goals are equivalent (i.e., that they are more concerned with achieving the objectives of their response than with maintaining or enhancing their relationship with the other person in the interaction, Linehan, 1984). Mary's goals in her assertive interactions would need to be clarified before she can decide on the type of assertive response most likely to result in reaching her goal.

As Mary learns that her new assertive skills can work effectively for her in the therapy sessions, experiments can be set up to help her test when this approach works and when it doesn't in the world outside of therapy. For example, Mary might be asked to predict the reaction to her complimenting a store clerk or classmate, expressing displeasure to a shopkeeper or waitress, or disagreeing with a friend about a movie or book. She would then be encouraged to test her predictions. As Mary becomes more successful in expressing herself assertively, it would be important to demonstrate systematically to her how each task she accomplishes challenges the idea that she cannot be competent. Left to her own devices, Mary has great difficulty in drawing connections between her actions and her level of competence.

## Cognitive Restructuring

Discussion of Mary's expectations during assertion training would provide an opportunity to begin to address the cognitions that elicit and maintain Mary's negative feelings. In a standard cognitive-behavior-therapy approach, the client is taught to recognize biases or cognitive distortions in thinking (e.g., dichotomous thinking, overgeneralization, personalization), to challenge these dysfunctional thoughts, and to substitute more adaptive ones. As Mary is likely to experience this as criticism of how she thinks, I would instead focus on describing Mary's cognitive processes and how her expectations of others may in fact set a self-fulfilling prophecy in motion. To help us both realize how easily Mary feels criticized, I might say, "You're 5'3", have black hair, and you're wearing jeans. Now, how do you feel when I say that?" I would expect to find that Mary experiences this as a criticism (i.e., she hears the other person saying, "You should be different than you are"). Again, we would draw on her social-learning history (e.g., "Even when your mom said, 'Your hair is getting longer,' that was a criticism, not a description, because she meant, 'You should get a haircut'"). I would encourage Mary to test how this expectation of criticism fits in interpersonal interactions outside her family. To try to check Mary's tendency to feel criticized, I might predict it (e.g., when I describe a cognitive distortion that I observe Mary engaging in and say, "It's interesting. You certainly think about things in an all-or-nothing way," I would follow it with "I bet you might have heard that as a criticism." After her reply, I would follow up with "It's interesting, you know I see it differently. An observation just describes, while a criticism has a judgment attached to it").

The rules guiding Mary's behavior and the standards by which she evaluates her behavior change will also need to be addressed. One of her rules seems to be "I should never feel angry at others." An important goal would be to help Mary alter this unrealistic rule. One technique I might use would be asking her to list the advantages and disadvantages of having this rule (Beck, Rush, Shaw, & Emery, 1979). Mary's view of herself and others tends to be quite dichotomous (e.g., she's either good or bad, competent or incompetent). Again, we would reflect on the historical antecedents of this cognitive pattern. Her mother had rigidly high standards for her and was intolerant of her failures to meet these standards. Mary's dichotomous thinking could be cautiously approached through the use of metaphor (Linehan, 1987: "When you look at a glass of water filled to the middle, most people see it as either half empty or half full. Everybody has probably told you that you should see it as half full when you've seen it as half empty. But, you know, I see it differently. It's both half empty and half full"). I would suggest that Mary is probably neither good nor bad, neither totally competent nor totally incompetent, but a blend of strengths and weaknesses. We would collect data that would, I expect, validate this assertion. This would allow us to begin addressing Mary's behavioral strengths and weaknesses in a descriptive, uncritical manner.

Therapeutically, we need to increase Mary's awareness that her current self-critical cognitions are an extension of her earlier experiences, implying that the feelings are understandable but may be unwarranted from the vantage point of today, and also to increase her tolerance for her personal failings. We would work to increase her willingness to be self-accepting, despite her shortcomings, through the use of supportive self-statements that Mary would generate herself (e.g., "That's quite a mistake I made. But don't forget how much I can learn from it. And making mistakes doesn't make me bad or stupid, just human and fallible").

A straightforward self-instructional training component (Meichenbaum, 1985) in which Mary is helped to generate more coping, competence-enhancing self-statements may confront many obstacles. It is possible that Mary will have difficulty giving up her self-critical attitude and continue to feel guilty. If so, the reinforcers or investments in the apparently aversive experience of feeling guilty will need to be explored (Klass, 1990). Possible hidden benefits include: guilt short-circuits the escalating cycle of anger; it reinforces Mary's self-schema that she is a mass of contradictions and couldn't possibly survive without the support, albeit shaky, of her parents; it allows her to maintain her attachment to her parents, regardless of how poor they were at carrying out basic parenting functions; and by feeling guilty and responsible for events at home (e.g., causing her mother's blood pressure to rise), Mary doesn't have to experience threatening feelings of dependency and neediness that her dysfunctional family has engendered. The successful challenge of these strong reinforcers for self-criticism and guilt may depend on Mary's developing new attachments outside of her family. As Mary's therapy progresses, it would be particularly important to encourage her to access new social systems that support adaptive autonomy and decrease the cues for dependency.

At a later point in therapy, Mary's expectations about men and relationships with men would be discussed. (There is no evidence that Mary is anything but heterosexual in her inclinations.) If, for example, she expects men to be critical and/or emotionally·abusive, she would be encouraged to test these expectations, using her new assertive skills. Through becoming involved in new activities where men are present and share interests with her, she would be able to broaden her experiences with men and perhaps avoid becoming involved in a dependent, abusive romantic relationship. If not, we would recognize the pattern in this relationship as a replication of an old experience whereby she revalidates her sense of herself as weak, helpless, and inadequate, as well as subjugating her own needs in order to maintain a relationship. We would discuss this relationship with frequent reference to her social-learning history by asking about familiar situations and feelings in this relationship. The replication of conflicting environmental incentives would be addressed. Together we would help her build her sense of what she wants and deserves in a relationship. The book *Women Who Love Too Much* (Norwood, 1985) might be recommended and discussed, and she would be encouraged to join a women's support group addressing this type of problem if her therapy group were not doing so.

## Stress Inoculation

I would also incorporate a stress inoculation program for anger problems (Novaco, 1975) to help Mary manage her anger and use it more constructively. Stress inoculation follows an immunization model (Meichenbaum, 1985). Given opportunities to deal effectively with mildly stressful stimuli, it is predicted that one will be able to tolerate stressful situations of greater intensity in the future. Novaco (1975) viewed anger as jointly determined by an initial provocation, mediating cognitions, the somatic-affective state of the individual, and behaviors that escalate the anger. We would begin by generating ideas about the functions of anger, both adaptive (e.g., anger is an energizer, a cue to tell us that something is unjust or threatening, and a potentiator of feelings of control) and maladaptive (e.g., anger disrupts thoughts and actions and instigates aggression). It would be suggested that Mary consider keeping a daily diary of her anger experiences to help us learn more about the specifics of her anger patterns. The diary may also help Mary distance herself from particular episodes and adopt the role of an outside observer by defining the situation as a problem calling for a solution rather than a threat calling for an attack that is forced to go underground because of fear of retaliation. From a review of these assignments, we would come to identify the persons and situations that most typically tend to trigger Mary's anger, and the typical interaction sequences. It is important to note that the goal of this intervention is to teach Mary socially acceptable ways to express her anger and not to stop her from feeling angry—in other words, help her to maximize the adaptive functions of anger and minimize its maladaptive functions.

Through discussion of information Mary brings in from her anger diary, she would be helped to discover that anger occurs as a series of stages (e.g. preparing for the provocation, reacting during the confrontation, coping with arousal, and reflecting on the experience, Novaco, 1975). Since Mary's indirect defiant-compliant behavior is actually a sequence of responses chained together, we will have a far greater likelihood of reducing the defiant indirect expression of anger if Mary's efforts at self-control occur early rather than late in the sequence. For instance, an early realization that she would like to make her own decisions about when to return home at night and an empathic assertive statement with a willingness to compromise might ward off the whole self-destructive sequence. When Mary's mother begins criticizing Mary upon her arrival home one night, Mary could say, "Mom, I know you really worry about me when I come home at this hour. I wonder if it might be helpful if, in the future, when I'm going to be later than midnight, I give you a call to let you know?" Spontaneously provided self-statements that help her cope with a provocation would be reinforced, and she would be encouraged to expand upon these. Both emotional controls (e.g., progressive muscle relaxation and humor, both of which are incompatible with anger) and behavioral controls (e.g., assertion) might be generated through problem solving as alternatives to the maladaptive expression of anger.

Mary would also be helped to understand the feelings of other people, using a role-reversal technique, and to become aware of her repeating interpersonal cycles (e.g., when she responds with hostility, even indirectly cloaked, this elicits further hostility in the other person). I would proceed cautiously in encouraging her to apply her new anger-management skills, first by means of imaginal and role-playing inductions of anger and later outside her therapy sessions. When Mary is ready, we could practice provocation simulations in a hierarchy ranging from minor annoyances to infuriating events. This hierarchical approach, aiming for gradual approximations of the desired behaviors, typifies cognitive-behavior therapy.

At a later point in therapy, after Mary's feelings and fears about getting a job were discussed and if she did decide that she wanted or needed to work, she would be encouraged to use stress inoculation procedures (Meichenbaum, 1985) to prepare for job interviews (e.g., viewing the stress as occurring in stages and generating self-statements to help her cope more effectively). Role-playing would be used extensively to prepare for this task. Her appraisals of the interview situation would be examined (e.g., "This is important to me, and if I don't get the job, I must be a loser"). By now, Mary would probably be able to describe cognitive distortions in her responses. If she could not spontaneously generate alternatives, "dispute handles" (Heimberg & Becker, 1984) that elicit coping self-statements might help Mary alter her view of the situation. (For example, she could ask herself: "How likely is it that I won't get the job? What evidence do I have that this means I'm a loser? Is getting this job really so important that my entire future or sense of self-worth should reside in its outcome?") Thus, she might come to view the interview situation as an experiment to try out her new assertive skills or as an opportunity to determine whether she is interested in this particular work environment. As with assertion, I would encourage Mary to set a goal other than the external environmental feedback of getting the job (e.g., maintaining eye contact, asking questions that she has prepared).

Thus, Mary's therapy would be long-term and consist of many forward and backward progressions. Therapeutic effectiveness would be monitored on an ongoing basis, prompting readjustments in the therapy as necessary.

## PREPARATION FOR TERMINATION

I would begin to prepare for therapy termination when Mary reached her stated goals and/or felt satisfied with the progress she had made. In planning for maintenance of her therapeutic gains, with Mary's collaboration, we would gradually withdraw the structure of the therapy program, perhaps by reducing the frequency of therapy sessions, and monitor the durability of behavior change. I would also use some relapse prevention tactics (Marlatt & Gordon, 1985). The first step in relapse prevention is having Mary identify situations that may tempt her to slip back into old patterns of indirect expression of defiance and compliance (e.g., an increase in stress, getting a new job, an indication of her mother's love withdrawal, higher levels of emotions such as anxiety or anger). Behavioral and cognitive rehearsal of how she could handle these situations more skillfully would ensue. We might make a relapse prevention card to remind her of specific steps to help keep a slip from becoming a relapse (e.g., remember the triggering stimuli, make an immediate plan for recovery from the slip, and specify ways to avoid the slip in the future). I would suggest that instead of seeing a slip as permanent defeat, it can be an opportunity for learning that indicates a mistake that needn't be repeated. Reattributing a slip to something in the situation for which one can be prepared is also a helpful tactic. Mary would be told that guilt over lapses may actually increase rather than reduce her self-defeating behavior (Beck et al., 1979). The importance of perseverance in the process of behavior change would be stressed, perhaps using an analogy (e.g., "Like walking down a road, you will find yourself at different places along the road as you move along, sometimes turning off for a bit, and then returning"). I would also schedule follow-up sessions. These would also provide me with information to evaluate the effectiveness and durability of my treatment strategies and indicate whether alterations in my own behavior would be needed in the future. Finally, I would let Mary know of my availability to her for any future therapeutic work should she so desire.

## DISCUSSION

We would expect that the therapeutic interventions introduced in the course of Mary's cognitive-behavior therapy would increase her awareness of her approach-avoidance conflicts and would increase her skills for making choices for herself and functioning in a competent, direct, and independent manner. We would also expect Mary's self-schema regarding her personal worth and her involvements with other people to become more flexible. In considering how other cognitive-behavior therapists might approach this case, we would expect numerous points of similarity but also differences. For example, the approach-avoidance conflict that Mary confronted is less commonly addressed in standard cognitive-behavior therapy. We suspect, however, that these differences would probably reflect individual variations in style rather than gender-related differences between therapists.

Through cognitive-behavior therapy, Mary was encouraged to acquire skills to help empower her, and in becoming assertive and independent, she was helped to consider herself, rather than the therapist, as her best guide. A female therapist may be a more direct model of an independently functioning woman to Mary than a male therapist, but male therapists certainly can model and reinforce independence and assertion in women clients. We speculate that Mary may have chosen a female therapist because of greater familiarity with and comfort in working with women, and because of her naïveté and discomfort with men, an issue that was addressed in therapy.

We might speculate that a male cognitive-behavior therapist would be somewhat less concerned with maintaining Mary's relationship with her family. He might place more emphasis on autonomy and separation from this rather destructive environmental setting. In the treatment that we outlined, Mary was helped to recognize and confront the conflicting familial and subcultural messages that created her maladaptive behaviors. She was taught how to dispute actively some of the more destructive messages that she had received. But we think it rather unrealistic to expect an adult female raised within the milieu discussed here to break off completely from her family. We would certainly encourage Mary to develop outside sources of support for her newfound independence but would teach her ways of communicating more effectively with her family (e.g., empathic assertion) and help her learn to receive many of the more critical messages less as a personal indictment. Thus, we would see autonomy and attachment as compatible. Whether cognitive-behavior therapists actually differ in their choice of target behaviors and techniques of intervention as a function of their own gender and that of their client is an empirical question that merits investigation.

In conclusion, the therapeutic approach used in Mary's case demonstrates many features of cognitive-behavior therapy. These include the educative, active, and directive stance of the therapist; the value on assessment and ongoing monitoring of change; specificity in problem assessment, definition, and treatment; and a gradual, incremental approach to change. The extent to which differences and similarities emerge within these areas when cognitive-behavior therapy is compared to the other treatment approaches presented in this volume will be of interest.

## NOTES

1. Readers are referred to Dobson and Block (1988), Goldfried and Davison (1976, pp. 3–78), and Masters, Burish, Hollon, and Rimm (1987, pp. 1–12) for more extensive discussions of these matters.

2. In the case analysis, the use of the pronoun *I* for the therapist will be used for ease of communication.

# REFERENCES

Alberti, R. E., & Emmons, M. L. (1970). *Your perfect right: A guide to assertive behavior* (2nd ed.). San Luis Obispo, CA: Impact.

Alexander, R., & French, T. M. (1946). *Psychoanalytic therapy.* New York: Ronald Press.

American Psychiatric Association. (1987). *Diagnostic and statistical manual of mental disorders* (3rd ed., rev.). Washington, DC: American Psychiatric Press.

Bandler, R., & Grinder, J. (1979). *Frogs into princes: Neurolinguistic programming.* Moab, UT: Real People Press.

Bandura, A. (1965). Influence of models' reinforcement contingencies on the acquisition of imitative responses. *Journal of Personality and Social Psychology, 1*, 589–595.

Bandura, A. (1977). Self-efficacy: Toward a unifying theory of behavioral change. *Psychological Review, 84*, 191–215.

Bandura, A. (1978). *Social learning theory.* Englewood Cliffs, NJ: Prentice-Hall.

Barbach, L. G. (1975). *For yourself: The fulfillment of female sexuality.* New York: New American Library.

Barlow, D. H. (Ed.). (1985). *Clinical handbook of psychological disorders.* New York: Guilford.

Beck, A. T., Rush, A. J., Shaw, B. F., & Emery, G. (1979). *Cognitive therapy of depression.* New York: Guilford.

Beck, A. T., Ward, C. H., Mendelson, M., Mock, J., & Erbaugh, J. (1961). An inventory for measuring depression. *Archives of General Psychiatry, 4*, 561–571.

Bernstein, D. A., & Borkovec, T. D. (1973). *Progressive relaxation training: A manual for the helping professions.* Champaign, IL: Research Press.

Bornstein, P. H., Hamilton, S. B., & Bornstein, M. T. (1986). Self-monitoring procedures. In A. R. Ciminero, K. S. Calhoun, & H. E. Adams (Eds.), *Handbook of behavioral assessment* (2nd ed., pp. 176–222). New York: Wiley.

Burns, D. D. (1980). *Feeling good: The new mood therapy.* New York: New American Library.

Chambless, D. L., Caputo, G. C., Bright, P., & Gallagher, R. (1984). The assessment of fear in agoraphobics: The Body Sensations Questionnaire and the Agoraphobic Cognitions Questionnaire. *Journal of Consulting and Clinical Psychology, 52*, 1090–1097.

Dobson, K. S. (Ed.). (1988). *Handbook of cognitive-behavioral therapies.* New York: Guilford.

Dobson, K. S., & Block, L. (1988). Historical and philosophical bases of the cognitive-behavioral therapies. In K. S. Dobson (Ed.), *Handbook of cognitive-behavioral therapies* (pp. 1–38). New York: Guilford.

D'Zurilla, T. J., & Goldfried, M. R. (1971). Problem solving and behavioral modification. *Journal of Abnormal Psychology, 78,* 107–126.

Ferster, C. B., & Skinner, B. F. (1957). *Schedules of reinforcement.* New York: Appleton-Century-Croft.

Fiske, S. T., & Linville, P. W. (1980). What does the schema concept buy us? *Personality and Social Psychology Bulletin, 6,* 543–557.

Garner, D. M., & Bemis, K. M. (1982). A cognitive-behavioral approach to anorexia nervosa. *Cognitive Therapy and Research, 6,* 123–150.

Goldfried, M. R., & Davison, G. C. (1976). *Clinical behavior therapy.* New York: Holt, Rinehart & Winston.

Goldfried, M. F., & Sprafkin, J. N. (1974). *Behavioral personality assessment.* Morristown, NJ: General Learning Press.

Heimberg, R. G., & Becker, R. E. (1984). *Cognitive-behavioral treatment of social phobia in a group setting.* Unpublished manuscript, State University of New York at Albany, Albany, NY.

Jakubowski, P., & Lange, A. (1978). *The assertive option: Your rights and responsibilities.* Champaign, IL: Research Press.

Kelly, J. A., Kern, J. M., Kirkley, B. G., Patterson, J. N., & Keane, T. M. (1980). Reactions to assertive versus unassertive behavior: Differential effects for males and females and implications for assertiveness training. *Behavior Therapy, 11,* 670–682.

Klass, E. T. (1990). Guilt, shame and embarrassment: Cognitive-behavioral approaches. In H. Leitenberg (Ed.), *Handbook of social anxiety* (pp. 385–414). New York: Plenum.

Lange, A. J., & Jakubowski, P. (1976). *Responsible assertive behavior: Cognitive/behavioral procedures for trainers.* Champaign, IL: Research Press.

Linehan, M. M. (1984). Interpersonal effectiveness in assertive situations. In E. A. Blechman (Ed.), *Behavior modification with women* (pp. 113–169). New York: Guilford.

Linehan, M. M. (1987, November). *Dialectical behavior therapy.* Workshop presented at the meeting of the Association for Advancement of Behavior Therapy, Chicago.

Marlatt, A., & Gordon, J. R. (1985). *Relapse prevention.* New York: Guilford.

Masters, J. C., Burish, T. G., Hollon, S. D., & Rimm, D. C. (1987). *Behavior therapy* (3rd ed.). New York: Harcourt Brace Jovanovich.

Meichenbaum, D. (1985). *Stress inoculation training.* New York: Pergamon.

Miller, N. E. (1959). Liberalization of basic S-R concepts: Extensions to conflict behavior, motivation, and social learning. In S. Koch (Ed.), *Psychology: A study of a science,* (Vol. 2, pp. 196–293). New York: McGraw-Hill.

Norwood, R. (1985). *Women who love too much.* New York: Simon & Schuster.

Novaco, R. W. (1975). *Anger control: The development and evaluation of an experimental treatment.* Lexington, MA: D. C. Heath.

Rathus, S. A. (1973). A 30-item schedule for assessing assertive behavior. *Behavior Therapy, 4,* 398–406.

Rogers, C. R. (1959). A theory of therapy, personality, and interpersonal relationships, as developed in the client-centered framework. In S. Koch (Ed.),

*Psychology: A study of a science*, (Vol. 3, pp. 184–256). New York: McGraw-Hill.

Romano, J. M., & Bellack, A. S. (1980). Social validation of a component model of assertive behavior. *Journal of Consulting and Clinical Psychology, 48,* 478–490.

Safran, J. D., & Segal, Z. V. (1990). *Cognitive therapy: An interpersonal process perspective.* New York: Basic Books.

Scharlach, A. E. (1987). Relieving feelings of strain among women with elderly mothers. *Psychology and Aging, 2,* 9–13.

Smith, J. C. (1985). *Relaxation dynamics.* Champaign, IL: Research Press.

Turkat, I. D., & Maisto, S. A. (1985). Personality disorders: Application of the experimental method to the formulation and modification of personality disorders. In D. H. Barlow (Ed.), *Clinical handbook of psychological disorders* (pp. 502–570). New York: Guilford.

Weiss, L., Katzman, M., & Wolchik, S. (1985). *Treating bulimia: A psychoeducational approach.* New York: Pergamon.

Wilson, R. R. (1986). *Don't panic: Taking control of anxiety attacks.* New York: Harper & Row.

Woolfolk, R. L., & Dever, S. (1979). Perceptions of assertion: An empirical analysis. *Behavior Therapy, 10,* 404–411.

# III

## WOMEN TREATING MEN

# 9

---

# The Case

## Karen Zager

---

## REFERRAL

It was an unusual referral for my practice. Rick had looked up my name in an insurance company's provider handbook and chosen me because my name, beginning with a Z, was last on the list and because I was a woman. There seemed to be no other reason he could identify for choosing me as his therapist. Although he had sought therapy several times before, he had never stayed in treatment for more than a few sessions and had never felt comfortable with the therapists, all of whom were men. In fact, he could recall neither when he had seen those therapists nor the names of the therapists.

## FIRST SESSION—PRESENTING PROBLEM

Rick opened up the first session with a brief but to-the-point description of his problem. He felt depressed, ugly, and bad. This set of feelings had come and gone throughout the years, and he wanted to be "off the emotional roller coaster" once and for all. Whenever he started treatment in the past (always because of these feelings), he had not felt comfortable enough to continue and had quickly ended the sessions. But once again he felt besieged with these terrible feelings and wanted to get his life straightened out, so he was willing to try therapy just once more.

The immediate situation precipitating these feelings was that Rick was in the process of getting divorced from his second wife. They had recently separated, and now that they were involved with lawyers and divorce proceedings, the relationship had become more bitter, and she was refusing to allow him to visit his 3-year-old daughter. He was drinking heavily, using cocaine regularly, and feared that he would lose his job because of his failing job performance. It was important that he keep his job though. He had been steadily employed as a U. S. Postal Service worker for the past 1½ years. He had never stayed at a job this long before, and he needed to keep this position to salvage what was left of his self-esteem. He knew that this job held the hope of a future for him, and he wasn't willing to ruin it.

This was the only information provided during the first session. Although the session was 45 minutes long, much of the time had been spent in silence. Rick was slow to respond to questions I asked, and every comment he made seemed to be agonizingly difficult. He was obviously very anxious, uncomfortable in talking about personal matters, and barely able to glance in my direction, much less look me in the eye.

## BACKGROUND INFORMATION

Over the next few months of therapy, the background information began to unfold. Rick was a Hispanic man in his midthirties who had been raised by his mother in the ghetto of a large southern metropolitan area. He had never known his father, and although he had two older brothers, he barely knew them. When he was a child, Rick's mother worked as a seamstress, and in order to support the family, she had to work day and night. She was barely able to provide enough money for food and shelter, and was so depleted by working to survive that there was almost no emotional nourishment for her sons. Rick's memories of childhood and adolescence were that his mother was always at the sewing machine and that his brothers were always out of the house. Rick did not feel a sense of family at all, and he grew up "on his own." The only family life he ever knew was when he visited friends and could see how other families ate dinner together, celebrated Christmas together, or went on vacations together. He could recall not a single incident of such a family life in his own home. In fact, he could not remember *ever* being hugged or kissed by his mother. He considered himself fortunate to have a roof over his head and food on the table.

Rick spent most of his childhood and adolescence "on the streets," involved with drinking, drugs, petty thefts, and occasionally crimes of a more serious nature. He had a small group of close friends, his "partners in crime," and he felt accepted by them. But he did not feel accepted in the larger peer group because he looked different from the other boys. His very dark complexion with shocking red hair and freckles made him feel isolated and ostracized, so even his agemates were never a family to him. The nickname given to him in school, "Red," was used to humiliate and embarrass him, and it served as a constant reminder that he did not fit in.

Nonetheless, Rick remained keenly aware of an intense desire to participate in a normal family like those he would see on TV. He had rushed into his first marriage impulsively when he was a teenager, hoping to make a family of his own. They had a child quickly, but the stresses of marriage and parenthood were overwhelming, and the relationship soon ended after a period of bitter arguing. Contact with his ex-wife continued to be hostile through the separation and divorce, but Rick had maintained close contact with his son over the years.

After the marriage ended, Rick became increasingly insecure about women. He could not date and would freeze at the idea of a relationship. He was dreadfully disappointed in himself for the failed marriage and was tempted to go back on the streets. Instead, he enlisted in the army to go to Vietnam rather than see his life go down the drain by returning to drugs and crime.

Unfortunately, he could not escape drinking and drugs in Vietnam either. Although he thought of himself as a tough ghetto kid, he was not prepared for the horrors of war, for seeing his friends killed, for facing the possibility of his own death. Rick resolved that if he made it through the war, he would do something positive with his life. He did not know what he would do or how he would do it, but he knew he had to do it.

After returning from the war, Rick felt utterly lost. He went from job to job, never lasting more than a few months in any position. He dated a few women but was overwhelmed with anxiety and insecurity each time. He became increasingly depressed, relying more and more on drinking and drugs to get through each day. Every time he became disgusted with himself, he decided to make another effort at getting off the streets and putting his life in order. This cycle of despair, drugs and drinking alternating with periods of pulling himself together and feeling more productive, was to continue for years.

Several years before I first saw him, Rick had made yet another major attempt at putting his life back on track. He enrolled in some college courses, started working full-time, met a woman he liked, and began to dream about establishing a family life and a sense of belonging. He married the woman, impulsively and without really knowing her, and they soon had a child. The relationship seemed to go well at first, but they were not strong enough to deal with the pressures of being parents, and after their girl was born, the relationship rapidly deteriorated. During this time, Rick lost his job, quit school, and felt generally depressed and anxious. He and his wife split up, but the crowning blow was that she moved out of the country, taking their daughter with her, and refused to allow him to visit the little girl. The destruction of his hopes for a family life made him feel worthless and desperate, and he decided to move north, for a fresh start, and to go into therapy as a last resort.

## COURSE OF TREATMENT

Rick has been seen in therapy once a week for the past 3 years. At first, he thought he was "going crazy": he didn't seem to know who he really was. He couldn't predict how he would feel or how he would behave from day to day. Some mornings, he would awaken feeling strong and positive, hopeful about working, meeting a new woman, being able to date without "freezing." Other days, however, he would feel miserable from the moment he opened his eyes, overcome with depression, unable to carry through the simplest of plans. Although he managed to go to work every day, his job performance varied tremendously according to his mood. He feared losing his job, which he was determined to keep. But he felt that he had so little control over his feelings, so little control over his behavior, that his own unpredictability scared him.

During the first year of therapy, it became increasingly clear that Rick had developed two identities. At times, he felt more closely identified with the "Red" side of himself—the street kid who was drinking, taking drugs, involved in criminal activities, not fitting in with anyone, tough, but a failure. At other times, "Rick" felt more real, giving him a sense of hope and purpose, allowing him to try and make something out of his life, to hold a job, to feel good about himself. The "craziness" he felt, the confusion over who he was, was directly tied in with his fluctuations between these two selves. Although Red seemed to be more of the bad side and Rick seemed to be more of the good side, neither identity was complete unto itself, and neither felt entirely comfortable to him. He had spent his life up to this point bouncing back and forth between these two identities, and it was only when he recognized how he had divided up his life that he began to feel reassured that he was not "crazy" at all, that there was some explanation for his variability.

The entire first year of therapy concentrated on identifying Red and Rick, and focusing on how each of these identities emerged at different times, how each affected his life. This was not a true case of multiple personality since Red was entirely aware of Rick and vice versa. However, as we discussed Red and Rick in detail, it became obvious that two different "lifelines" had developed, with quite separate existences and separate needs. As he bounced back and forth between the two, he felt that he could not control his own life but that at least he had some sense of what was happening to him and why.

A few typical vignettes will serve to illustrate the major themes and issues as they surfaced during this first year of therapy.

## Work

On the job, Rick was able to perform adequately well, showing up for work on time, achieving some measure of success. Red could not tolerate this easily, because he viewed Rick as having sold out, a spineless wimp trying to please his boss. When he became eligible for a promotion, Red neatly sabotaged the progress by "taking over," initiating a long drinking-drug binge. Not only was the hope of a promotion dissolved, but he could no longer feel deserving of a promotion because he had proven to himself that he was incompetent, a failure. Red was victorious, and only after hitting rock bottom was Rick even allowed to fight his way to the top again.

## Relationships

### Women

Red typically prided himself on not trusting anyone, not loving anyone, not allowing anyone to love him. Sex was fine; caring was unacceptable. Red had never really experienced tenderness, and the women with whom he usually became involved were drug users, alcoholics, women he met in late-night clubs. Rick, however, craved a family, a sense of stability, and above all, love. Rick was the one who got married, but Red was the one who had chosen the woman from the streets. Red had wanted someone to have sex with, to do drugs with. Rick wanted to read books together, to go to college together, to have children together. Not only could the woman that Red had picked not deal with Rick's desire to be a homebody and a family man, but Red couldn't accept such behavior either. To make the relationship even more confusing, Rick felt that love was pure but that sex was dirty and that therefore *he* was dirty and bad. So Red picked the woman; Rick got married. Red wanted out of the marriage; Rick wanted out of the sex. Not surprisingly, they quickly got divorced. Then Rick was overwhelmed with guilt and deep depression at losing his wife and child.

## Men

Simply put, Red's friends hung out on street corners and in bars, and lived in the ghetto or in jail. Rick's friends were from work and were responsible, upstanding, honest. There was no overlap between the two sets of friends.

## Therapy

Only Rick came to therapy during the first year. Red wouldn't consider it for a moment. Red didn't need help. Red didn't need anything from anybody. In fact, when Red was at his strongest, weeks would go by with one canceled appointment after another since Red wouldn't set foot in my office. Red was horrified by Rick's admissions of feelings, of vulnerability. When Rick was at his strongest, he was able to tell me about Red's exploits and adventures, of which he was deeply ashamed, but it was a long time before I got to meet Red.

During the second year of therapy, the focus of our work shifted dramatically. Rick decided he had to stop drinking and using drugs altogether. He wanted to straighten out completely, including putting an end to his criminal activities. He wanted to control Red. He had been at his job for 2½ years and was getting worried about his drug usage jeopardizing his career. His employer was instituting random drug testing, and Rick was getting scared. Although I was reluctant to take sides with only one part of his personality, it was clear that the drinking and drugs had to stop. I actively sided with Rick in getting control over Red. He refused to go to AA or Narcotics Anonymous, so we did it alone. Rick was successful. No more drinking, and no more drugs. Period.

Finally, in the third year of therapy, Rick and Red started to become integrated. Partly because Rick had established greater control during the previous year, he could allow Red to come to sessions on occasion without feeling too threatened. I actually "met" Red for the first time during this third year of therapy. He was tough, angry, hateful, violent. Red thought that Rick was a "faggot" and a "wimp" for coming to see me, but apparently he felt trusting enough to tell me about it instead of just not showing up for his appointments. Where Rick had often told me of the love he felt for his teenage son, Red was able to tell me of the fury and the beatings. Clearly, Red was scared to feel many of the tender and loving feelings that Rick desperately craved, and Rick could not experience any of the anger that was relegated to Red.

In this third year in therapy, Rick and Red were put together, so to speak. Red learned to accept a compliment; Rick learned to get angry. Red learned to accept a hug; Rick learned to give up some of his unrealistic self-protective fantasies of creating a purely loving world. Together they began to experience life as sometimes tough, sometimes tender and loving. Rick stopped setting himself up for failure by setting his expectations unrealistically high; Red no longer had to sabotage every forward step. He applied for and received a major promotion at work. He met a woman who had also grown up in the ghetto but had put together a successful life for herself, with no drinking and no drugs. They have been dating for 6 months now and are thinking of getting married in about a year. He is spontaneous without being impulsive, cautious without being "frozen" in a relationship, realistic without seeking refuge in his fantasies.

Rick continues in therapy, though he no longer has sessions every week. He feels good enough about his life and his inner strength to "live in his life" instead of only in his therapy. Red and Rick are increasingly integrated, not only in my office but in the outside world. Recently, I have been thinking about what to call him. Neither Rick nor Red seems to fit entirely. I find myself thinking of him as "Ricardo," the Spanish equivalent for Richard, the name given to him by his mother. He hasn't been called Ricardo since he was a young child, before he was split into Red and Rick. It seems fitting to me that Ricardo is back now, not as a child but as a full-grown man.

## EPILOGUE

When I first saw Rick, I was doubtful about his potential either to stay with therapy or make any substantial changes in his life. There was such a history of deprivation and such a powerful influence from the streets that I didn't feel I had a chance. But his sense of resolve and his remarkable will to live were undaunted.

His progress has been remarkable, and of course I have been pleased. I feel a sense of warmth and fondness for him that was difficult to imagine just a year ago.

Just recently, though, when I was beginning to think our work together was about finished, a new twist occurred. Rick called me to have a joint session with his teenage son. Although I was reluctant to alter the "ground rules" of our individual therapy, I also realized that I'm probably the only therapist that he would trust, and as such I am not only his therapist but also his family's therapist. Several months ago, his son had come to live with him. For all these years, the boy had been living in the South with his mother, who is a drug addict and a thoroughly neglectful parent. Rick had maintained contact with his son since he and his wife divorced, and he finally decided that he was emotionally ready to have his son live with him. The boy had recently become a truant, failing his classes, hanging out on the street corner. Rick saw the boy on the path that he had taken as an adolescent, and he was determined to save him.

The mother was more than happy to have the problem kid taken off her hands, and the boy was not given a choice. Rick felt ready and able to step in and offer the boy a new home. The few months of having his son live with him have been trying. Rick is now suddenly facing all the difficulties of parenthood, plus the difficulties of disciplining and dealing with a teenager who is not without ambivalence about living there. I expect that the months ahead will be difficult ones. I can only hope that Rick and Red can maintain their integration in the face of this new set of problems.

# 10

## An Analyst Views
## the Case

### Judith L. Alpert

## INTRODUCTION

I indicated two concerns in my chapter on women treating women. I have these concerns for this chapter as well. First, it is difficult to analyze psychoanalytically when the material was not derived from a psychoanalytic treatment. A psychoanalyst would have presented more material focusing on free association, dreams, fantasies, transference, and countertransference. Second, it is difficult to present *the* psychoanalytic perspective when there are many psychoanalytic perspectives. Given restraints posed by the nonanalytic material presented and space, the analysis of Ricardo's case is limited.

In my chapter on women treating women, I briefly reviewed drive theory, ego psychology, object-relations theory, and self psychology, and indicated how these theoretical stances are used in clinical work. Then I discussed Mary's case with respect to two theoretical perspectives, drive theory and object-relations theory. I selected drive theory and object-relations theory because feminists have been most critical and excited about these theories, respectively.

While the theoretical consideration in my first chapter is broad, in this chapter it is focused. I will elaborate on theory dealing with gender issues. Specifically, I will consider (1) the coexistence of psychoanalysis and feminism; (2) the contributions of feminist psychoanalytic thinking to our understanding of men and women; and (3) treatment differences as a function of the analyst's gender. In the second section, I will discuss Ricardo's case from the theoretical perspective of drive theory, one of the two theoretical perspectives I considered in my previous chapter. I select drive theory again because of its relative familiarity to the reader and to illustrate that the theory can be helpful to feminist psychoanalysts. As I did in my previous chapter, I will consider aspects of the theory most relevant to the case. While I may agree with the views of the case presented by the other contributors, here too I will focus on what is most different. In this way I may clarify the unique contribution of psychoanalysis.

## THEORY

I would like to state at the outset that I am a feminist. Consequently, how I see, understand, and interpret has been informed by an understanding that girls and women in this culture have occupied a restricted place. I am also a psychoanalyst. The point is that my feminist perspective and my psychoanalytic theoretical orientation coexist quite comfortably, and this is generally true for my analytic colleagues who are feminists.

When I mention that I am a feminist and a psychoanalyst, people sometimes look perplexed. Their confusion is relieved only when I respond to the question "Do you believe that girls experience penis envy?" My response is that for some girls it is a relevant concept, and for some it is not. I believe that some boys envy the female capacity to bear children. I can recall one clear example that indicated a 3-year-old girl did not have penis envy. It was the first time the girl saw a male naked. She looked horrified, pointed to his penis, and exclaimed, "He's lucky that it did not grow on his face."

In this section I will consider the coexistence of psychoanalysis and feminism, the contributions of feminist psychoanalytic thinking to our understanding of men and women, and some treatment differences as a function of the analyst's gender.

## Coexistence of Psychoanalysis and Feminism

There is a developing literature that clearly indicates that a psychoanalytic point of view can be a feminist one and that multiple perspectives within psychoanalysis can coexist with feminism. While the issue of the coexistence of psychoanalysis and feminism is not the focus here, I refer the reader to several recent books (e.g., Alpert, 1986; Baruch & Serrano, 1988; Bernay & Cantor, 1986; Chodorow, 1978; Dinnerstein, 1976; Fogel, Lane, & Liebert, 1986) that exemplify some of the positive contributions that a feminist outlook gives to the psychoanalytic study of human behavior. These writings indicate that there is a growing number of analysts with a feminist orientation; that they are beyond critiquing psychoanalytic theory or indicating that it is based on male development; and that they are writing about our analytic experiences, identifying treatment issues, reformulating definitions and conceptualizations, and placing new ideas into analytic currency.

Let me be clear. Without question, we are witnessing an integration of feminist thinking into mainstream psychoanalysis. While Karen Horney, Clara Thompson, and Erich Fromm were among the few early feminist voices, there ware many feminist voices representing different theoretical orientations within psychoanalysis today. These voices are contributing to our understanding of female and male development. These voices are acknowledging differences between women and men without equating "difference" with female "inferiority."

As I have indicated elsewhere (Alpert, 1989), contemporary psychoanalytic theorizing of female psychology has been influenced by theoretical psychoanalytic formulations that emphasize object relations and the concept of the self rather than instinct. Cultural changes, research on infant observation, and feminist criticism of Freudian theory have also been influential.

Freud's "story" about the development of femininity and masculinity is well known. The reader is referred to *Three Essays on the Theory of Sexuality* (Freud, 1905), *Some Psychical Consequences of the Anatomical Distinction between the Sexes* (Freud, 1925), and *Female Sexuality* (Freud, 1931). The 1905 article contains Freud's early ideas about the development of female and male sexuality as parallel processes; the latter two references contain his later thinking about the more complicated development of female sexuality.

From his theory on male sexuality, Freud derived his theory about female sexuality. This theory emphasized organs, bodily sensations, reactions to the discovery of anatomical differences between the sexes, penis envy, feelings of inferiority, and the Oedipus complex. According to Freud's theory of female sexuality, girls blame mother for their castration. Consequences of the castration discovery include turning to father, relinquishing masturbation, and becoming passive, masochistic, and narcissistic. The girl "cannot win" in this theory. Her desire to be mother is theorized as a conversion of penis envy and a desire to be masculine. In the oedipal period, her task is to become heterosexual. According to Freud, this task involves a change of object, a change from activity to passivity, and a shift from clitoris to vagina as the primary organ of sex gratification.

Freud's theory has been reformulated. According to Fast's (1984) reformulation based on drive theory, masculinity and femininity are parallel constructs that occur through the process of psychological differentiation. In this theory, young children are not aware of sex differences or the limitations imposed by one's gender. Interest in sex difference begins with this recognition. Boys recognize their inability to bear children, and girls recognize their inability to have penises. Fast defines success as coming to terms with these limits. Thus, while Freud pointed to girls' lack and envy, Fast points to envy in both sexes. Fast draws implications for the oedipal process resulting from the initially overinclusive perspective of boys and girls. Penis envy in a girl is viewed as a recognition of her limits. The wish for daddy's baby is viewed as a turning away from mother as well as an identification with mother. Castration anxiety in boys is viewed as repudiated wishes for the characteristics of females as well as a derivative from rivalry with father. The task for boys is to accept their limitations and relinquish claims to female attributes. Fast has revised the objectionable Freudian views about female development while staying within the broad outline of basic Freudian theory.

Most of the contemporary psychoanalytic theorizing on female psychology, however, is based on object-relations theory. The psychological dissimilarities between men and women have been accounted for by Chodorow (1987), a sociologist who utilizes object-relations theory and considers the sociopolitical context. According to her theory, differences between men and women are due to women's dominance of child care and the differential effects of the mother's gender on preoedipal boys and girls. The reason girls experience themselves as continuous with the related to the external world is that they had their first social relationship with a woman. A consequence of this early female identification is that girls have more trouble separating and individuating from their mothers than boys. The task of separation is particularly difficult because mothers experience their daughters as extensions of themselves and unconsciously communicate this sense of connection and identification. Based on this revised conception of the preoedipal relationship, the oedipal conflict has been reconceptualized. The girl's oedipal attachment to father is conceptualized as an attempt to experience a sense of self and to free self from mother. Engagement with father, therefore, fosters separation and individuation. In contrast, it is believed that in boys the preoedipal attachment to mother extends to an oedipal one.

While separation-individuation is more problematic for girls, establishing intimate relationships is more problematic for boys. Chodorow attributes both the interpersonal orientation of women and the impersonal orientation of men to women's dominance of child care. According to Chodorow, boys and girls have different early experiences. While Freud believed that there was an identical (masculine) preoedipal phase for boys and girls, the more recent gender theories that utilize the work of Money and Ehrhardt (1972) and Mahler (1963) as a base indicate that the core gender identity evolves from the child's emergence from symbiosis with mother. For girls, the primary identification with mother continues. For boys, there must be disidentification with mother. Girls need to learn that they are not mother. They do, however, grow up with a sense of continuity and similarity to mother because they are female like her. They, in turn, can be more related. They do not have to deny as many early feelings related to mother and femininity. Boys need to learn, as girls do, that they are not mother. Boys have an additional task at those early ages: They must also learn that they are not female like mother. Thus, boys must disidentify from mother in order to develop their sense of maleness. This results in males' having to deny their early feelings, which they experience as relating to mother and femininity. There is a denial of feelings such as dependency and relational needs, and a resultant personality development that is more impersonal.

## Contributions of Feminist Psychoanalytic Thinking to Our Understanding of Men and Women

A number of general and overlapping themes emerge from my recent collection on psychoanalysis and women (Alpert, 1986). I state them briefly here. One theme is the importance of the preoedipal experience. In general, it is no longer believed that all children are originally masculine, that girls desire to mother is a conversion of penis envy and a wish to be male, and that genital differences determine destiny. Rather, contrary to Freud's belief, contemporary thinking is that the earliest gender differentiation is the result of sex assignment and that the behavior of infant males and females differs before sexual distinctions are known. The knowledge that one biologically belongs to one or the other sex is irreversibly established by age 3 for both sexes, rather than as a consequence of the oedipal conflict.

Without question, some of Freud's views that are demeaning to women and reflect the androcentric model have been revised. While there is an acknowledgement of the validity of the oedipal experience and the oedipal father, the role of penis envy is no longer viewed as central to female development. What is seen as critical to female development is the preoedipal experience and the experience of a female-dominated infancy. Separation-individuation in the mother-child relationship and male repudiation of mothering are important concepts. Also important is the influence of the early preoedipal relation with the mother and how this results in the female tendency to be more affiliative and nurturing and the male tendency to be more concerned with separation and autonomy.

A second theme is that women and men are different and are perceived differently. While individuals vary enormously, some characteristics seem to be more common to one gender than another. Also, the feminine aspect of both men and women has been derogated in the past and needs to be valued by society and further developed in women and men. In general, the authors in my book point out that women are more intimate, personal, connected, and related, while men are more detached, abstract, and reasoned, and approach problems in a more objective fashion. Further, they point out that women and men have different experiences, relationships, and concerns, and that the material they present in analytic sessions differs. Female and male analysts also differ in what they bring to analytic session and how they are perceived. Many of the contributors conclude that analysts must understand and work with this difference in order to attain analytic goals.

A third theme is that the experience of women and the circumstances of women's lives need consideration. The authors in my anthology, and in other contemporary psychoanalytic collections (e.g., Bernay & Cantor, 1986), consider the interaction between the intrapsychic and the social reality of women's lives. There is work to discover new phenomena, redefine concepts, and reformulate theories based on the unique development and experiences of women. There is an attempt to view women directly rather than infer what women are like from a study of men. Clearly analysts in general no longer view male development and behavior as the norm from which all else deviates.

A fourth important theme is that a feminine orientation can enrich men's lives as well. While relationships are central to women's lives, males in general have more difficulty with relationships. Intimacy, caring, and connectedness are not central to men's lives as they are to the lives of women. A developing theme in much of the contemporary psychoanalytic literature is that men might experience less alienation if they were enable to develop their more feminine qualities.

While one theme indicates that a feminine orientation can enrich men's lives, another theme indicates that it can enrich psychoanalysis. There is an effort to enrich psychoanalysis by accepting and valuing feminine characteristics and visions, specifically by focusing more on maintenance and improvement of interdependency, intimacy, empathy, nurturance, and caring for others, and less on separation, autonomy, individuality, self-assertion, and independence. Traditionally, psychoanalysis has mirrored Western society and has devalued women's more nurturant and affiliative style, and valued men's more autonomous stance. Some analysts are working toward changing the structure and technique of psychoanalysis, so that it will be more reflective of these feminine characteristics and visions.

## Treatment Differences as a Function of Analysts's Gender

A much-debated question in the analytic literature is whether treatment differs as a function of analyst's gender. Prior to the last decade, this question received little attention. Presently, it is receiving a great deal of attention. Two major questions have been addressed: (1) Does treatment *outcome* differ as a function of analyst gender? (2) Does analytic *process* differ as a function of analyst gender? The results of a large body of research focusing on outcome are inconclusive and inconsistent (e.g., see Gornick, 1986).

The literature concerning process focuses on transference, an important concept in analytic work. *Transfer* means "to generalize." *Transference* is the process in which the patient transfers to the analyst experiences from early relationships. As the transference evolves, the analyst learns of the past through the present and by working through these transferences, enables the patient to approach new relationships without the "baggage" from early ones. The transference is evident in material presented in fantasies, dreams, associations, memories, acting-out, and direct verbalizations of thoughts and feelings.

In theory, over the course of a complete analysis, the analyst's gender makes little difference since both paternal and maternal transferences are established and worked through; the analyst becomes mother, father, sister, and brother. Regardless of the analyst's gender, the transference allows significant early object relations to be experienced and unconscious fantasies to be transferred to the analyst. The current thinking is that the analyst's sex has a greater effect on the *course* of treatment than had been previously acknowledged in the analytic literature (e.g., see Gornick, 1986; Kulish, 1989; Meyers, 1986). Further, the effects of the analyst's sex are believed to be greater under certain conditions, as with more regressed patients and in therapy as opposed to analysis (Meyers, 1986). The reasoning for the greater effect is that regressed patients need to cling to reality more than the less regressed and that therapy is more reality linked than analysis.

In general, the sequence, intensity, and inescapability of certain transferences are believed to differ as a function of analyst's gender (Meyers, 1986). These differences are believed to be due to both the reality of the analyst's sex and the analyst's greater ease in seeing self as a same-sex object of transference. For example, some male analysts may not work well with maternal preoedipal transferences, given difficulty in acknowledging that they are perceived and responded to as if they were female. On some level, they may still be dealing with concerns around passivity, castration fear, and merger with the engulfing all-powerful mother. Similarly, some female analysts may not work as well as some male analysts with paternal oedipal transferences. Thus, there is a developing body of literature focusing on gender-linked countertransference as well as transference (e.g., see Fogel et al., 1986). Some examples of frequently noted beliefs: (1) regarding sequence, in contrast to male analysts, female analysts might pull for preoedipal issues sooner; (2) regarding intensity, the transference to the maternal, in contrast to the paternal, may be more intense with a female analyst; (3) regarding inescapability of certain transferences, maternal transferences may be more difficult to avoid with female analysts (Kulish, 1989; Meyers, 1986).

For some patients, the therapist's sex seems to be an important variable in selecting a therapist. The preference for a male or female therapist, motivational patterns that contribute to this preference, and ways in which preference is related to internal object world and characterological defensive organization have received attention in the literature. In general, in making referrals, analysts respect these preferences as they affect initial resistances (Fogel et al., 1986; Kulish, 1989). While women used to prefer males as analysts, more women presently seek out women analysts, and more referrals to female therapists are made.

## CASE DISCUSSION

Two comments must be made at the outset. First, there must be recognition of the power of drugs, particularly cocaine. Some of Ricardo's instability may be due to drugs. Second, it is important to reiterate that Ricardo is not suffering from a split personality. Dr. Zager refers to Rick and Red as metaphors, as a means of conceptualizing the case. I will too.

## Drive Theory and Case Discussion

Ricardo suffers from an unstable balance among his impulses; there is a conflict between the pleasure principle and the reality principle. The problem is that Ricardo's instinctual energy (or id) is very strong and that he has a primitive, sadistic, and insistent superego combined with a weak ego. The id is persistently rebelling against the superego, and the superego is reinforced by an ego ideal. Thus, there is a major ongoing battle in Ricardo's unconscious. The warring nations are on the one side, the id, represented in the person of Red, and on the other, the ego and superego, represented in the person of Rick. When Red was in power, the id had rebelled against the superego. Red obeyed the pleasure principle only and was seeking endless gratification; he wanted to stay in power and overthrow the superego. Red represents drinking, drugs, violence, lust, toughness, social irresponsibility, and the street-kid side, with impulses seeking immediate expression. In contrast, when Rick was in power, Rick had overtaken the ego, and the ego was striving for the ego ideal. While the superego is the internalized voice of the parents, the ego ideal is based on parental influences and is enforced by the policing of the superego. Rick represents postponement, deprivation, inhibition, tender feelings, and abstinence.

How did Red lose power to Rick? The superego had made the id wish unpalatable to the ego through guilt and shame. How did Rick lose power to Red? Red—the id drive—appears when Rick—the ego—is weakened by constant battle. The point is that there is not a stable balance. Rick tries to keep Rusty under lock and key, while Red keeps pressing for release. The press for release leads to shame, guilt, and more defensive action.

How did this conflict between the pleasure principle and the reality principle come to be? While it is known that there are in general two sources for pathological superego formation, we do not have enough material about this case to identify the source of his conflict. We can, however, make some suppositions. One source of pathological superego formation is the specific, individual quality and intensity of the child's instinctual state. Red, without question, represented a great deal of anger. The second source is the nature of the material available for internalization. The superego is the internalized voice of the parents. The absence of either parent leaves the child at the mercy of the present parent. Rick identified with his mother's abstinence and dutifulness. His mother represented one picture that was important for him. The problem, however, is that this picture did not leave room for his instinctual energy. He had a spartan ideal in which sex and aggression were not included. Stated simply, his mother represented too much abstinence;

she was hardworking, seemingly celibate, and inhibited. These characteristics were what he internalized. He valued and deified his self-sacrificing mother who did so much for her children. The core of his
problem is that within this internalization there was no place to integrate his aggression and his sexual needs.

One analytic effort would be to help this young man accept his feelings and the various parts of himself. We would want to help him to release the energy bound up in the defense structure. Once released, it
would rejoin the personality. Rick's tender feelings, for example, are not
acceptable to Red, whose anger serves the important function of ener-
getically warding off Rick's tender feelings. Similarly, Red's sexual feelings are not acceptable to Rick, who wanted "out of the sex" in his
marriage. We see Rick attempting to defend against his sexual impulses
by denying and repressing them. This splitting in order to deny the two
parts of himself would be considered in treatment. His self-punish-
ment, atonement, and unintegrated self would be dealt with by analyzing and reliving Red's absence and Rick's presence in the treatment.
Later in the treatment, Rick's tender feelings toward the analyst and
Red's concern about those feelings would also be analyzed. The treatment framework would be our knowledge of his central conflict, which
concerns the pleasure principle and the reality principle; the focus
within that framework would be what he says and does in a particular
session.

The treatment goal would be to attain a stable balance. The id energy
needs to be released, and an ego ideal is needed that allows for contrasting parts of his nature. A stronger ego is needed, one that can
make compromises between his conflictual feelings. The effort would be
to move toward assimilating all his complicated feelings as part of his
identity; there would be an effort to free Red to come out more and to
free Rick to experience some joy.

In addition to the conflict between the pleasure and the reality principles, treatment would focus on his fixation to a previous state. There is
a fixation to the trauma, to the experience that started the illness. This
fixation represents the ego's attempt to restore the relatively satisfying
stage that existed prior to the trauma. Thus, there is an effort to master
the traumatic experience by compulsively repeating it. In this case we
see two fixations, one at a developmental state and the other on loss.
Rick/Red is fixated at the oedipal stage when the superego, the internalized voice of the parents, emerges. He is fixated at this stage in that he
is trying to integrate his superego severity with his angry and sexual id
impulses. He wants to redo this integration because it has not worked.
Therefore, he tries to combine his id and his superego—his Red and his

Rick—in an effort to make an integration and a realistic internalization and identification.

He is also fixated on loss, the loss of his father and the "loss" or absence of his mother. He attempts to master this loss in two ways. First, he perpetuates a reidentification with the role of victim by provoking women to leave him. He does this in the hope of finally restaging the traumatic theme as he wished it to be. His wife and child leave him alone as his mother, father, and brothers did.

Also, he attempts to master by identification with the aggressor. Through his identification, *he* is the leaver, and he is attempting to gain active mastery over the passively experienced trauma of being left. He reenacts, but this time he is assuming an active role. We see this leaving behavior in relation to his child and his male therapist. He leaves himself as well, as we see from his drinking and drugging behavior. This behavior represents a defensive denial rather than a creative assimilation of the traumatic experience. One analytic effort, then, would be to help him to end this reenactment by reliving and working through the trauma of his paternal and maternal "abandonment."

Thus, the analytic work would focus on (1) the unstable balance between his impulses, (2) the developmental fixation in which he attempts to integrate his superego severity with his angry and sexual impulses, and (3) his fixation on loss, which he deals with by identification with the aggressor and reidentification with the role of victim. According to drive theory, neurotic symptoms and character traits, as well as all psychic activity, are determined by conflict and compromise formation. In Rick/Red, the cycle—that of despair, drugs, and drinking alternating with periods of trying to be and feel more productive—is so determined.

Ricardo's treatment was tremendously therapeutic. There were at least two important improvements. He developed the capacity to relinquish drugs and alcohol, and the ability to have a seemingly meaningful and long-term relationship. It appears that he is no longer fixated at an earlier state of development. With Dr. Zager's help, he has been able to integrate his childhood trauma. Dr. Zager concludes, "It seems fitting to me that Ricardo is back now, not as a child but as a full-grown man." I see it differently. Ricardo was never there. Rick/Red was never Ricardo. Through treatment with Dr. Zager, Ricardo has evolved. Through his relationship with Dr. Zager, Ricardo moved from his fixations, experienced developmental stages which he previously missed, and in this way, *evolved*.

Finally, how might Rick/Red's therapy have differed if he had been in treatment with a male therapist? Ricardo had been in treatment previously with male therapists. He reported that he never felt comfortable with them and could not recall basic information about them. While Ricardo experienced a relatively stable and trusting early relationship with a woman, apparently he had not experienced any early closeness with males. Given that both his father and brothers were unknown to him, he did not develop early trusting relationships with men. Thus, it is understandable that he wanted a woman therapist.

It was easier for him to be with a female therapist. With a woman therapist, he could begin to talk about the meaning of his poor recall with respect to his male therapists and his choice of a woman therapist. This would be the beginning of understanding the effects of the absence of his father and the presence of his mother on his development and present relationships. Thus, the major point here is that it appears that Ricardo could initially trust only a woman therapist. Therapy could not proceed with a male therapist. The initial resistance with a male therapist would have been too great and would have mitigated against the development of a working alliance. In order to begin a therapeutic voyage, it appears that Rick/Red needed to be in treatment with a woman.

A second reason that it may have been easier for Ricardo to be treated by a woman concerns the sequence of the transference. The analyst's gender tends to influence the earliest transference reactions. While one experiences both maternal and paternal transferences with both male and female analysts, generally it is more difficult to escape a gender-linked transference. In contrast to treatment with a male therapist, treatment with a female therapist will lead to more intense, compelling, and clear maternal transferences. Further, the initial transference reactions of a man in treatment with a woman are related to a woman (mother). It may be that Rick/Red needed to deal first with issues related to mother. While he had issues to work out with his absent father as well, these issues may have been less compelling to him at the time of treatment or too threatening.

Let me be specific. Ricardo had some issues he needed to work out with his mother. Initially he could show Rick to his mother; Red was hidden. He probably anticipated a negative response to Red. As his "therapist-mother" expressed acceptance and interest in Red, he was able to bring the id side of himself to her and to work on the integration of the two parts of himself.

I cannot state with certainty that the issue emerged only because the analyst was female. The working-through of a maternal transference and subsequent integration of Rick and Red may have come up with a male therapist *if* Rick/Red had been able to develop a working alliance with a male. The point is that the issue of his mother's abstinence and his need to submit to her and to internalize her assumed demands or to rebel and produce Red could not be avoided with a female analyst. While both maternal and paternal transferences can be experienced with a female analyst, there is no escape from the female transference with a female analyst.

# REFERENCES

Alpert, J. L. (Ed.). (1986). *Psychoanalysis and women: Contemporary reappraisals.* Hillsdale, NJ: Analytic Press.

Alpert, J. L. (1989). Contemporary psychoanalytic developmental theory. In H. Tierney (Ed.), *Women's studies encyclopedia.* Westport, CT: Greenwood Press.

Baruch, E. H., & Serrano, L. J. (Eds.). (1988). *Women analyze women in France, England, and the United States.* New York: New York University Press.

Bernay, T., & Cantor, D. W. (Eds.). (1986). *The psychology of today's woman: New psychoanalytic visions.* Hillsdale, NJ: The Analytic Press.

Chodorow, N. (1978). *The reproduction of mothering: Psychoanalysis and the sociology of gender.* Berkeley: University of California Press.

Dinnerstein, D. (1976). *The mermaid and the minotaur: Sexual arrangements and human malaise.* New York: Harper & Row.

Fast, I. (1984). *Gender identity.* Hillsdale, NJ: Lawrence Erlbaum.

Fogel, G. I., Lane, F. M., & Liebert, R. S. (Eds.). (1986). *The psychology of men: New psychoanalytic perspectives.* New York: Basic Books.

Freud. S. (1905). Three essays on the theory of sexuality. *Standard edition* (Vol. 7, pp. 125–353). London: Hogarth Press, 1962.

Freud, S. (1925). Some psychical consequences of the anatomical distinction between the sexes. *Standard edition* (Vol. 19, pp. 253–260). London: Hogarth Press, 1961.

Freud, S. (1933). Femininity. *Standard edition* (Vol. 22, pp. 112–135). London: Hogarth Press, 1964.

Gornick, L. K. (1986). Developing a new narrative: The woman therapist and the male patient. In J. L. Alpert (Ed.), *Psychoanalysis and women: Contemporary reappraisals* (pp. 257–286). Hillsdale, NJ: Analytic Press.

Kulish, N. M. (1989). Gender and transference: Conversations with female analysts. *Psychoanalytic Psychology,* 6(1), 59–71.

Mahler, M. (1963). Thought on the development of the individual. In *The psychoanalytic study of the child* (Vol. 18, pp. 307–332). New York: International Universities Press.

Meyers, H. (1986). How do women treat men? In G. I. Fogel, F. M. Lane, & R. S. Liebert (Eds.), *The psychology of men* (pp. 262–276). New York: Basic Books.

Money, J., & Ehrhardt, A. A. (1972). *Man and woman boy and girl.* Baltimore: Johns Hopkins University Press.

# 11

# A Feminist Therapist
# Views the Case

## Lenore E. A. Walker

## INTRODUCTION TO FEMINIST THERAPY WITH MEN

Feminist therapy with a man! No way, say numerous feminists as well as other therapists. A major goal of feminist therapy is the empowerment of women. How can such a goal be consistent with meeting most men's needs? Why would a man choose a feminist therapist? How could a focus on women's issues be helpful to Rick, the tough, street-wise, aggressive, and sometimes violent man presented in this case? Why should a woman therapist who has developed skills in helping women advance toward their true potential divert her energies to treat men too? These are important questions to consider, even before any man, including Rick, steps through the feminist therapist's door.

In fact, many feminist therapists choose not to treat men, either with their women partners or individually, as Rick was requesting. Some will agree to treat a man in a couple or a family situation, but only when the woman is identified as the primary client. Still others, like myself, will treat men who are aware of my theoretical orientation and prefer to work with a woman-identified woman therapist who is not a man hater.

I believe it is possible to be a women's advocate and like men, want them to be mentally healthy, and devote time and energy to help them achieve their goals. There are a number of reasons why feminist therapy would be beneficial for many men, including Rick.

The first is the likelihood that a feminist therapist would be less likely to assume the typical woman's role of nurturing. In therapy, nurturance is often played out by taking over handling too much of the man's pain for him, reinforcing the stereotype that men cannot handle their emotions. Much like the male therapist who becomes the beneficent but authoritarian arbiter of the female client's choices, the nonfeminist-oriented female therapist often presents emotional choices to male clients in a watered-down version, as though he cannot handle his own feelings. Men often choose women therapists as a way to get someone else to do this emotional work for them. Most men yearn to be nurtured by a woman, and they see a woman therapist as someone to provide them with nurturance or teach them how to relate better to other women so they can get these needs met. A feminist therapist, using the same techniques used to teach women self-nurturance, can teach a male client how to nurture himself. Men can then be free to relate to women as equals rather than repeat the socialized pattern of dominance in some areas and dependency in others.

A second benefit for a man working with a feminist therapist is the attention paid to a man's expression of anger and violence. Men are typically trained to turn all unpleasant feelings into anger, skipping the experiences of sadness, upset, pain, hurt, and other unpleasant emotions. This has been commonly found in exaggerated form in batterers' backgrounds (Dutton, 1984; Ganley, 1988; Walker, 1979, 1984, 1989). In Rick's case (when he was acting as Red of course), there are a number of important clues to believe that he was both a victim of child abuse as well as a batterer in his relationships with women. Men are often socialized to react to angry feelings with action, often aggressive action. In some cultures, little boys are socialized into fighting before they are even 2 years old. The emphasis placed by feminist therapists on eradicating family violence and other forms of interpersonal violence between men and women has gained them skills that can be helpful to men in learning to acknowledge a wide range of emotional feelings that get masked as anger and how to express them in a nonviolent way (Sonkin, Martin, & Walker, 1985). Further, incorporating an understanding of domestic violence into therapy assists men who may not have been physically or sexually abusive but whose behavior could be defined as psychologically abusive to recognize and change their coercive techniques. For Rick, his inability to conform his behavior to his desire for a commitment to a woman would be further analyzed using this perspective (Dutton & Painter, 1981; Ehrenreich, 1983).

A third benefit is the political-gender analysis through which all of the man's psychological problems will be filtered. Similar to the process in feminist therapy with women, the man's disturbing intrapsychic problems will be separated from those problems that are commonly experienced by men raised to feel they must follow the norms to be dominant. There are numerous sex-role stereotypes that men are socialized into believing that limit their potential to be their own person in much the same way as women (Goldberg, 1976, 1983; Pleck, 1981; Pleck & Sawyer, 1974). One of the major stereotypes is man's natural position of power over women. This feeling of entitlement fuels the battle between Rick's and Red's character values. Thus, it is not individual pathology that causes the split in the two personalities but the difficulties most men have with following the stereotyped male values and those wanting to be expressed by their gentler side. Helping men learn how to feel interdependent with women in a more equal way reduces the pressure to conform to the male stereotypes that also limit many men's ability to relate to other men (Lyon, 1978; O'Neal, 1981; Sonkin et al., 1985). Sometimes, the acceptance and support for their gentle, less macho values is the very hook that is needed to keep men like Rick in therapy. Feminist therapy's open and direct principles supporting the eradication of these sex-role stereotypes (for men as well as women) as a means of promoting equality can help men learn to change faster than more traditional therapies that do not take an open stand on these social issues.

A fourth benefit is the clear understanding that blaming the man's mother for his lack of childhood nurturance is not useful in helping men learn not to expect women to meet all of their emotional needs. In this case, the picture of Rick's childhood focuses on his mother's being so busy with work that she could not pay attention to his emotional needs. What is missing from the picture is the additional impact of poverty, racial and ethnic discrimination, and the absence of a relationship with his father on Rick and the rest of his family. Also important is the difficulty women have supporting a family, including the general inability of women to earn wages equal to a man's in most jobs and the impact such poverty has on a woman's mental health (Belle, 1984). A feminist therapist would help a male client learn to balance the burdens of being a single mother with an individual woman's inability to pay sufficient attention to a child's developmental and emotional needs. A feminist therapist would try to see that Rick's mother would not be blamed for more than her fair share of the responsibility for his child-hood deprivations (Cammaert, 1988).

Fifth, the attention paid in feminist therapy to the effects on mental health from the oppression experienced as a member of a racial or ethnic minority is helpful with clients who are members of minority groups (Carillo, 1989). In fact, many attempts have been made to assure that feminist-therapy theory will not be developed only for the benefit of a white, middle-class, verbal, and affluent dominant culture. Instead, inclusion of a multicultural diversity has been emphasized (see Brown & Root, in press). In this case, Rick is a Hispanic male whose culture is not one I share. His shocking red hair and dark complexion make him physically different from other Hispanic males, and therefore some further cultural analysis is needed to understand how his appearance of being interracial affected his identity and relationships with peers. My own experience—growing up in a large, racially mixed, urban neighborhood—and subsequent knowledge of Hispanic culture for males is sufficient for me to accept him as a client, knowing I will seek consultation or even ongoing supervision if we get into areas in which I am not knowledgeable or competent.

Sixth, feminist therapy's educational approach permits the nonpathological analysis of Rick's problems. Those features that a therapist of another orientation could label as pathology would be considered skill deficits in a feminist analysis. Subsequent therapy would concentrate on teaching Rick ways to learn the skills he is missing. Rick's many strengths would be analyzed and strengthened initially, and the deficits would be remedied, using some adapted cognitive-behavioral skill training (Fodor, 1988; Frank & Houghton, 1982; Ganley, 1981; Gondolf, 1985; Sonkin & Durphy, 1982).

The issue of Rick's use of drugs and alcohol is generally beyond the knowledge base of most feminist therapists who have not sought additional training in the area of chemical dependence. Therefore, consultation with or even referral to a specialist may be necessary. Some addiction specialists have popularized the philosophy of codependency, which would suggest that Rick's wives may have encouraged or at least accepted his misuse of drugs and alcohol for their own needs. While this may or may not be true, feminist therapists have begun to challenge the notion of codependency, suggesting that it is an additional form of women blaming since it is usually applied to wives of alcoholics. The danger of applying such a notion to Rick's wife is that it will divert his attention from claiming responsibility for his maladaptive behavior rather than focusing on what his wives did or did not do to help him. To stop abusing drugs and alcohol, he will have to feel in control of his own thoughts, feelings, and behavior.

# OVERVIEW OF THE CASE

## Feminist Analysis

### Presenting Information

Rick comes into therapy in a great deal of pain that appears to be set off by the separation from his second wife and child and his impending divorce. However, he is clear that this is not the first time he has experienced the feelings of being "depressed, ugly, and bad." It is interesting that he used the analogy of being on an "emotional roller coaster" to describe his perception that he does not have control over his emotions. It is often this chaotic up-and-down experience with feelings that is a clue to violent behavior. Rick's admission of using cocaine and alcohol (one stimulates and one depresses feelings) suggests that he has more ambivalent feelings about giving up the emotional roller coaster than his pain now lets him admit. It is certainly a strength that Rick is able to admit to excessive use of drugs and alcohol in the first session, one that indicates his strong motivation to control his chemical usage. Of course, it was not known initially that another side of his personality, Red, did not want to stop the drug abuse and would undermine the control Rick wanted.

Rick also admits to trying therapy several times previously, each time prompted by the same feelings he is experiencing this time. Often, clients who come in with similar presenting problems have what is sometimes called a flight into health after a few therapy sessions that take the edge off their pain and make it more bearable. Given this history, a feminist therapist (or for that matter, a therapist of any orientation) would do well not to help him remove his motivating symptomatology, at least initially. Rick's ability to identify his roller-coaster emotional experiences can be seen as a strength, but more work will be needed for him to connect them with the familiarity of his childhood chaos.

As in any feminist-therapy analysis, it is important to identify as many of Rick's strengths as possible so that they can be acknowledged, validated, and supported. Very little information has been provided at this time. It will be difficult to cut through his depression to get him to talk about things he likes about himself. In this case, he has already separated the good and bad sides of himself that appear to be at war, hence the emotional roller coaster. It is interesting that each side gets named: "Rick" for the gentler, more positive part of his personality desiring love and nurturance and "Red" for the tough, street-smart, violent part of his personality. Although he comes in yearning to be more Rick, it is Red who has better developed skills to have things his way. Thus, until Rick feels more competent about himself, he will be unable to give up those negative behaviors ascribed to Red that get in his way of forming intimate and fulfilling relationships.

Such a clear but integrated split is diagnostic of a dissociative disorder, although neither side seems to be totally fragmented or whole enough to be a separate personality as would be seen in a true multiple-personality disorder. However, as in multiple-personality disorders, dissociative states often result from severe physical, sexual, and psychological abuse during early childhood. Those personalities that remain intact although split, like Rick and Red, frequently result from an emphasis on severe abuse during the middle rather than the early childhood years (early abuse is more likely to produce separate multiple personalities). Although sexual abuse may have occurred, sometimes it is remembered, more often it is not. Another pattern of childhood abuse that can result in such splitting occurs when there is some nurturance that offsets the extreme cruelty. Sometimes this comes from the same person who does the abusing; sometimes it is another person, frequently the other parent or a grandparent.

The battle between Rick and Red can be expected to deal with more than their different personalities. It will be a metaphor for the male and female roles that cannot be expressed except by gross stereotypes in Rick's world. Neither personality trusts a woman, however, or believes that she can be there for him. Each personality obviously has different relationships with women; Rick desiring to create the idealized family he never had, Red refusing to allow any intimacy with a woman. In feminist therapy, the goal will be for Rick to learn how to relate in a genuine way to a woman. The relationship with a therapist who needs to be a constant support for either Rick or Red, even if she must place external controls on his behavior should it get out of control, will be an important way to reestablish basic trust in women.

Rick's relationship with his mother is an area that needs more information. It is clear that he wanted more from her than he was able to get and that this is part of the source of his lack of trust in women. Yet she apparently gave him some nurturance and support, or he would not have developed a yearning and hope that more is possible in a relationship. It is interesting that he does not search for more nurturance from males, only women. Although his mother may have been abusive (there is not enough information to make any further inference about the origin or nature of his abuse), his descriptions of the males in his life suggest that they were abusive.

This absence of gentle male role models has been filled in by cultural and ethnic stereotyped male models. Thus, it will be important to establish Rick's, as well as Red's, views about being male in his world. This includes a further analysis of what it was like to be a male, even a tough street-wise male, in the Vietnam War. It is often difficult for women to listen to tales of violence and horror in war, but sometimes it is easier for men to admit their fears, terror, and personal horror to a woman rather than face the potential scorn of another man for not living up to the macho image expected of soldiers. There are materials published by former Vietnam combat veterans to educate both the therapist and the client (see Figley, 1985, 1986). It is also important to understand what images Rick or Red has of a nurturing male so that treatment can focus on increasing those skills.

In addition to Rick's and Red's views about men in general, it is necessary to gather more information about his views about women and how he treats them. From the data already gathered, it is probable that he views women with the same kind of split that he uses for himself: the idealized madonna or unworthy whore concepts. The information tells us that Red has chosen the women to date, often street-wise drug users like himself. Rick tries to idealize the relationship. Red intervenes to make it impossible. Although there is no analysis for domestic violence, much of the information strongly suggests that Rick (Red) has been a batterer. Most women who flee to another country, refusing to allow their former husbands to see their children, are battered women who fear continued control and abuse by the men. Furthermore, most battered women describe their abusive partners as having a dual personality, sometimes using the characterization of Dr. Jekyll and Mr. Hyde. The description of Rick and Red fit such descriptions. Further clues of possible violence include Rick's fear of abandonment and idealized image of marriage and the family.

It will be important for the therapist to question Rick about physical confrontations with his wife without excusing the behavior if he admits it has occurred, also giving him hope that the behavior can be changed. If Rick admits to abusing the child too, the therapist is faced with the need to make a child-abuse report to the appropriate authorities. This needs to be handled sensitively. It is assumed that disclosure of the legal requirements for breaking confidentiality (in most states, in includes the therapist's judgment that the client is a danger to himself and the reasonable suspicion of child abuse) would have been explained to Rick at the initial session. For example, in Colorado, the law requires disclosure of the boundaries of confidentiality and the illegal nature of any sexual acts between therapist and client, as well as the address of the state grievance board. If Rick disclosed child abuse after he learned of the legal requirements for mandatory reporting, it can only be surmised that he was aware the therapist had no choice about reporting and that something would have to be done to protect the child.

Rick's level of intellectual competency and his ability to work and provide a living for himself and his family demonstrate strength at this time. His history suggests that he can blow it all, but one of the major motivating factors of his entering therapy at this time is his fear that he will lose his job. The desire to keep this job is a positive strength and can be used to keep him in treatment.

## Treatment Process

### *Setting the Stage*

Helping Rick engage in therapy can be expected to be a difficult process, for several reasons. Certainly his method of choosing a therapist, selecting an unknown woman who is at the end of the referral list, is a clue to his ambivalence about getting help. However, his previous attempts at treatment with male therapists were unsuccessful, so selection of a woman this time is a sign of his desire for things to be different. It is clear that for Rick the relationship with the therapist will be a significant part of the corrective experience. He will need to feel control over the relationship yet will also need to learn how to set limits on his behavior.

It is important to find out what Rick liked and didn't like about his previous therapists and to see if he can enumerate his expectations of how a woman therapist might be different. His difficulty in talking during the initial therapy hour suggests that he will have a difficult time staying in therapy and will probably use any excuse to leave until the therapeutic bond is formed. That he sought therapy while feeling depressed suggests that Rick's depression was of recent origin, yet his prior therapy experiences were helpful in some way to permit his to reach out for help again. Thus, it can be assumed that he is afraid of becoming even more depressed and is hoping that therapy will stop the slide downward. It would be appropriate, then, to discuss some of the usual effects of a depression and give him several suggestions to try to control it, such as activity and contact with friends, even if he doesn't feel like it.

It is important to strike the proper balance of being professional yet warm with Rick during the initial visits. Negotiating a treatment contract is one way to accomplish this task. From the information gathered during the initial period, it is apparent that Rick wants help with several areas of his life. First, he does not want to feel so bad about himself. Second, he does not want to lose his job. Third, he wants to understand the loss of his wife and child, and put it in its proper perspective. Fourth, he wants to control his drug and alcohol use. And fifth, he wants to learn how to control his roller-coaster feelings. This gives a feminist therapist with a cognitive-behavioral orientation sufficient information to begin to negotiate a treatment contract.

There is little information given about Rick's strengths except that he appears to be good at building a life, including his jobs, until he lets his emotions get in the way and then blows it. Some information suggests that Rick is bright, ambitious, responsible, and a hard worker. There is further suggestion that he has some good social skills and has a good friendship network, but little is known about the kind of friends he likes other than the fact that they are divided into two sets—one from his childhood neighborhood and one from his adult work environment. And there is a suggestion that he is capable of falling in love, experiencing intimacy, and making a commitment, although he does not seem to understand what went wrong with the relationship when it ends.

The interaction between the client and therapist during the initial session reinforces his reports of discomfort when talking with women or about his feelings. To keep the relationship as gender-neutral as possible, it is important to make sure Rick understands the limitations and boundaries in a therapy relationship. In Colorado, this would be dealt with through the mandatory disclosure statement that therapist and client sign during the first session. The printed disclosure statement informs clients that confidentiality will be broken only if the therapist perceives the client to be a danger to herself or others or if child abuse is suspected. There is also a statement concerning the illegalities of a sexual relationship between client and therapist that affords the opportunity to discuss the benefits to the client of such professional restraint. The name and address of the state grievance board are provided, letting the client know that there are remedies should a therapist attempt to break these ethical boundaries. In Rick's case such a routine disclosure would help him differentiate the relationship with the therapist, particularly the female therapist, from his other relationships with women. It also gives him information about the limits of confidentiality so that if any need arises to break it, he will have had the option and known the consequences.

My initial suspicions are that Rick has been physically violent with his wife and perhaps his child. I would also be concerned about the potential for suicidal behavior during one of his emotional roller-coaster experiences. Given that his employment might be jeopardized by any breaches in confidentiality, it is important that Rick understand the legal obligations of a therapist. However, it is also important that he not set up the therapist to hurt him if he is feeling unworthy and down on himself. Thus, this is an area that needs to be handled very delicately during the entire treatment process, and the initial discussion needs to be done with compassion and sensitivity.

## Therapy Sessions

Therapy needs to begin slowly, allowing the therapeutic relationship to develop. It is anticipated that Rick will be unable to tell whether the therapist approves of and likes him, which is important for him to know if he is not to become wary of the developing relationship. Thus, overt signs of approval—including smiling, occasional laughter and display of a sense of humor, and attention paid to places where approval is appropriate—need to be emphasized in the beginning. Later on, these gestures can be pointed out to Rick so that he can learn other ways of knowing when someone likes him. The fact that the therapist is willing to be there for the long haul will help Rick be more forthcoming about his negative behavior committed under the personality of Red. If the therapist can still be there even after she learns his terrible secrets, that relationship will be a critical factor in integrating Rick's and Red's personalities.

Feminist therapy is a more active therapy, so there will be less opportunity for Rick to sit with long silences during the therapy session, although if he needed to do that, it would certainly be permissible. It is more likely that the feminist therapist would do some exploring with him to find areas that he would be more willing and able to share. This is a part of gathering data about his strengths, and such areas would be noted as important sources of self-esteem and gratification. I would move back and forth between asking for data about things he liked talking about and things that were more difficult for him. Although I would like to gather an abuse history as early as possible, if I pushed too hard, then Rick might not be truthful or stay in treatment. However, it would be important for him to know my views that violence is not acceptable behavior and that there are other ways he can learn to deal with his anger, frustration, and upset. This statement of values should convey an acceptance of the past along with hope for change in the future.

It will also be essential to deal with Rick's childhood. Again, timing will be determined by Rick's ability to deal with these issues. The areas that need to be covered include his relationships with his mother, his brothers, and his social system. The issues about Rick's relationship with his mother, his feelings of not getting enough from her, need to be tempered by his understanding of how she dealt with life as a woman who had lots of social and cultural barriers. These descriptions would guide the feminist therapist as she and Rick explore the past. There is less information given about Rick's brothers, so little can be assumed

about their role in his life other than their providing some male modeling, even if they were out of the house much of the time. It would be interesting to know if they all had the same father or the physical
characteristics that set Rick apart from the other Hispanic kids. Rick's
red hair and dark skin is, of course, a giveaway that he comes from two
cultures, and the place of this in his emotional development would be
an issue to discuss in therapy. There is a body of literature on interracial
children that might be appropriate to suggest to Rick, so that he identi-
fies with others who are dealing with carrying the overt physical characteristics of two cultures.

## Dealing with Feelings

The need to deal with feelings will be important early in the treatment
process and will continue throughout most of the therapy relationship.
Initially, Rick seems more willing to discuss his bad feelings about himself. His depression and drug and alcohol use may also be rooted in the
need to keep himself from feeling the really bad feelings he has buried
and tries to keep from his awareness. However, they are obviously
breaking through the denial and repression he has used and need to be
dealt with directly by the therapist. It will probably be necessary first to
teach Rick to differentiate the different emotions he experiences, a difficult task when they are as intense as they appear to be when he is on
his emotional roller coaster. Therefore, a matching of the early experience of the same feeling later identified in an intense mode is a critical
cognitive exercise to help Rick learn to control the feelings by recognizing them before they get too intense. This will take time and may need
to be approached slowly, using material he brings into the sessions for
discussion, as abstract concepts and generalizations come later on. The
cognitive and emotional sides of abused and neglected children fail to
develop fully or integrate together, which suggests that the steps necessary for Rick to relearn how to identify his emotions will be at an early
developmental stage (Gabarino, Guttman, & Seeley, 1987). Thus, little
generalization of feelings from one event to another should be expected
until later in treatment.

One of the positive interventions for helping Rick learn how to deal
with his feelings is for him to learn to make himself feel good—self-nurturance. There are various techniques to assist in the development of
self-nurturance with men, and it is considered more difficult for men
than women as most women already have developed the ability to provide nurturance to others and they need to learn how to do the same for
themselves. Men, particularly those like Rick who have not experienced

much nurturance or given it, may have to start with the basics even to recognize how to take care of themselves emotionally.

Rick's feelings of *anger* will probably reflect a number of different emotions mixed together. It is not unusual for a variety of negative feelings to be expressed as anger to protect feelings of vulnerability. Both abuse victims and street kids learn to exaggerate the male stereotype of not permitting themselves to perceive, acknowledge, or express emotions. Those that include tenderness, love, and positive feelings are shut off, while those that deal with vulnerability, upset, hurt, and interpersonal difficulties are turned into anger and expressed aggressively. If too much anger is allowed to build up, violent explosions can occur. Sometimes the anger builds up internally until it becomes rage, and when it is unleashed, it is very destructive. Rick's need to divide his angry side (Red) and his more compassionate and rational side (Rick) suggests that there is a great deal of rage buried inside him. The origins of this rage probably go back to his childhood and the injustices he experienced. His experiences in Vietnam added more rage, and the experiences with two failed marriages added more. Obviously, some of the rage gets discharged periodically, often causing total disruption to his life. Rick's fear of this intense anger's exploding is probably a part of the depression and drug and alcohol use.

Helping Rick deal with getting rid of the accumulated anger and rage in a nondestructive way is a particular skill of the feminist therapist, who has learned how to work with women violence victims who also have long-term accumulated anger and rage from injustices they have lived with. The use of *cognitive and educational approaches* is particularly helpful when working in this area. A cognitive grid must be established, much like that used for a rape victim or battered woman where the experiences of injustice are acknowledged and explored, and the anger is slowly expressed intellectually, the feelings following. Cognitive controls such as the ability to acknowledge anger yet not express it destructively are in place when this work begins. Steps are taken to protect family or friends, including bringing them into a session to discuss the difficulties they can expect over a period of time. Use of anger workbooks such as Sonkin and Durphy (1982) help foster anger-management techniques and positive expression of the angry feelings. Sometimes use of guided imagery helps to express the feelings and fantasize revenge and retaliation in a safe situation.

The therapist must expect to help provide the controls when the man is not able to do so himself. This includes additional sessions and permission for more telephone contact between sessions if necessary. The emphasis is on developing Rick/Red's self-control while teaching him to recognize legitimate angry feelings and differentiate them from other negative emotions that make him feel vulnerable. The content used in Rick's case would be his childhood memories of being hurt and vulnerable; his wartime combat experiences of being frightened, unprepared, and in danger of being killed; and his failed marriages. Obviously, feelings of loss and abandonment will be dealt with in addition to the ones already described.

## Abuse Issues

Rick's relationships with his two wives need to be analyzed from both his and their perspectives. Although I believe he could be labeled as a batterer, before I would give him that label, I would probably ask him if he thought his wife would say that about him. It would be important to get an abuse history to be able to help him understand his impact on women and children. However, most batterers do not understand their women's fears about being hurt. They believe that they are in control when they hurt the women and usually justify their actions by tying it to some wrongdoing that she commits. The batterer believes that the woman does whatever upsets him, knowing that if she does it, he will hurt her. So when they act violently, they believe she deserves it and knew it would happen; otherwise, she would have conformed her behavior to his wishes. They do not understand that they do not have the right to demand she conform her behavior to their wishes, nor do they recognize that they do not have to follow up on the woman's behavior by trying to make her conform. It may be that Rick will want to attend a men's treatment group to help him deal with sex roles and anger-management techniques, simultaneous with his individual therapy. In Denver, a relationship with the facilitators of the AMEND program would make such an adjunct to treatment possible.

This perception that he can assume expectations of what the woman will provide for him, without negotiation is often referred to as male entitlement. While feelings of entitlement are present in most socialized males, batterers use them to justify their abusive behavior. It would be important to explore Rick's entitlement beliefs and help him learn to negotiate expectations, personal commitments, and better conflict-resolution skills, so that he doesn't have to use violence when he believes a commitment is broken.

Rick's entitlement beliefs consist of socialized expectations of behavior between men and women as well as personal expectations that he needs to make him feel good as an individual. The socialized expectations come from his role models as a child as well as the stereotyped male cultural values he absorbed in place of a father and other important males in his family. Further, they come from Hispanic cultural beliefs about male behavior as well as those operating in the minds of peers with whom he grew up. Add in the male values that come from men who experience war together, and there is a lot for a feminist therapist to work with. It is interesting that Rick appears to believe that his tough ghetto-kid experiences would prepare and protect him through the war experiences. He will need to learn to accept his fears and performance as normal, even for a street kid. The personal expectations come from his disappointment as a child that he didn't have close family relationships, including his feeling a lack of love from his mother, the only significant adult mentioned in his life. If the therapist helps him understand the values and belief systems of the women in his life, then Rick may understand how situational forces as well as his own behavior contributed to the demise of his marriages.

Rick will probably need to look at how his behavior provoked his wife to leave him as well as setting up situations where he could be the aggressor and then leave her. It is probable that he learned that violence is power and control. The feminist analysis is that he has developed poor strategies to get the emotional responses he wants from his wife, so he ensures that he will not have a stable relationship through his own behavior rather than chance her abandonment of him. It also seems that he has boundary issues between himself and his wife and child that need to be addressed during this part of treatment.

My own experience in the field of domestic violence leads me to believe that fear of further physical, sexual, and/or psychological abuse underlies Rick's wife's refusal to allow him to see his daughter and her decision to leave the country. Certainly, the later admissions of his sporadic abusive behavior with his son supports this hypothesis. It may be appropriate for the therapist to help Rick understand how his wife might interpret his behavior and help him learn new ways to communicate with her, should that still be an option. If not, then an analysis of his positive and negative communication patterns with his wife could be useful to develop behavioral techniques as he begins to date again.

## Competence Issues

Rick's feelings of competence will be strengthened in different areas through feminist therapy. First, the area of his present strength is his job performance and his ability to keep his job. Second, using *cognitive-restructuring* techniques, many of his prior experiences can be redefined to demonstrate his competence in a difficult situation rather than his believing them to be evidence of incompetence because they were not perfectly performed as he expected. For example, Rick presents himself as fearful that he will lose control over his behavior, yet his presentation indicates he usually does have control, except for some lapses that cause major disruption of his life. This reframing of his ability to control his behavior helps encourage even more personal responsibility during the difficult times.

The issue of who is in control when Red is around is an interesting one for the feminist therapist. Obviously, Red's womanizing and violent behavior pose some difficulties for a feminist therapist to deal with, as safety needs would be a prominent issue. Red would probably have a difficult time dealing with a feminist therapist, and not until a positive therapeutic relationship was established with Rick would he chance letting his "dark" side become visible. By that time, Rick would have perceived that he had more control over Red and would not allow those negative behaviors to jeopardize the positive gains he had already made in treatment. (It is assumed there were sufficient positive gains to permit Rick to stay in therapy during this time.) Once the safety issues are under control, the feminist therapist can help identify the strengths in Red's personality and encourage their integration with the other positive features already identified when the Rick side is present. The use of a different name, Ricardo, his given name, is an interesting way to encourage the integration of Rick and Red.

## Friendship Patterns

Rick comes into therapy describing his friendships as nonintegrated, like the two sides of his personality. Rick and Red both have a set of friends representing their split values: Rick's friends seem to be middle class, competent, and work-related, while Red's friends are lower-class, drug- and alcohol-addicted, and street smart. Although he has strengths in being able to make friends and spend time with them, there is a suggestion that he may have difficulties really feeling that he belongs in either group's world, given his childhood experiences of feeling he was not really like the other Hispanic kids because of his red hair.

The therapy relationship can be an effective tool for Rick to learn how to evaluate whether he is respected, appreciated, valued, and loved for himself as well as learning how to relate with emotional intimacy in a stable and consistent relationship. The bond formed between himself and a woman therapist who can help provide some external limits and controls on his behavior will stick with him during the rough times and can provide some of the relationship and social-skills training he lacked as a child. As he develops a new love relationship, it will be important to help him learn how to keep his relationship with his friends to meet some of his needs, so that he does not overload the relationship with the new woman. The ability to get his many needs for nurturance as well as affiliation met from different sources will help this new relationship get off to a less intensive and more positive start.

## CONCLUSIONS

Successful feminist therapy with Rick/Red/Ricardo will be measured by a number of factors. First, it would be important to go back and measure whether the original goals that were contracted for were met. In fact, if the treatment lasted several years, it is probable that those original goals would have been modified and revised several times before the termination, so all the goals need to be reviewed. Second, it would be important to measure whether the therapy was able to empower Rick so that he could set boundaries and place limits on his violence, chemical abuse, and criminal behavior. Third, successful feminist therapy would have helped Rick work through the abuse issues and resolved some of the dissociative behavior, particularly the split in his self-perception. The integration of Rick/Red/Ricardo would be a positive outcome. Fourth, Rick would have learned to identify and deal with his full range of feelings without ignoring them until they become so strong that they take over or turning the more painful ones into anger and violence. In order to reach this point, he will need to have dealt with his early childhood and mourned the loss of the idealized mother he wished for as well as the failed dreams of family from his adult life. Fifth, successful feminist therapy will have helped him feel more competent, especially if he was able to hold on to his job through the difficult times. He also will have come to terms with his identification as a Hispanic male with red hair! And sixth, successful feminist therapy will have helped Rick develop his friendships with men and women to meet some of his emotional needs for affiliation and have less need for control and power in his intimate relationships with women, so that he can choose a woman with whom to develop a positive love relationship, leading to the emotional stability he seeks.

## REFERENCES

Belle, D. (1984). Inequality and mental health: Low income and minority women. In L. E. Walker (Ed.), *Women and mental health policy* (pp. 135–150). Beverly Hills, CA: Sage.

Brown, L. S., & Root, M. P. P. (Eds.). (in press). *Diversity and complexity in feminist therapy*. New York: Haworth Press.

Cammaert, L. P. (1988). Nonoffending mothers: A new conceptualization. In L. E. A. Walker (Ed.), *Handbook on sexual abuse of children* (pp. 309–325). New York: Springer Publishing Co.

Carillo, R. (1989, June). *Domestic violence in the Hispanic community: Treating men*. Presentation at the Interamerican Congress on Psychology, Buenos Aires, Argentina.

Dutton, D. (1984). An ecological nested theory of male violence toward intimates. In P. Caplan (Ed.), *Feminist psychology in transition*. Montreal: Eden Press.

Dutton, D., & Painter, S. (1981). Traumatic bonding: The development of emotional attachments in battered women and other relationships with intermittent abuse. *Victimology: An International Journal, 6,* 139–145.

Ehrenreich, B. (1983). *The hearts of men: American dreams and the flight from commitment*. Garden City, NY: Anchor/Doubleday.

Figley, C. R. (Ed.). (1985). *Trauma and its wake: Vol. 1: The study and treatment of post traumatic stress disorders*. New York: Brunner/Mazel.

Figley, C. R. (Ed.). (1986). *Trauma and its wake: Vol. 2: Theory, research, and therapy*. New York: Brunner/Mazel.

Fodor, I. G. (1988). Cognitive behavior therapy: Evaluation of theory and practice for addressing women's issues. In M. A. Dutton-Douglas & L. E. A. Walker (Eds.), *Feminist psychotherapies: Integration of therapeutic and feminist systems* (pp. 91–117). Norwood, NJ: Ablex.

Frank, P., & Houghton, B. (1982). *Confronting the batterer: A guide to creating the spouse abuse educational workshop*. New York: Volunteer Counseling Service of Rockland County.

Gabarino, J. K., Guttman, E., & Seeley, J. W. (1987). *The psychologically battered child: Strategies for identification, assessment, and intervention*. San Francisco: Jossey-Bass.

Ganley, A. (1981). *Court mandated counseling for men who batter: Trainers guide*. Washington, DC: Center for Women Policy Studies.

Ganley, A. (1988). Feminist therapy with male clients. In M. A. Dutton-Douglas & L. E. A. Walker (Eds.), *Feminist psychotherapies: Integration of therapeutic and feminist systems* (pp. 186–205). Norwood, NJ: Ablex.

Goldberg, H. (1976). *The hazards of being male*. New York: Nash.

Goldberg, H. (1983). *The new male-female relationship*. New York: Signet.

Gondolf, E. W. (1985). *Men who batter: An integrated approach for stopping wife abuse*. Holmes Beach. FL: Learning Publications.

Lyon, H. (1978). *Tenderness is strength: From machismo to manhood*. New York: Harper & Row.

O'Neal, J. (1981). Patterns of gender role conflict and strain: Sexism and fear of femininity in men's lives. *Personnel and Guidance Journal, 60,* 203–210.

Pleck, J. (1981). *The myth of masculinity*. Cambridge, MA: MIT Press.

Pleck, J., & Sawyer, J. (1974). *Men and masculinity*. Englewood Cliffs, NJ: Prentice-Hall.

Sonkin, D., & Durphy, M. (1982). *Learning to live without violence: A book for men*. San Francisco: Volcano Press.

Sonkin, D., Martin, D., & Walker, L. E. A. (1985). *The male batterer*. New York: Springer Publishing Co.

Walker, L. E. A. (1979). *The battered woman*. New York: Harper & Row.

Walker, L. E. A. (1984). *The battered woman syndrome*. New York: Springer Publishing Co.

Walker, L. E. A. (1989). *Terrifying love: Why battered women kill and how society responds*. New York: Harper & Row.

# 12

## A Family Therapist
## Views the Case

### Sandra B. Coleman

## INTRODUCTION

Within the framework of systems theory (see Chapter 7), the family is expected to alter some of its transactional patterns as it wrestles with marriage, birth, childrearing, midlife, retirement, old age, and death. Consistent with this concept, Carter and McGoldrick (1980) view the life cycle in terms of "the meaningfulness of intergenerational connectedness in the family." They focus on the emotional tasks that the family must satisfy at each passage point in the life cycle. They are particularly concerned with the intersection between contemporary developmental events and historical family patterns, and suggest that family dysfunction is most apt to result when normal developmental tension collides with transgenerational stress. Carter and McGoldrick are particularly interested in the entry and exit points that disturb the family's balance. They note that adaptive reorganizational changes are a result of the family's ability to process its emotions at each transitional juncture. For example, to cope maturely with the empty-nest period of life, both parents and children must prepare themselves for the contingencies associated with their physical and emotional separation. As children embark on their adult tracks, parents need to realign themselves in a new dyadic marital relationship. Should this not occur, profound systemic problems may develop in one or both generations.

Despite some necessary struggle, families usually succeed in accepting the exigencies of their normal life cycle. Sometimes they do not. For approximately 30 years, family theorists and practitioners have been developing explanations and treatment methodologies for those families whose systems have difficulty incorporating change. Attention has recently been drawn to the family's psychosocial experience of death and traumatic loss. Since loss is a basic component of life, no family escapes its vicissitudes. Over time, however, it is usually accepted vis-à-vis the family's amalgam of interpersonal coping devices. In the case of loss due to death, cultural-religious rites such as the funeral, wake, and prescribed mourning period generally facilitate this process. Other types of losses may not have accompanying rituals, and in the case of severe reactions, this may contribute to the development of pathological conditions. Substance abuse is one behavior that often appears to be a function of the family's incomplete, unresolved loss of a member.[1]

## THEORETICAL UNDERPINNINGS OF CASE

The following case is embedded with factors associated with drug-addict families. My major research focuses on families amazingly similar to Rick's; thus, it is important to note that the hypothetical treatment of this case derives from a theoretical study supported by a National Institute on Drug Abuse Research grant award (DHHS Grant # R01-DA-02332-02). A review of the relevant literature will serve as a background for the case material.

### Death, Loss, and Separation

Within the context of family-systems theory, compulsive drug use can be viewed as a function of intrafamilial transactional patterns. From this perspective, drugs play a significant role in maintaining family balance or homeostasis. By adapting the major tenets of family-systems theory to the drug-abuse field, several authors cogently explain how the family encourages, reinforces, and sustains drug-seeking behavior (Harbin & Maziar, 1975; Klagsbrun & Davis, 1977; Seldin, 1972; Stanton & Coleman, 1980; Stanton et al., 1978; Steinglass, 1976). For an elaboration of these constructs and concepts, the reader is referred to the publications cited. The focus here is on one particular dimension of family life—death, separation, and loss—that appears to have a significant etiological effect on drug abuse, given the necessary addiction-producing elements of family behavior. Specifically, the incomplete-mourning theory of drug abuse (Coleman, 1980a, 1980b; Coleman & Stanton, 1978) suggests that addictive behavior is related to an unusual number of traumatic or premature deaths, separations, and losses that occur in critical or transitional stages of the family's developmental cycle and are not effectively resolved or mourned. The homeostatic family processes and interlocking transactional patterns make drug abuse a likely response for coping with the overwhelming stress associated with the loss experience. Drug use also serves to keep the abusing member helpless and dependent on the family, a process that unifies and sustains family intactness (Stanton, 1979). Within the complex set of interpersonal relationships is an overall sense of hopelessness, despair, and lack of purpose or meaning in life.

The early foundation for the theory of incomplete mourning lies in a pilot study of the prevalence of death among 25 recovering heroin addicts and their families (Coleman, 1975). At least one traumatic or untimely death in either the addict's family of origin or family of procreation had been experienced in 72% (N = 18) of the families. The investigation was limited to those deaths that were premature, unexpected, and not a function of illness associated with the normal aging process. Thus, the majority of deaths reported took place during the addicts' or parents' developmental years. Further findings revealed that 68% (N = 17) of the families had an alcoholic parent or sibling in either of the two generations studied. It is interesting to note that in addition to heroin addiction, death and alcoholism were common variables among these families.

In the years since this early work was completed, much additional support for the connection between unexpected death and/or traumatic loss and drug abuse has appeared in the literature (Coleman, 1980a, 1980b; Coleman & Stanton, 1978; Stanton & Coleman, 1980; Stanton et al., 1978).

Of further significance in Rick's case is the fact that in addition to separation caused by real death, any type of disengagement is found to be particularly difficult for addict families. Stanton (1979, 1980) and Coleman (1978, 1979) have written extensively about the conflictual elements of separation, expressing doubt that it is mere coincidence that drug use becomes intensified during adolescence when separation conflicts are at a peak. As Stanton et al., (1978) point out, drug abuse is a "paradoxical resolution" to growing up and leaving the family. The drug permits the user to leave, as a means of establishing some independence, but it also facilitates the return to the hearth when it is time to "crash." This perpetuates the cyclical pattern of leaving and not leaving, keeping the addict straddled between home and the outside world of drugs. The profound conflict that separation presents for these families has been discussed extensively in other publications and will not be repeated here.

## The Role of Religiosity in Drug-Addict Families

Akin to exploring the role of death in addict families is the investigation of the function of religion in family life.[2] The family's religious beliefs or philosophical systems are apt to be the major interface between death and the family's adaptive behavior. A sense of faith may either alleviate or exacerbate the sorrow, rage, and guilt that accompany or follow the loss of a loved one.

Feifel (1959) feels that one's religious orientation, coping mechanisms, and personal reaction to death are all related. The major thesis underlying Frankl's (1963) logotherapeutic system is that man's primary life force is the search for meaning. Frankl suggests that the loss of meaning creates an "existential vacuum" in which one lacks a rationale for living, thus creating hopelessness and despair. He explains alcoholism as a function of the "existential vacuum" and further suggests that the frustrated will to meaning may be compensated for by the substitution of a will to pleasure. Could one then suppose, in view of such a theoretical premise, that drug addition is also a means of coping with the spiritual void?

Drug experimentation may be seen as part of the individual life cycle since the initial experience with a drug is usually associated with the adolescent stage of development. Like acne or other age-related phenomena, the predisposing factors have long been present. However, it is the family's relationship patterns and feedback system that determine whether this initial drug use develops into serious drug abuse. A circular homeostatic model has been developed by Stanton et al. (1978) and Stanton (1980) that explains how drug use is reinforced and maintained. This model is based on a complex set of feedback mechanisms that involve, at a minimum, a triadic family subsystem—most likely mother, father, and drug abuser. In contradistinction to the linear or causal chain of family events, the circular model suggests that the incomplete mourning of a deceased member (or other loss experience) keeps the family in a continuous grieving process. Because the loss has not been mastered, the drug abuser becomes the "revenant" of the deceased and is encouraged to stay close to the family. When he attempts to leave home, a family crisis ensues, and he will be "called back." These families would rather have the addict dead than lose him to outsiders (Stanton et al., 1978). The "moving in and moving out" of the addict serves a family-maintenance function and preserves the homeostasis. It is part of the cycle of interlocking behaviors, and if the addict should die, another member will probably start to use drugs, ensuring the family's enmeshment in an endless cycle of mourning, loss, and mourning.

Thus, the incomplete-mourning theory is based on the premise that death, separation, and loss are significant etiological factors in drug-abusing families. Although death and some types of loss are stage-related predictable events in all families, among-drug-abusing families, death and loss are expected to occur at unpredictable, unexpected points on the life-cycle continuum. The theory emphasizes that the idiosyncratic orientation that these families have toward death and loss makes it extraordinarily difficult to accomplish the emotional "completion" of mourning. Thus, the death and death-related variables become integral parts of a homeostatic pattern that keeps the drug-abusing member helpless and dependent on staying at home with the family. Within the complex set of feedback mechanisms involved in the drug-sustaining cycle of family interactions lies an overall sense of family hopelessness and lack of purpose or meaning in life.

More recent research support for the theory of incomplete mourning derives from a study on the function of heroin addiction as a family-learned method of coping with death, separation, and loss across the life cycle. (Coleman, Kaplan, & Downing, 1986; Coleman, Kaplan, Gallagher, Downing, & Caine, 1982). Subjects in this study (N = 111) consisted of heroin addicts, psychiatric patients, and a population designated as normal. Each of these subjects was given an individually administered series of tests and an extensive structured interview covering a broad range of family life-cycle experiences. The latter, *The Coleman Family Background Questionnaire* (CFBQ) (Coleman, Kaplan, & Downing, 1982), the major instrument of the study, includes questions on demography, living arrangements, religion, meaning in life, experience with pain, attitudes toward death, addictive behaviors of three generations of family members, relationships with parenting figures, and children and incest. It also provides a retrospective overview of major life events, the subject's responses to those events, and her perception of family members' reactions.

Questions about family composition over time lead to a "map" of the subjects' homes and of all those who have lived with the subjects. For every deceased family member or significant other, details are elicited as to the cause of death; age of subject and deceased; closeness of the relationship; emotional and practical impact of the death; extent of mourning by the subject, parents, and siblings; and whether the subject attended the funeral and its impact. Each permanent and temporary separation from a family member is also explored to determine its timing, cause, and effect, and whether the subject was reunited with this person.

## Summary

The incomplete-mourning theory as developed by Coleman (1980a, 1980b; Coleman et al., 1982; Coleman et al., 1986) views drug addiction as a means of coping with traumatic family experiences. It is much like Bowen's (1978) "emotional shock wave," which he describes as a network of underground "aftershocks" of serious life events that occur anywhere in the extended family system in the months or years following a serious emotional family event. He feels that these usually occur after the death or threatened death of a significant family member but suggests that they could follow other types of losses. Bowen relates the reaction to denial of emotional dependence among family members and feels that it most often occurs in families with a significant degree of denied emotional "fusion."

The misuse of drugs is viewed as a structural or functional imbalance in the family rather than a problem experienced by a single individual (Steinglass, 1976). Thus, the initiation of drug abuse cannot be ascribed to a linear cause-and-effect model. Rather, drug abuse is part of a family cycle in which each family member's behavior affects and is affected by another member's behavior in reciprocal fashion.

## Treatment Implications

The extension of the incomplete-mourning theory to clinical practice is best accomplished within the context of family therapy. For more than a decade, this approach has taken hold in the drug field. A national survey of drug abuse and family treatment (Coleman, 1976; Coleman & Davis, 1978) reported that 93% of the respondent clinics (N = 2012) were providing some form of treatment to families. Stanton's (1979) review of the literature on family treatment of drug problems indicates that this approach and its variations (e.g., multiple family therapy, marital therapy, etc.) are both "beneficial and effective." Thus, the application of family-systems theory and its related treatment techniques is a logical and effective means of dealing with the case of Rick.

## RICK'S FAMILY BACKGROUND
### Ethnic Confusion and Loss Issues

Rick came from a family background embedded with loss issues. This was a Hispanic family living in the ghetto of a large U.S. city. Although one might assume that such a location is an attempt to maintain ethnic identity, Rick's lack of strong family ties and his physical uniqueness (red hair, freckles, and a dark complexion) suggest that there was enormous difficulty creating a bond with either the Hispanic community or with the larger assimilated metropolitan city.

Clearly, looking like an "Irish Spaniard" did not allow for easy identification with any group. Rick's loss of a father, from whom he may have inherited his red hair, prohibited him from forming an identity or a relationship with him. Because of his mother's heavy work load, she was only marginally available to him. In addition to her preoccupation with the financial support of her three sons, she too may have experienced considerable conflict about her youngster's unusual appearance. Also, one might hypothesize that Rick was born out of wedlock, the result of a momentary attraction between her and a handsome Irishman. Rick could have been a constant reminder of such a liaison—one she might rather have forgotten. It is not possible to know whether Rick's appearance affected his relationship with his two siblings, but he clearly felt abandoned by them also since his only recollection of them during his childhood was that they were always "out of the house."

Rick's early life was thus a blend of abandonment and isolation, and he obviously served as the "carrier" of his family's burden of disenfranchisement. In his attempt to search for a family, Rick in a sense continued the family theme by abandoning his own family and becoming a member of the outside community. He found a strange kind of kinship with peers, drugs, and booze on the streets, which ultimately led to the same cycle of alienation and rejection that existed in his family. Overall, the repetitive pattern, reinforced from birth through Rick's developmental years, was one of emotional deprivation in family and friendships. Attempts to cope by "hanging out" with substance-abusing street people led only to a continuous recycling of previous disappointments.

In late adolescence and adulthood, Rick experienced another series of losses, and his effort to escape through an early marriage and parenthood ended in divorce and estrangement. This was followed by joining the army, which led him to Vietnam and more loss, this time of buddies through death. Rick's suffering continued after the war when he reentered society. His matriculation at a college and a second marriage were thwarted when this marriage also dissolved. There was despair and depression as a consequence of losing his daughter when his former wife took her out of the country.

It is evident that in every situation where Rick was systemically connected, he experienced loss, despair, and abandonment. His intrapersonal relationship with himself was no different. In his "split" between the "good" Rick and the "bad" guy Red, the same themes prevailed. Thus, his individual system merely recapitulated what dominated his interpersonal ones.

## Relationship Conflicts

Attempts to resolve his problems through therapy mirrored his former failures. It is predictable that he would be unable to connect more easily with a therapist than with family or friends. His therapists were all men, and despite his obvious need for a male relationship, this posed enormous conflicts for him. Indeed, for brief periods he had been able to relate to women, but his experiences with men were infused with drugs, alcohol, and war. Even his sibling relationships had left only a hopeless void. Thus, there was little reason to expect that meeting individually with a man would result in anything less than overwhelming anxiety. Again, on an intrapersonal level, his insecurities about his masculinity and his lack of ever having a strong male with whom to identify might introduce an element of homophobia to threaten further any opportunity to develop intimacy with men, even therapists.

The manner in which Rick finally came to select his only successful therapy sadly reflects his vacuous view of relationships. The impersonal use of an insurance company's provider list and his choice of the "last" person on the list were a desperate yet impersonal "last" attempt at rehabilitation. Rick's "split" between wanting to live and wanting to die became apparent in his choice of a female therapist. Surely his other "doctors" had faded, like the rest of his life, into nameless, faceless oblivion, so he approached his last selection in similar manner: almost a chance situation, with just one more identityless psychotherapist, except that he ruled out a man, the absolute fatal probability, so this time he chose a woman. Thus, the healthier part of him, the part that "hoped," prevailed. And fortunately this therapy shifted the pattern. In my opinion, had this not worked, suicide would have resulted, either directly through a self-inflicted act of violence or indirectly in a drug-induced state.

## Gender Confusion, Drugs, and Violence

Because of Rick's lack of a father and the deficit he experiences with regard to male identification, Rick seems to have formed a negative identification with the drug-abusing subculture. Here, among drugs and violence, as Red, he embraces the pseudo-masculine image—machismo—that causes conflict with the "good" guy Rick.

## Case Summary

Rick's family is living in a subsection of American life in the Hispanic ghetto of a large metropolitan city where ethnic conflicts prevent his family from integrating with the larger culture. Rick's physical differences from his neighbors only accentuate the problem. Developmentally, Rick is unable to go beyond the adolescent phase, and unfortunately his family cannot help him because they are stuck in the same phase of development. As a system, they are unable to master the passage of growing-up and letting-go. Rick's mom has never remarried or successfully moved beyond a particular stage of her development, and although she has had relationships with men, she has never created a bonded, committed union. She works obsessively, perhaps even addictively, and by doing so avoids other areas of life that might offer her healthy opportunity and challenge. Rick's developmental delay merely reflects the impasse in his family's life cycle. Since we know little about his brothers, we can only assume that they are stuck in a similar fashion.

Rick had no positive models for marriage, and although he married twice, neither was a success. As with his mother's workaholism, Rick was too obsessed with using and dealing drugs to provide adequately for his son or daughter. Consequently, his tenuous connection with his children reinforced his concept as a loser. Alarming too is the fact that Rick's absence from his children's lives recapitulated his own father's abandonment of him, clearly suggesting that the intergenerational transmission of the pattern of loss and despair will invade their future.

Thus, major systems hypotheses center around a family background of confused mixed-cultural identity and an intergenerational lack of adequate role models, leaving the whole family stuck in their developmental process. Rick's family could neither resolve their ethnic issues of belonging nor cope with their multiple losses and disappointments. There is no evidence that either Rick or his family have any religious affiliation or supportive belief system. This unfortunately leaves the whole family in a despondent hopeless situation. Within such a context of powerlessness and despair growing up, the responsibilities of adulthood for Rick could only appear overwhelmingly formidable.

## A FAMILY-THERAPY APPROACH

As a family-systems therapist I would begin treatment with Rick by having him construct (with my assistance) a family genogram (Bowen, 1960, 1978) with as much richness of detail as possible. This would immediately reconnect him with his roots and, with my support, give him the courage to explore what he had too much fear to do alone. It would be readily obvious that Rick's knowledge of his family lineage was limited, and thus, when his therapeutic bond with me was strong enough, we would bring in his family of origin (his mother and two brothers).

There is no question that he knew where they were. My job would be to help him feel safe enough to approach them.

## Phase I: The Past—Rick's Family of Origin

Family therapy with Rick's mom and siblings would focus on three time dimensions—past, present, and future. Initially, the past would be represented by the work with the genogram. This is a relatively non-threatening way to reveal both family history and pockets of unresolved emotional distress. Since my major hypothesis about this family system is that there is an intergenerational theme of loss and despair on both cultural and transactional levels, the construction of the genogram is an essential aid to treatment. Also, if in fact Rick's father was Irish, he would learn this. He might also learn how the Irish continuously struggle for identity and how all too often their methods for dulling the pain of cultural inadequacy and suffering involve the pervasive use of alcohol. This new knowledge would provide Rick with a significant understanding of his heritage and the previously missing ethnic connection. Further, any family history of substance abuse or other addictions would be exposed and thus could be dealt with supportively and directly. The hope here is that this could lead Rick ultimately to acknowledge his need for working with an AA program, a vital ancillary treatment.[3]

Rick might also be encouraged to search for his father and face what for too long he had avoided. Rick's work in this area would ultimately reinforce his relationship with his mother, who might at first be overwhelmed with apprehension, but in the presence of an understanding therapist, she would have an opportunity to complete her own unfinished business with regard to Rick's father, her family of origin, and perhaps her relationships with other significant persons in the past. If her two older sons had had a father or fathers other than Rick's (which I strongly suspect), we would also explore this and expose the family secrets that have perniciously contributed to the long term disengagement and cutoffs.

The way men in the family dealt with their sexuality is an important area to examine. Particularly significant is how the men handle their anger and whether their relationships with women are too often a blend of sex and violence. Healthy ways of handling these emotions would be an important therapy goal. Related goals would include looking at gender-specific roles and behaviors, and the "stakes" of giving up cultural stereotypes.

This work, along with the shedding of the family secrets, would permit the brothers to develop sibling relationships that would create bonds with men of their own generation and a sense of extended family, particularly if these siblings had married and had children.

## Phase II: The Present and Future—Rick's Family of Procreation

This phase of treatment would occur after Rick and his family of origin had resolved their interpersonal conflicts to the extent possible. Certainly, family therapy would have created a safe laboratory for Rick's mom and brothers to talk to one another in an open, trusting manner. Because few families ever reach an absolute end point, therapy affords an opportunity to continue the process long after formal sessions are completed.

After the family-of-origin work, I would encourage Rick to look at his issues with his former wives and children. Again, I would begin this part of therapy by helping Rick deal with the emotions associated with both marriages and divorces, and the births of his son and daughter. If Rick is emotionally blocked and fearful about doing this, I would encourage his to bring in any memorabilia connected with the relationships. Photographs, family movies, and any other articles that evoke memories of significant relationships can be helpful therapeutic materials.

I would next ask Rick to begin a search for each former wife and child, with the ultimate goal of bringing them to a few sessions. Although at times a former spouse has too much residual anger to make a potential conjoint session productive, if the couple has had a child together, there may be some motivation to cooperate. If necessary, I will follow up the client's request to a former spouse with a personal phone call or letter from me. In most instances, I gain sufficient trust to effect a more mature relationship among the estranged members.

It is important to note that the major purpose of working with former marital partners is not to attempt reconciliation but to open a path for more effective child-parent connections. If Rick could maintain ongoing relationships with his son and daughter, it would serve as an important preventive for his offspring, who are both at risk for substance abuse and emotional disorders. In addition, by giving them a meaningful experience with open communication, they can learn respect for their father, perhaps even develop some love. Regardless of what ultimately happens to the relationships, Rick will know that he reached out to his family. This will elevate his self-esteem, giving him a chance to know himself at a deeper level of awareness.

Finally, if direct contacts with significant family members were not possible, I would create well-conceived therapeutic rituals to face the conflicts and resolve the incomplete mourning patterns. The incorpora-tion of family members into these rituals would again offer family mem-bers an opportunity to form personal liaisons with the present and the future, thus shifting the pattern from one of perpetual loss to that of po-tential family loyalty, trust, and interpersonal gain.

Theoretically, our therapy would establish a family bond that would foster Rick's sense of self-worth, previously nonexistent. In addition to family therapy, when Rick was ready, I would recommend that he join a men's group. Here he could learn to trust men and develop a more posi-tive, nonviolent sense of masculinity. From such a base, he could then move forward through his life cycle, developing more stable associa-tions with significant others and his career.

## FINAL NOTE

Rick's case clearly demonstrates how a family becomes developmentally stuck when its history is threaded with unresolved losses. Consistent with the theory of incomplete mourning, Rick's family could not effec-tively "empty its nest" when so many ghosts hovered over it. By treat-ing Rick within the context of a family-systems model, the family's growth mechanisms would be released, allowing Rick to achieve per-sonal identity and his children a chance to become better integrated.

Whether my gender would produce special results is a moot point since we cannot do more than speculate. For Red, a woman family psy-chologist would certainly be "safer" initially since he never succeeded in previous therapies with men. Rick's ambivalence about whether to love or hate women could be resolved by learning to trust me. My re-spect for him would also nourish and improve his self-concept. Rick's mother would certainly benefit from having an experience with a strong female role model, and because I could share some of my own experi-ences as a mother of three adult children, two of whom are sons, she might learn how to relate more effectively with Rick. As a woman, I might be more successful in encouraging Rick's former wives to attend therapy, for they would probably feel less threatened in a room with Rick and another woman than in a male-dominated session.

The problems inherent in Rick's life are complex and multifaceted. Whether the route I would take would succeed cannot be known. How-ever, if I was given the opportunity to treat Rick and his family, my knowledge of Rick's particular intergenerational patterns, both theoreti-cally and clinically, makes me feel that I could make the connection to his family. Thus in this case, family psychology might be the "difference that makes the difference."

## NOTES

1. The term *substance abuse* is interchanged with *drug abuse,* and each refers to the habitual use of drugs to the extent that physical and psychological dependency occur, with resultant symptoms of withdrawal syndrome upon cessation of use. Although the term *addition* usually implies a compulsive preoccupation with drugs, it is used interchangeably with *abuse* since neither word is as yet universally differentiated. This theory has been largely developed from heroin-abusing populations, but evidence suggests that it also pertains to alcoholics and serious abusers of other drugs.

2. *Religiosity* or *religion,* as used here, extends beyond formal doctrine and includes any system of philosophical belief that represents a specific view about the meaning of life. Thus, the term *religion* embraces a sociological view of weltanschauung that includes the conceptualization of the purpose of one's existence. This is considered one of the motivating forces that guide purposive behavior—an internal determinant, to some extent, of one's life process.

3. The 12-step program is the central recovering process associated with Alcoholics Anonymous. Entry into a 12-step program is representative of a person's desire and commitment to making a serious effort to sustain sobriety.

## REFERENCES

Bowen, M. (1960). A family concept of schizophrenia. In D. D. Jackson (Ed.), *The etiology of schizophrenia.* New York: Basic Books.

Bowen, M. (1978). *Family therapy in clinical practice.* New York: Jason Aronson.

Carter, E., & McGoldrick, M. (Eds.). (1980). *The family life cycle.* New York: Gardner Press.

Coleman, S. B. (1975, September). *Death—The facilitator of family integration.* Paper presented at the American Psychological Association, Chicago.

Coleman, S. B. (1976). *Final report: A national study of family therapy in the field of drug abuse.* Grant No. 3H81-DA-01478-0151. Document available through National Institute on Drug Abuse Library, Rockville, MD.

Coleman, S. B. (1978). Sib group therapy: A prevention program for siblings from drug addict programs. *International Journal of Addictions, 13,* 115–127.

Coleman, S. B. (1979). Siblings in session. In E. Kaufman & P. Kaufman (Eds.), *Family therapy of drug and alcohol abuse.* New York: Gardner.

Coleman, S. B. (1980a). Incomplete mourning and addict family transactions: A theory for understanding heroin abuse. In D. Lettieri (Ed.), *Theories of drug abuse.* Washington, DC: National Institute of Drug Abuse, Research Monograph 30, DHHS, Pub. No. (ADM) 80-967, Government Printing Office.

Coleman, S. B. (1980b). The family trajectory: A circular journey to drug abuse. In B. Ellis (Ed.), *Drug abuse from the family perspective*. Washington, DC: National Institute of Drug Abuse, Office of Program Development and Analysis, DHHS, Pub. No. (ADM) 80-910.

Coleman, S. B., & Davis, D. I. (1978). Family therapy and drug abuse: A national survey. *Family Process, 17,* 21–29.

Coleman, S. B., Kaplan, J. D., & Downing, R. W. (1982). *The Coleman Family Background Questionnaire*. Copyright registration number TXu 258–477.

Coleman, S. B., Kaplan, J. D., & Downing, R. W. (1986). Life cycle and loss—The spiritual vacuum of heroin addiction. *Family Process, 25*(1), 5–23.

Coleman, S. B., Kaplan, J. D., Gallagher, P. R., Downing, R. W., & Caine, C. (1982). *Heroin—A family coping strategy for death and loss: Final report 1979–1981*. Washington, DC: National Institute on Drug Abuse, Grant No. R01-DA-02332-02, Achievement Through Counseling and Treatment.

Coleman, S. B., & Stanton, M. D. (1978). The role of death in the addict family. *Journal of Marriage and Family Counseling, 4,* 79–91.

Feifel, H. (1959). Attitudes toward death in some family and mentally ill populations. In H. Feifel (Ed.), *The meaning of death*. New York: McGraw-Hill.

Frankl, V. E. (1963). *Man's search for meaning*. New York: Beacon Press.

Harbin, H. T., & Maziar, H. M. (1975). The families of drug abusers: A literary review. *Family Process, 14,* 411–431.

Klagsbrun, M., & Davis, D. I. (1977). Substance abuse and family interaction. *Family Process, 16,* 149–173.

Seldin, N. E. (1972). The family of the addict: A review of the literature. *International Journal of Addictions, 7,* 97–107.

Stanton, M. D. (1979). Family treatment approaches to drug abuse: A review. *Family Process, 18,* 251–280.

Stanton, M. D. (1980). A family theory of drug abuse. In D. Lettieri et al. (Eds.), *Theories on drug abuse*. Washington, DC: National Institute on Drug Abuse, Research Monograph 30, PHHS Pub. No. (ADM) 80-967, Government Printing Office.

Stanton, M. D., & Coleman, S. B. (1980). The participatory aspects of self-destructive behavior: The addict family as a model. In N. Farberow (Ed.), *The many faces of suicide*. New York: McGraw-Hill.

Stanton, M. D., Todd, T. C., Heard, D. B., Kirschner, S., Kleiman, J. L., Mowatt, D. T., Riley, P., Scott, S. M., & Van Deusen, J. M. (1978). Heroin addiction as a family phenomenon: A new conceptual model. *American Journal of Drug & Alcohol Abuse, 5,* 125–150.

Steinglass, P. (1976). Family therapy in alcoholism. In B. Kissin & H. Begleiter (Eds.), *The biology of alcoholism* (Vol. 5). New York: Plenum.

# 13

---

# A Cognitive Behaviorist
# Views the Case

## Ellen Tobey Klass and Joann Paley Galst

---

Rick presents with serious problems in the affective, behavioral, and cognitive realms, along with social stressors. Thus, treating him would challenge the cognitive-behavior therapist to develop a multifaceted approach that would encompass many problem areas. The treatment that we portray illustrates the cognitive-behavioral use of assessment and case formulation to select priorities for intervention and the clinical practice of assessment at turning points in therapy. Our treatment also illustrates cognitive-behavioral interventions to maintain therapy with a client who finds it difficult to stay in treatment. As in Chapter 8, where necessary for the exposition, we have added details to the case. Our final section discusses questions that our case analysis raises about women as cognitive-behavior therapists.

To review briefly our summary of cognitive-behavior therapy in Chapter 8, a basic premise is that learning processes play an important role in the origin, maintenance, and change of thoughts, feelings, and actions. The causal model emphasizes the contributions of *social-learning history* (past learning) and *current maintaining conditions* to the client's problems. Assessment focuses on *proximal* (immediate) and *distal* (more removed) antecedents and consequences of target problems. A *functional analysis*, or formulation of the controlling conditions, guides the choice of treatment methods, which generally focus on relatively specific areas that are viewed as proximal causes. With a skills-learning model of treatment, interventions are designed to provide specific new learning experiences. The therapist takes an active, directive, and educative stance and encourages the client to collaborate in treatment. As an environmentalist theory that has not extensively elaborated on inherent or normative aspects of personality, cognitive-behavioral theory views sex differences as the product of the individual's social-learning history and current conditions. Depending on their impact on the individual client's functioning, sex role issues may or may not require attention in therapy.

## INITIAL ASSESSMENT

### First Interviews

Like many therapists of other schools (see Wachtel, 1978, p. 109), I[1] would first explore the specific referents of Rick's initial complaints of feeling depressed, bad, ugly, and on an emotional roller coaster. Rick feels worthless and has little enjoyment in life. Although he has had these feelings for as long as he can remember, they have worsened since his second divorce and the struggle over visitation of his daughter. I would ask Rick for his sense of how things changed from the top to the bottom of the roller coaster. Rick might respond that the changes came out of nowhere.

Based on Rick's inexpressiveness and labored presentation as we began the first session, I would identify two crucial clinical needs: to develop rapport and to assess for severe mental disorder. In keeping with our task-oriented stance, cognitive behaviorists generally intervene in long silences. I would comment on Rick's seeming difficulty with talking and encourage him to tell me about it. As Rick did speak, I would respond emphatically and sympathetically to reinforce verbal behavior, but beyond saying it was hard he offered little to work with. To soften my numerous diagnostic questions, I would use the disarming communication tactic of apologizing in advance in this case for any pressure that my questions might create. I would also inquire into Rick's earlier therapy experiences. As he haltingly told me that his prior therapists had set off feelings without helping him handle them, I would differentiate my approach by emphasizing the coping orientation (e.g., "An important part of therapy as I see it is to help you learn to handle strong feelings without getting overwhelmed") and my commitment to his remaining comfortable enough to be able to stay in therapy. I would ask if

Rick had specific hopes about a female therapist, but he could not explain this choice. I would make sure to conclude each assessment session by asking Rick how he had felt in the session, encouraging questions, and answering them as directly as possible. (Cognitive behaviorists generally directly respond to clients' questions rather than exploring fantasies or motives [Sloane, Staples, Cristol, Yorkston, & Whipple, 1975].)

In the first two sessions, I would assess whether Rick met the diagnostic criteria of the *Diagnostic and Statistical Manual of Mental Disorders* (*DSM-III-R;* American Psychiatric Association, 1987) for endogenous depression, bipolar disorder and hypomania, and psychosis. Given Rick's presentation, I would want to evaluate whether alternatives to outpatient psychotherapy (e.g., medication, partial hospitalization) are needed. Clearly, Rick meets diagnostic criteria for a major depressive episode. I would inquire into physiological signs of endogenous depression, such as sleep and appetite disturbances, for which medication might be indicated. Except for difficulty sleeping (but not early-morning waking) and possibly mild psychomotor retardation, Rick does not show or report symptoms of endogenous depression. I would be concerned about manic and hypomanic episodes because of Rick's self-reported mood swings, but his highs are short-lived (less than a day) and usually involve cocaine use. Rick denies symptoms of psychosis. He reports recently wishing he were dead, but says that he has no plan for suicide or past suicide attempts.

I would consider the possible role of alcohol and cocaine use in Rick's presentation and symptoms. I would reserve detailed assessment of this area for further sessions, but I would ask when and how much he had last used alcohol and cocaine in order to rule out possible current intoxication. To determine if intervention was urgently needed, I would inquire into negative feedback about drinking and drug use. Rick's fears were based solely on his discomfort with occasional lateness to work, hangovers, and difficulty concentrating, so I would defer further inquiry until there was more rapport.

## Additional Assessment Sessions

In the next several sessions, I would assess the S-O-R-C variables (stimulus, organismic, response, and consequence) that cognitive behaviorists draw on to make a functional analysis. I would also work on safeguarding the therapy.

### *Safeguarding the Therapy*

As in treatment of borderline personality disorder patients, I would define safeguarding the therapy as a top priority (Linehan, 1988). I would introduce this by emphasizing Rick's hope and courage in again seeking therapy, both to defuse any sense of criticism and also to begin to establish myself as a source of positive social reinforcement (praise, concern, and respect). I would also introduce a contract of addressing threats to the therapy: "If there is something I'm doing that makes therapy difficult for you or a way that I could help you be more comfortable, I hope you will let me know. Also, if there are things that you are doing that I think are making it difficult for therapy to be of use to you, I will let you know. This way, we can try to come up with solutions."

To develop specific safeguarding methods, it is advisable to heighten client involvement through the technique of problem solving (Goldfried & Davison, 1976)—generating many solutions with the client in a brainstorming, nonevaluative fashion, selecting ones to implement, and evaluating implementation. If I encouraged Rick to give ideas and he said that he had none, I would propose several. Rick might let me know as soon as his feelings seemed even slightly unmanageable, or if this seemed too difficult, he could raise his hand or a finger as a signal. (In line with our step-by-step approach to change, cognitive behaviorists often restructure tasks to make them easy enough for clients to accomplish.) I would tell Rick that I would respond to these signals by clarifying the source of his discomfort and explaining or suggesting alternatives. I would also propose that I ask Rick about his feelings from time to time. In the hope that he would express dissatisfactions in the therapy context, I would describe ways that I would handle issues around termination. I would ask that Rick let me know if he was considering stopping therapy, so that we could explore possible remedies. If he did decide to terminate, I would tell him, I would be asking him to come for a last session to tie up loose ends and enable him to move on. As long as Rick thought these suggestions were "all right," which was the extent of his enthusiasm at this point, I would begin to implement those that were currently pertinent.

## S-O-R-C Assessment

Among the stimulus variables that might be immediate antecedents to Rick's emotional symptoms, I would attend in most depth to alcohol and drug use. This would not, however, be my first area of extensive inquiry, because of threats to rapport that it might present. Rather, I would begin by exploring Rick's current life context, asking about satisfactions and difficulties with work and his current relationships. I would ask Rick what his brothers and his son were like as people and about the frequency and nature of their contacts. Rick sees his son at least once a week for an all-day outing and talks to him on the phone almost every day. He has phone conversations with his brothers, whom he could describe only vaguely, on two or three holidays a year; he last saw them 5 years ago. I would ask Rick about his relationship with his mother and the circumstances and status of his current divorce.

With regard to organismic variables, I routinely ask about general health and results of a recent physical examination. Given my questions about possible abuse and dependence on psychoactive substances, I would follow up (with Rick's consent) with his physician. I would also assess Rick's health habits, including exercise, which may relieve anxiety (Long, 1985) and depression (Fremont & Craighead, 1987), and caffeine use, which may exacerbate anxiety conditions (Charney, Heninger, & Jatlow, 1985). Rick is mildly hypertensive and does not show physical signs of drug withdrawal, such as tremor. He never exercises, and he drinks approximately six cups of coffee and cola a day, an estimated 400 mg of caffeine, which substantially exceeds recommended levels.

Organismic variables also include psychosocial history, such as upbringing, education, work, military service, and intimate relationships. Rick describes the severe emotional deprivation in his family life and his experiences of intense involvement with a wild group of boys who courted trouble with the law. Despite his disrupted adolescence, Rick had managed to graduate from high school. When Rick expressed horror about his Vietnam experience, I would inquire into specific symptoms of posttraumatic stress disorder, such as flashbacks. (Although Rick did not meet diagnostic criteria, I would plan to inquire further into his combat experiences later in therapy, as they may relate to intimacy fears [Glover, 1984; Keane, Fairbank, Caddell, Zimering, & Bender, 1985a].) I would ask what he felt had gone wrong and right in his prior relationships with women and be told of his repeated disappointments with how little they had to offer. Cognitive behaviorists also evaluate the client's strengths. Rick's repeated efforts to improve his life (through completion of high school, military enlistment, enrollment in college, and prior therapy), the fact that he had held his job for a year and a half and wanted to keep it, and his continued relationship with his son suggested his persistence and ability to act in a goal-directed fashion at times.

Response variables involved Rick's chief complaints of unpredictable depression and anxiety. I would observe Rick's interactions with me when topics become more personal. He frequently becomes unexpressive and terse at these times, suggesting difficulty tolerating emotionality and intimacy. In considering consequence variables, I would note that unlike the situation with some clients, Rick's expression of symptoms did not appear to obtain direct rewards from other people (e.g., attention and sympathy for reports of depression) that might reinforce symptoms in an operant fashion. The role of negative affect reduction as a consequence that maintains alcohol and cocaine use is discussed below.

A major focus of the initial assessment would be psychoactive substance use. Since this was not Rick's presenting complaint, I would raise this topic carefully, but its possible role in creating and maintaining negative affect would make detailed assessment essential. Following McCrady's (1985) assessment guidelines, I would ask Rick to tell me about his experiences with drinking and drugs, including variations over time in the amount and circumstances of use, and any efforts to reduce or stop either activity. As McCrady recommended, I would explicitly recognize the difficulty in talking about such behaviors and give credit to his efforts at self-disclosure. I would aim to reflect the positive as well as negative impacts he perceived.

I would learn that Rick began drinking as a young teenager, started smoking marijuana a few years later, and first used cocaine when 18 years old—all with his street friends. He smoked marijuana continually while in Vietnam, but he now finds it too depressing and stopped a few years before. He tried to cut down on drinking three times, but he had felt isolated and tense, and he therefore returned to his usual level each time. Currently, his heaviest drinking (two six-packs of beer a night) is on weekends with buddies, and he says he has three or four beers most evenings to unwind after work. He claims he gets intoxicated only two or three times a year. On weekends with heavy drinking, he and his friends occasionally "get a little excited" (i.e., tease each other almost to the point of provoking a physical fight). Rick's cocaine use is episodic, on weekends, and involves inhaling cocaine, which he and his buddies take turns buying for the group. Rick spends most of his discretionary income on this expense. He has not tried to stop using cocaine. At this point, Rick definitely meets diagnostic criteria for alcohol abuse (maladaptive use of the drug without clear evidence of physical dependence), as he had unsuccessfully tried to reduce intake and drinks steadily. While his sleep disturbance might reflect depression or anxiety, it might also be due to alcohol and cocaine use.

## Functional Analysis

In formulating the controlling conditions for Rick's mood difficulties, my initial working hypothesis would be that use of alcohol and cocaine maintains and exacerbates his problems. Clearly, psychoactive substance abuse is only one of many immediate causes of his mood difficulties. (I would conjecture that other proximal causes include difficulties in managing negative affect and intimacy, along with his limited and negative social network, and that these areas in turn reflect more distal causes in his extremely deprived upbringing.) However, substance abuse appears to be the most immediate aggravating cause of Rick's intense problems at the time that he seeks treatment. Alcohol is a depressant, although its immediate effects at low doses are subjectively experienced as positive. In addition to its direct effects on mood, hangovers (and sleep difficulties that might be drug-related) had begun to affect work and thus to threaten a major source of Rick's self-esteem. Although Rick did not show definite physiological tolerance of alcohol, his pattern of steady drinking in evenings and heavy weekend drinking without feeling intoxicated might reflect some degree of tolerance. Moreover, cocaine triggers depression in a well-known rebound effect and thus might contribute to his out-of-control mood swings.

Some additional clinical considerations would argue for an initial focus on substance abuse. The clinical picture might change dramatically when the acute adverse effects of substance use were eliminated. Ignoring substance abuse and treating Rick's other difficulties in their own right could be problematic in that alcohol and cocaine would continue to affect these areas. It is also possible that state-dependent learning would limit therapeutic gains. In state-dependent learning, behaviors that are acquired when the organism is under the influence of a psychotropic drug are not demonstrated when the individual is drug-free. The status of state-dependent learning in human beings with respect to alcohol and cocaine is unclear, but I would want to err on the side of caution.

My functional analysis of psychoactive substance abuse would consider distal causes in Rick's upbringing. I would note in particular the lack of nurturance and harsh demands for conformity on the part of Rick's mother, who virtually ignored him except for stinging criticisms of perceived transgressions (e.g., not doing household chores). These experiences resulted in both a vulnerability to experiencing negative affect and a deficit of skills for regulating it. Drug use can serve as a chemical means to reduce negative affect without requiring actual behavioral or cognitive skills. In addition, Rick's adolescent street buddies regularly used alcohol and drugs to excess, providing positive reinforcement in the form of social interaction and also modeling substance use as a desirable behavior.

These distal causes led to several more proximal causes of substance use. Alcohol and cocaine provided immediate negative reinforcement through reductions in anxiety and depression, along with immediate positive reinforcement in aiding social interaction. When an immediate stressor arose, such as job difficulties or relationship issues, Rick's major way to reduce unpleasant feelings was drug use. Since he did not effectively cope with the stressor, it remained or grew worse. Thus, a cycle had evolved in which alcohol and cocaine use led to immediate relief of distress and immediate pleasure, but also to later dysphoria. Rick self-medicated his dysphoria with the same drugs, resulting in immediate relief but subsequent return of dysphoria. Due to the well-known primacy of immediate over delayed reinforcement, substance abuse is maintained despite delayed undesirable effects. Cognitive factors might also play a role in that Rick did not connect his mood difficulties with alcohol and cocaine use.

## Initial Treatment Recommendation

Having decided that intervention with substance abuse was needed, I would have to choose alcohol abstinence or controlled drinking as the specific goal and decide whether outpatient or inpatient treatment should be attempted. (It seems self-evident that controlled use of cocaine is not an appropriate goal, given the legal risks, financial impact, and rebound effects.) Rick's several unsuccessful attempts to moderate alcohol use on his own, along with his early and long exposure to abusive drinking, are negative prognostic signs for controlled drinking (McCrady, 1985). Many specialists in behavioral treatment of alcohol abuse (e.g., McCrady, 1985) have advised that except in research settings, controlled drinking is extremely difficult to manage and that the potential for relapse is great.[2] I would conclude that abstinence from alcohol as well as cocaine was the appropriate treatment goal. With respect to treatment setting (outpatient or inpatient), the indications are mixed, but on balance they favor an initial effort at outpatient treatment. Rick's lack of physical withdrawal symptoms, his commitment to keeping his job, and the fact that he is not drinking at work support outpatient treatment. Also, his cocaine use is episodic and involves inhaling rather than the more addictive smoking. Certainly, the lack of social support for abstinence is a major factor that outpatient treatment would need to address (McCrady, 1985). I would also note the need to track Rick's physical symptoms as he reduced alcohol in the event that medical intervention was needed.

In some circumstances, the therapist must prepare the client for a treatment recommendation. I would see Rick's situation in this light, for substance use is not his self-defined chief complaint. (Rather than viewing Rick as in a state of denial, the cognitive behaviorist would attribute Rick's lack of focus on drug use to reinforcement contingencies such as delayed adverse effects of drug use and conflicting incentives regarding it.) To prepare Rick and to test my hypothesis about the role of drug use, I would return to Rick's initial complaint of unpredictable mood swings and suggest a self-monitoring task. I would ask Rick to record, every morning for 2 weeks, his mood, his activities the previous night,

and how he had slept. These data might show that his worst moods almost always follow heavy drinking or cocaine use and disturbed sleep.
As Rick and I reviewed the self-monitoring, I would ask him to note patterns, reinforce any connections he made between substance use and
dysphoria, and point out the patterns that I saw.

Cognitive behaviorists typically provide the client with a rationale for
treatment that summarizes the functional analysis, explains the selection
of goals, and gives some indication of specific treatment methods that
will be employed. I would sympathetically predict that Rick might be surprised and upset by my ideas, and I would tell him that he does not have
to make an immediate decision about them. In a simplified version of the
functional analysis presented above, I would tell Rick that it seems that
bad feelings were left over from the difficult time he had growing up, his
Vietnam experience, and his unhappy marriages. He has only two ways
to deal with these very painful feelings—his job and getting rid of the feelings with drinking and drugs, which also provide his only pleasant social
contacts. "Yet as the self-monitoring shows us, alcohol and cocaine create
a roller coaster of negative feelings, including anxiety and depression." I
would explain the rebound depressant effects of cocaine and point out financial stress and lowered sense of competence as additional effects of
substance use. I would explain the cycle of negative reinforcement: "With
these painful feelings, you want to get high again because it stops the bad
feelings, and the cycle keeps going. I'm not saying that alcohol and cocaine are the only reason you feel bad, but I do think that they are part of
the reason and a very immediate part. When you stop, your other problems may change dramatically." I would let Rick know that I viewed abstinence as the goal, but I would not ask that he contract for abstinence at
this point. As McCrady (1985) discussed, recognizing the need for abstinence is a step in active treatment. Because cognitive-behavior therapy is
both directive and open with clients about therapist goals, there is a risk
that therapist and patient can become adversarial about the stated goals. I
would therefore be careful to describe my recommendation of abstinence
as my own view of Rick's needs, which could be modified as we gathered
more information. I would frame our next task as further exploration of
the role of substance use in Rick's life.

## INITIAL PHASE OF THERAPY: TREATMENT OF SUBSTANCE ABUSE

### Safeguarding the Therapy

Beginning in the initial interview, the need for special attention to maintaining Rick in therapy and helping him use it constructively has been

evident. This area would continue to be a focus as active treatment begins. My attention to moment-by-moment process during assessment might have helped Rick tolerate therapy without the frequent cancellations noted in the presentation of the case (Chapter 9). If not, I would remind Rick of our contract to address threats to the therapy and explore the specific sources of cancellations in a problem-solving fashion: "What feelings and thoughts did you have just before you decided not to come last week? How else could you and I have handled these issues?" If cancellations continue, I would use assertive communication techniques (Jakubowski & Lange, 1978), beginning with empathic assertion (reflecting the other party's experience) about Rick's difficulty with therapy and then discussing drawbacks of missed sessions, such as disruptions in continuity and in the development of trust. With realistic nonangry discussion, Rick could begin to express his difficulties with therapy more directly and to believe that I would take these seriously and work to remedy them. I would also be careful to maintain a nonadversarial stance about substance use through use of communication tactics and a fact-gathering stance.

## Treatment of Substance Abuse

My interventions with Rick's use of alcohol and cocaine would adapt McCrady's (1985) treatment of alcohol abuse, which applied social-learning principles to accomplish the goal of abstinence. Central phases of treatment are identification of the need for abstinence and training in abstinence strategies and tactics.

### Identification of the Need for Abstinence

Since Rick doubted the need to address his substance use, I would be prepared to spend considerable time in this phase. Drawing on the assessment data already gathered, I would encourage Rick to review both the adverse consequences and the advantages of his substance use. I would also help Rick to reconstruct a daily history of his drinking and drug use for the last 3 months and discuss with him the immediate stimuli for substance use that it revealed. Based on these sources, we would list the advantages and disadvantages of alcohol and cocaine use for Rick. I would ask him to review the list several times daily during a high-frequency activity like eating or talking on the telephone as a way to heighten his awareness of factors that he tended to ignore. I would also tell Rick that I see him as in conflict about whether to drink and use cocaine. (Giving a process a name can help the client orient to it, and the notion of *conflict* may reduce the chances of Rick feeling dismissed or judged.) Throughout, I would not argue that controlled substance use is impossible, but with McCrady (1985), I would suggest that Rick needs to have a period of total abstinence as a provisional choice before he can make an informed decision about future substance use: "After all, you haven't experienced a drug-free period since you were a child. Also, because substance use may be creating some of your symptoms, we need to clear the air so that the issues that do need separate treatment become evident."

## Abstinence Skills

If Rick decided to experiment with abstinence, I would start by teaching him to analyze the "behavior chains" involved in incidents of alcohol and cocaine use (McCrady, 1985, p. 272). As in the cognitive behaviorist's S-O-R-C analysis, the client is guided to identify the immediate "trigger" for substance use of urges, the intervening thoughts and feelings, actual substance use (if any), and positive and negative consequences of the results. The behavior-chain analysis thus conveys that triggering events do not inevitably lead to substance use. As Rick began to make behavior-chain analyses in daily life, the act of doing so provided a first alternative to yielding to his urges. In discussing behavior-chain records, I would pinpoint successful strategies for withstanding temptation, with an emphasis on specific actions rather than trait-like attributions such as "I used willpower." In this way, I would hope to help Rick see that he could use these coping strategies in the future. To encourage self-reinforcement, I would ask Rick his feelings about specific accomplishments he reported, and I would emphasize Rick's efforts and honesty. Rick clearly has difficulty being enthusiastic about his successes. With the treatment focus on abstinence, I would not engage in specific therapy of this cognitive style. Instead, I would use the pragmatic tactic of brainstorming for anything that Rick could say to himself that did feel encouraging.

The review of behavior chains showed that the proximal stimuli for substance use include boredom and loneliness as well as anxiety and depression, underlining the need to access alternative social supports (McCrady, 1985). I would use problem solving to help Rick generate social activities in which drinking and drug use were not central. I would suggest that he gather information on social options, and I would help him plan his approaches and discuss his experiences. My suggestions would include Alcoholics Anonymous, and if he objects, I would explore Rick's specific thoughts about the weakness of depending on others and the importance of will. I would share my philosophy that will is largely the result of skills and support. If he continued to object, I would indicate that it is not important *what* he does but that it is important *that* he does non-drug social activities. I would also suggest groups that might help Rick manage his immediate life stresses, such as self-help groups for divorcing fathers and for Vietnam combat veterans.

For management of negative affect, I would strongly encourage Rick to develop an exercise program, preferably in a competitive sport. Such activity could have antidepressant effects (Fremont & Craighead, 1987) and relaxing effects (Long, 1985) and would also provide drug-free interaction with male peers. I would suggest that Rick gradually decrease caffeine as a way to reduce any direct anxiety-producing effects. I would also teach Rick a relaxation method for stressful situations. To increase Rick's sense of collaboration, I would devote a session to giving Smith's (1985, pp. 9–18) "grand tour" of relaxation techniques, which involves brief experiences with nine relaxation methods and questions to clarify the client's preferences. Training in Rick's preferred technique would include cue-controlled relaxation, in which an association is developed between the relaxation induction and a verbal cue (e.g., the word *relax* or *calm*) that Rick could use to elicit the relaxed sensation in daily life. Rick would be asked to practice his relaxation method daily. I would also encourage Rick to develop nondrug methods to reduce boredom and loneliness. The Pleasant Events Schedule (MacPhillamy & Lewinsohn, 1982), which lists 331 pleasant activities, could help Rick experience potentially pleasant activities other than hanging out and getting high. I would suggest that he try items when he has urges to substance use and at other times. Self-management techniques such as distraction (McCrady, 1985) would also be suggested.

My approach to incidents of breaking abstinence would be nonpunitive yet nonpermissive. I would label these events "lapses" rather than "failures," to reduce negative self-evaluation, anxiety, and guilt reactions. This abstinence violation effect (Marlatt & Gordon, 1985) may be so unpleasant that the client's only effective avoidance method is to resume abuse. I would ask, "How can we learn from this experience to try to keep it from happening in the future?" This approach would also lessen the chances that Rick would avoid therapy or lie to me. I might reflect the paradox of his difficulties: "It's ironic and sad, isn't it, that even though alcohol [or cocaine can] cause you [such] problems, you're drawn to it again and again" (Lipp, 1986, p. 138).

As we processed successes and lapses, Rick could develop a set of workable coping skills to avert immediate temptations. I would introduce stress inoculation training (Meichenbaum, 1985) to enhance Rick's ability to apply these skills. We would develop a list of potential temptation situations, and in session Rick would vividly imagine each situation in order of increasing difficulty. I would prompt Rick to imagine himself using his coping skills (including the cue to relax, self-statements developed in problem solving, and self-management techniques), recognizing his success, and congratulating himself or at least telling me about his accomplishment.

Over several months, with setbacks along the way, Rick attained consistent abstinence and also reported fewer urges to drink and use cocaine. At this point, I would introduce relapse prevention tactics (Marlatt & Gordon, 1985), explaining them as part of the transition to dealing with other issues in therapy. From a cognitive-behavioral perspective, the risk for relapse in substance abuse resides in environmental conditions and the client's prior learning experiences; in particular, in the facts that some antecedents of substance abuse have not yet changed and that drugs have immediate dysphoria-reducing properties. Expanding on our list of temptation situations, we would identify stressors that might tempt Rick to use alcohol and/or cocaine (e.g., conflict with an ex-wife, loneliness), and we would generate methods to handle each one. I would discuss abstinence as a process, rather than an all-ornone end point, so that if he did break abstinence, he could resume his abstinence strategies as soon as possible. I would explain the abstinence violation effect and help Rick generate alternative views of breaks in abstinence. We would plan ways to monitor his alcohol and drug use in the rest of the therapy.

## SECOND PHASE OF THERAPY: TREATMENT OF DYSPHORIA
### Assessment and Functional Analysis

When Rick's abstinence from psychoactive substances stabilized, I would review with him the status of his initial complaints of negative mood and mood swings, along with other current difficulties. We would observe that Rick's depression, anxiety, and mood swings had substantially moderated. His blood pressure was normal, and he slept well, got to work on time, and found it easy to concentrate. I would note dramatic improvement in his functioning in therapy sessions: His mental status was clearly normal, and we had a relatively smooth working relationship. When it was disrupted by Rick's occasional irritation or falling silent, we could process the incidents and move on. These changes certainly confirm the value of first safeguarding the therapy and treating substance abuse. Nonetheless, at this point Rick still feels depressed and unhappy about himself, and he expresses little pleasure in life or his accomplishments. He brushes aside apparent successes and dwells on failures to meet his standards, castigating himself as bad and ugly. He also complains that in some ways, he misses getting high and thinks that all this good behavior is weak and boring. Despite a growing circle of pleasant acquaintances, Rick does not have any new close relationships.

My functional analysis of Rick's continuing dysphoria would draw on the psychosocial history I originally gathered and observations from therapy to date. Rick's difficulties appear to reflect two contrasting patterns. Cognitively, he views himself both as failing to meet conventional standards for good behavior and also as failing to be tough and socially deviant. Behaviorally, a similar split is evident between overcontrol (e.g., his upstanding manner and rigid conformity) and undercontrol (e.g., his temper and the kinds of women to whom he is attracted), although the abstinence treatment has somewhat reduced the intensity of undercontrol.

I would consider several distal causes in Rick's early social-learning history with family and peers. First, Rick experienced virtually no nurturance in his family and did not have models of emotionally nurturant behavior for observational learning of how to treat himself supportively. Second, his family life taught him harsh standards for compliance and conformity. It appeared that obeying these standards could prevent intense maternal criticism for perceived transgression. Third, Rick's intense involvement with street buddies in adolescence (his only source of positive social interaction) had several adverse effects. It was the context for substance abuse and for direct reinforcement and observational learning of undercontrolled behavior. The hostile interaction style of the peer culture was particularly unsuited to the development of intimacy. In addition, Rick was cruelly teased about being physically different (his dark skin and red hair). This teasing not only taught him the specific belief that he looked strange and ugly, but also led to respondent conditioning of shame and embarrassment about his appearance. He also learned that he would be ostracized unless he was completely tough. (The absence of a father figure might have contributed to any or all of these difficulties.)

These distal causes created three more immediate and interrelated causes of Rick's current dysphoria: (a) negative cognitive processes; (b) deficient skills in self-nurturance and emotional expression; and (c) deficient intimacy skills. Pertinent negative cognitive processes differ in generality and accessibility to conscious self-report: (a) *negative self-statements*; (b) *dysfunctional attitudes*; and (c) *the self-schema*. Negative self-statements are specific, relatively retrievable thoughts and images with self-derogating or pessimistic content (DeRubeis & Beck, 1988). Rick's negative self-statements include harsh self-evaluations for failing to meet conventional standards and also for being weak and overly con-

forming. Dysfunctional attitudes are rigid implicit beliefs as to the conditions for attaining self-worth and relatedness (DeRubeis & Beck,
1988). Rick's dysfunctional attitudes seem to include beliefs like "I must
be perfectly conventional to be worthwhile" and "If I have feelings, I am
weak and unacceptable." The self-schema is conceptualized as organized knowledge of oneself, implicit and based on past learning, by
which new experiences are assimilated to old (Segal, 1988). It thus provides more efficient cognitive processing but reduces the impact of
potentially inconsistent contemporary events (Segal, 1988). The self-
schema may also have motivational properties, in that it may be tied to
attachments to significant others (see Safran, 1990). Rick's self-schema
appears to involve a split between elements of personal identity—being
a solid citizen and an unconventional delinquent—along with a sense of
inadequacy in establishing himself in either sphere and a devaluing of
both.

Rick's deficits in self-nurturing and emotion expression have been
somewhat improved by the abstinence treatment. He uses cue-controlled relaxation to interrupt negative feelings and sometimes does a
pleasant activity as an alternative to substance abuse. On the other
hand, he rarely enjoys these activities, and he often expresses emotion
indirectly through anger and sarcasm. Rick's behavioral and cognitive
skills for intimacy are also limited. He often shows discomfort with my
supportive responses. An additional source of intimacy difficulties may
be Rick's Vietnam combat experiences. Glover (1984) and Keane et al.
(1985a) suggested that the death of combat buddies can create intense
fears that renewed intimacy will again end in loss. I would explore this
area, using the combat exposure section of Keane et al.'s (1985b) Structured Interview for Posttraumatic Stress Disorder.

While each of these proximal sources could lead directly to dysphoria,
they also maintain each other. For instance, due to Rick's rigid self-evaluation, he screens pleasant experiences for whether he deserves them
and rarely finds himself eligible. At the same time, his avoidance of
pleasant activities and of emotional expression supports beliefs that
such experiences are unacceptably weak. His behaviors when relationships might become intimate are often guarded and alienating, and
therefore people often do withdraw or criticize him. Rick's standards for
conventionality have probably fostered his current work stability and
helped him attain and maintain abstinence, but their rigidity triggers
frequent negative self-evaluation and inhibits spontaneity and pleasure.
In childhood, and possibly in adulthood, Rick's delinquent angry side
may have prevented overwhelming feelings of depression and powerlessness. On the other hand, the split between conventionality and deviance has created a situation in which Rick cannot stably feel good

about himself, because conforming to either set of tacit rules inevitably means falling short on the other. With these vulnerabilities, when Rick faces life stressors (divorces, Vietnam combat) to which his difficulties may have contributed, he lacks adequate coping skills, and the experiences further exacerbate his dysphoria.

Effective therapy would therefore require developing both alternative, more constructive cognitions and also more effective skills for self-nurturing and intimacy. I would view these as interrelated processes rather than seeing any one as primary for causality or treatment. Although I present each treatment focus separately for ease of exposition, in practice I would interweave these areas as clinically appropriate. Moreover, as with any client who has been an active substance abuser, monitoring of urges to drink and use drugs would continue.

## Rationale to Client

My treatment rationale would emphasize our success to date and the relevance of skills-oriented interventions to Rick's current difficulties: "In treatment so far, through both of us working hard, we have relieved your most glaring mood difficulties and also found ways to work together. It is clear that there is another level to the negative feelings, which it seems is fed by several things—the ways you talk to yourself and see yourself [using examples from our work to date], the fact that you still could learn more about taking care of yourself, and your difficulty with getting close to people and feeling safe. These problems are certainly understandable, considering the ways you grew up." I would link the planned therapy approach to the treatment methods used for substance abuse. I would emphasize that at this point, the goal was to help Rick feel good, "not just feel not bad." I would also recall the need for continued monitoring of substance use.

## TREATMENT

### Modification of Negative Self-Statements

A central premise of cognitive therapy (Beck, Rush, Shaw, & Emery, 1979) is that changing negative self-statements to neutral or positive ones can improve mood and alter beliefs about the self, the world at large, and the future (the negative cognitive triad). There are three steps in changing negative self-statements (*cognitive restructuring*) (DeRubeis & Beck, 1988): (a) identification of specific self-statements linked to negative affect, (b) examining the validity of specific self-statements through discussion and sometimes through behavioral experiments to evaluate their current truth, and (c) developing more adaptive self-statements to use when experiencing negative self-statements or affect.

I would introduce the identification phase by tracking Rick's negative feelings in sessions and asking him to reconstruct the thoughts that may have preceded them. DeRubeis and Beck (1988, pp. 283–284) described three techniques for discussing the validity of self-statements: (a) *the three questions*, (b) *the downward arrow*, and (c) *cognitive distortions*. The three questions treat negative self-statements as hypotheses to be evaluated: "What is the evidence against this belief? What other interpretations of the event could there be? What would it really mean if this thought were true?" The downward arrow pursues the self-referential implications of the last question by asking, "What it would mean about me if this idea were true?" until a statement whose truth can be evaluated is reached.

Cognitive distortions are defined as biased inferential processes that result in inappropriately negative interpretations of experience (Beck et al., 1979). Because the term is sometimes experienced as highly judgmental, I would not use it with Rick. Rather I would draw on Beck et al.'s (1979) and Burns's (1980) lists of such biases as a guide to describing Rick's cognitive style (e.g., "You're really good at not counting the elements of success in what you did") and its functional impact (e.g., "What are the pluses and minuses of looking at it that way?"). When a discussion-oriented technique seems to have impact, we would develop it into an adaptive self-statement to use in relevant situations. As Rick becomes more adept at cognitive restructuring, I would encourage him to apply it in daily life, with the help of the Daily Record of Dysfunctional Thoughts (Beck et al., 1979). On this self-monitoring form, the client notes the upsetting event along with associated emotions and self-statements, and then generates alternative adaptive self-statements and rates his or her subsequent degree of emotionality.

My specific approaches to negative self-statements would include tactics to introduce flexibility into Rick's rigid and dichotomous standards for self-worth. I would discuss the continuum approach to self-evaluation (Beck et al., 1979): "What if you rated your actions as a matter of degree, rather than as all good or all bad?" With people like Rick, for whom sports are an important part of life, sports analogies (e.g., "What is a good batting average?") can be helpful. I might use my role redefinition exercise (Klass, 1990) to help Rick moderate his standards in areas that are central to his self-definition, such as being a father. After identifying the role (e.g., "Seems like you have to be a perfect father to feel good about yourself"), the therapist elicits the client's requirements for the role (e.g., "What does a perfect father have to do?"). Discussion of the validity and functional impact of these requirements follows (e.g.,

"How does that work for you and your son?"), along with consideration of alternative standards (e.g., "What would a good-enough father do?"). We would then devise behavioral experiments in which Rick could try in small ways to act in accord with the new standards and examine the outcomes.

Rick's extensive discounting of positive experiences would also receive attention, especially through behavioral experiments. The "count-what-counts" exercise (Burns, 1980) asks the client to record every desirable activity engaged in for a whole day and to note feelings and productivity compared to a day when recording perceived failures. In session, I would underline Rick's accomplishments, whether or not he views them positively, and elicit the self-statements with which he reacts. A role-playing exercise in which I complimented Rick might be the basis for processing cognitive, emotional, and behavioral reactions to positive input and for developing alternatives with which he could experiment in session and later in daily life (e.g., maintaining eye contact; saying thank you).

I would also specifically address Rick's sense of physical unattractiveness, adapting techniques that cognitive behaviorists devised to foster body image acceptance in women with sexual dysfunctions (Barbach, 1975) and eating disorders (e.g., Weiss, Katzman, & Wolchik, 1985). In the body mirror exercise (Barbach, 1975), the client is asked to look (privately, at home) closely and nonevaluatively at each body part until comfortable, while talking aloud about "what I like about my body." Given Rick's intense sense of unattractiveness, I would present this exercise not as an assignment but as "something that I'd like to know your reaction to, just hearing about it." He might become extremely upset, which would of course be consistent with the conditioned emotional reactions to his appearance that he had acquired in adolescence.

Unlike some cognitive-behavior therapists, who would immediately conduct cognitive restructuring of specific beliefs about physical appearance, I would sympathetically encourage Rick to express his feelings in some depth. This experience would provide exposure to avoided content (on the rationale of allowing extinction of conditioned emotional reactions), and the emotionality might also facilitate needed change. I would then ask Rick how he learned to feel so ugly and would trace the feelings associated with specific incidents. Since Rick was so unquestioning about his unattractiveness, I would hope that this emotional and historical framework could help him truly to entertain the idea that these self-evaluations were learned rather than necessarily factually correct. I would suggest that as a child and teenager, Rick had little choice but to think his peers were right. "As an adult, you may be able to learn other ways to feel about your attractiveness, hard as it is to believe that right now."

Further challenges to Rick's beliefs about his appearance would rely on behavioral and cognitive modalities. When his upset subsided, I would suggest that doing the body mirror exercise at home might be very interesting, and I would help him devise tolerable hierarchical steps to do so. I would also try to broaden Rick's view of the basis for attractiveness (Weiss et al., 1985) by asking him to list all the things that he feels make up attractiveness, with an emphasis on attractive behaviors rather than immutable physical traits. I would suggest that Rick experiment with systematically doing an attractive behavior for a week to see how it feels and what kind of interpersonal feedback he gets. As Rick becomes less upset about his appearance, I might use reframing by wondering aloud if he can imagine seeing himself as looking interesting or as someone whose looks some people would find acceptable.

## Self-Nurturing and Emotional Expression Skills

Two interventions already described would enhance Rick's skills at emotional nurturance and expression: the modulation of emotional intensity in safeguarding the therapy and the expressive aspects of working on his sense of unattractiveness. I would also ask Rick to consult the Pleasant Events Schedule (MacPhillamy & Lewinsohn, 1982) to develop a set of things to give himself each day noncontingently (whether or not he had been deserving; Weiss et al., 1985). Rick's response, "I have to earn pleasure," would be explored with a social-learning analysis: "How did you learn that good things have to be earned?" I would encourage affective expression, on the view that expressing grief for his lost childhood is a step in recovery as in other mourning (Brasted & Callahan, 1984). Affective expression would not, however, be an end in itself. I would encourage Rick to experiment by giving himself noncontingent pleasures, letting himself enjoy them, and applying alternative self-statements, and I would follow up with discussion of his experiences in doing so.

## Intimacy Skills

In point of fact, work on intimacy skills began during the initial assessment phase through dealing with Rick's in-session reactions as a way to safeguard the therapy. Tracking and addressing Rick's feelings in sessions had begun to teach him that one could negotiate difficulties in a relationship rather than simply leaving it. In the current phase of therapy, I would want to help Rick learn that he is acceptable with his intimacy needs and vulnerable feelings. I would recommend Zilbergeld's (1978) lay-oriented book on male sexuality, which discusses male needs for intimacy along with sex role definitions that distort men's ability to recognize and meet these needs. Zilbergeld also presented exercises that can facilitate change. A men's therapy group that could reinforce changes in Rick's interaction style would also be important, given the typical environmental contingencies in our culture for male expressiveness. I would also encourage Rick to find ongoing activities, like college classes, in which he might get to know both women and men through common interests. As Rick brought in Daily Records of Dysfunctional Thoughts about these experiences, cognitive restructuring would be conducted around his intimacy fears and his all-or-none views of women (e.g., "She could be a wife" versus "She's no fun"). Behavioral exercises in appropriate intimacy would also be used in therapy and as assignments (e.g., admitting a weakness, complimenting someone, divulging personal information). An assignment of collecting rejections might serve paradoxically to lessen Rick's pain when others did not wish to pursue interactions that he initiated.

If assessment had indicated that Rick's intimacy fears were related to survivor guilt from his Vietnam combat experiences, I would work to change guilt to regret (Klass, 1990). In this process, I would ask Rick to make a detailed review of his specific circumstances, thoughts, and feelings at the time of the loss. I would then ask, "Recognizing all this, if you had it to do all over again, would you do the same thing?" Whether his answer was yes or no, I would suggest that since the past cannot be undone, the issue is how to move on now. Problem-solving techniques would be used to generate meaningful personal responses, which for combat-related guilt may include developing methods of atonement and reparation (Klass, 1990).

## Moderation of Dysfunctional Attitudes and the Self-Schema

As discussed above, another goal of therapy would be to help Rick moderate and integrate his sharp differentiation between conventionality and deviance, as expressed in his dysfunctional attitudes and self-schema. The standard cognitive-behavioral techniques presented above can have constructive impact by instigating inconsistent behavior and highlighting its personal relevance. Methods that involve more affective arousal may facilitate change in these less accessible cognitive processes by rendering them more accessible (see Goldfried & Hayes, 1989). Affective arousal may also make disconfirming events more distinctive and salient. Conflicting motivations are also important to consider, since stable change may require that the client develop alternative sources of reinforcement.

To work toward these goals, I would include *addressing the implicit themes* and *affective expressive methods*. I have elsewhere (Klass, 1990) described a method for addressing implicit themes in which the client is strongly invested, consisting of (a) *establishing the theme*, (b) *social-learning analysis*, (c) *exploration of conflicting incentives*, and (d) *direct change efforts*. In establishing the theme, I would identify processes as I perceived them in Rick's reports of events from daily life and in his reactions in therapy (e.g., "perfecting yourself," "thumbing your nose"). The naming process can facilitate communication and begin to introduce a sense of controllability (e.g., "There it is again"). I would encourage self-monitoring of theme-relevant experiences in daily life to enhance awareness of controlling variables and aid in cognitive restructuring. Data on reliable relations between inner experience and environmental cues would aid in later direct change efforts.

The social-learning analysis would explore the historical antecedents for Rick's contrasting self-definitions and behaviors. I would move back and forth from the current theme to historical experiences. For instance, "So when you suddenly feel like a wimp, it's as if you're right back on the corner, carrying your schoolbooks, and your friends are mocking you." I would emphasize emotional, not merely intellectual, connections by encouraging Rick to imagine the experiences vividly as if they were happening today. My "no-wonder responses" (as in, "No wonder you do this now, given what you learned back then") would be the basis for creating adaptive self-statements. Rick's sharp distinctions between conformity and deviance reflect the conditions under which these patterns were acquired. A rigidly upstanding image could prevent punishment at home, but it was bound to fail in his aggressive peer culture. The strongly differential reinforcers would establish sharply distinct response patterns and views of self. I would explain this analysis to Rick. For instance, "In some ways, how we see ourselves depends on what we see reflected in other people's eyes. At home and on the street, what you saw in people's eyes was two completely different yous, except that in both places, people mainly saw you as defective."

Conflicting incentives for change and staying the same would also be explored. I would emphasize Rick's understandable attachments to both his home and street identities. The split may have helped Rick to feel more acceptable in each childhood context than if his view of self had been more integrated. I would suggest that Rick does not need to say goodbye to either aspect but simply recognize and make use of the contributions of each. I might ask him to list the advantages and disadvantages of change (Beck et al., 1979). In addition, Brown (1988) suggested that successful challenges to affect-laden core beliefs may depend on the development of new attachments to the therapist or others. In this regard, Rick's experiences in a men's therapy group would be an important resource. I would also use affective expression techniques for conflict resolution, as discussed below.

Direct change efforts would draw on the preceding steps and reframe conflicting incentives (e.g., developing adaptive self-statements like, "In some ways it's convenient to be split, but it sure can hurt"). I would also encourage recognition of valid needs (Bandler & Grinder, 1979), as in the question, "How can I meet the valid needs involved in wanting to be both perfectly upstanding and completely wild without so many negative effects?" Rick and I could generate answers using standard problem-solving techniques (Goldfried & Davison, 1976). I might suggest that on both sides of the split, Rick is conforming to other people's desires, although the people differ, and raise the question, "What about Rick and what he really wants?" I would instigate behavioral experiments with acting "in shades of grey" or as "a mix" of his different aspects. I might suggest that Rick collect data on how much conformity other people do expect by purposely engaging in mild deviations in conduct and observing the results.

For *affective expression*, in addition to emphasizing emotionality in the social-learning analysis, I would use Gestalt therapy techniques (see Stevens, 1971). For instance, the two-chair technique can aid in conflict resolution (Greenberg & Safran, 1987). The client takes the roles of the opposing aspects of self and carries on a dialogue between them, physically changing seats as he or she assumes each role. This experience can be intensely emotional and sometimes leads spontaneously to synthesizing the previously split aspects (Greenberg & Safran, 1987). It can also be followed by problem solving. Compared to cognitive-behavior therapy, Gestalt therapy makes more use of fantasy and emphasizes emotional expression as an end in itself. Nonetheless, the active, directive therapist style and the use of specific technical interventions to accomplish affective arousal are compatible with a cognitive-behavioral stance.

## Use of the Therapeutic Relationship

In this second phase of therapy, I would move beyond safeguarding the therapy to dealing with in-therapy incidents as in vivo samples of Rick's difficulties. They yield vivid data on relevant affective, behavioral, and cognitive processes, especially his interpersonal perceptions and dysfunctional attitudes. As Goldfried and Hayes stated (1989, p. 58), these incidents can provide evidence of how the client "interacts with significant others and what [he or she] in reality expects and desires from them." I would use such experiences as the medium for direct change efforts as they afford opportunities to pinpoint specific processes and provide compellingly immediate corrective feedback. Moreover, the intensity of the here-and-now situation can create an affectively arousing learning context. I would encourage Rick to delineate his interpersonal assumptions and help him to frame ways to test their accuracy, including experiments with alternative behavioral and cognitive responses in sessions. It is likely that the content elicited through exploration of in-session incidents would include Rick's perceptions of me and of women in general as withholding and judgmental. I would hope to moderate these perceptions (along with any others linked to Rick's view of women) through the feedback and hypothesis-testing approaches described here.

## Substance Abuse

At the beginning of this phase of treatment, Rick might occasionally struggle with urges to drink and use cocaine. As he developed more complex cognitive analysis and coping skills, we could apply them to temptation situations, along with previously developed relapse prevention tactics. Rick attained the ability to manage to withstand almost all temptations, and his few lapses were brief. By the end of this phase of therapy, abstinence was integrated in his lifestyle.

## Preparation for Termination

Over time, as a result of these varied interventions, I would expect Rick's mood and sense of self-worth to become increasingly positive and stable, and that he would show more flexibility, spontaneity, and involvement in satisfying relationships, both romantic and friendly. With such results, we would plan for termination of therapy, recognizing of course that Rick could return at any time. As in relapse prevention for substance abuse, we would identify potential stressors that could activate difficulties and plan behavioral and cognitive methods to cope with them.

## DISCUSSION

The multifaceted treatment that we have presented illustrates many core characteristics of cognitive-behavior therapy as generally practiced. For instance, targets for intervention are specified on the basis of assessment of controlling conditions for the client's difficulties. A sequential approach is used in which focused treatment of psychoactive substance use is followed by additional assessment and cognitive-behavioral treatment of dysphoria. The therapy is described in terms of specific technical interventions that are construed as methods to provide particular learning experiences. There is an emphasis on linking therapy to the rest of the client's life, including self-monitoring of pertinent daily experiences, in-session exercises, and the development of extra-session assignments for behavioral and cognitive change. Exercises and assignments are seen as providing the performance-based feedback that, it is believed, can most powerfully alter the patterns the client has developed in his or her prior social-learning history. An active, directive therapist style characterizes treatment, including safeguarding of the therapy through communication tactics, contracting, problem solving, and social reinforcement. Some of our interventions (e.g., addressing implicit themes, affective expression) appear to overlap with psychodynamic and experiential approaches. We believe there is a different emphasis in that cognitive behavior therapists use these techniques to heighten awareness of controlling variables and follow them with explicit change efforts.

Turning to the question of gender differences in treatment formulation and methods, we expect that most cognitive behaviorists, regardless of gender, would view Rick's use of alcohol and cocaine as an acute cause of his difficulties at the beginning of treatment. Consequently, they would recommend treatment of substance use before treating Rick's other problems. Our approach may differ from some cognitive behaviorists in greater use of affective expression, historical reconstruction (through social-learning analysis), and the therapeutic relationship. It is not clear, however, that these differences are related to therapist gender. Recently, male and female cognitive behaviorists have discussed the role of affect in the change process (see Goldfried & Hayes, 1989) and the possible contributions of historical reconstruction and exploration of the therapeutic relationship (e.g., Klass, 1990; Safran & Segal, 1990).

With regard to sex role issues, we considered some particularly male difficulties with intimacy and emotional expression, along with the desirability of providing a more reinforcing context for new patterns through a men's therapy group. Eisler (1989) discussed methods by which male therapists can help male clients address dysfunctional aspects of masculine sex role requirements for competitiveness and inhibition of emotions other than anger. These methods include delineation of masculine norms and discussion of the pros and cons of rigid adherence to them, along with assignments to engage in "activities . . . [the client] might enjoy, but which add nothing to our knowledge of the universe or the gross national product" (Eisler, 1989, p. 60). Eisler also recommended that the male therapist use self-disclosure with male clients, not only to model emotional expression, but also to inform the client about acceptable choices to violate rigid masculine role norms. The latter option clearly is not available to women therapists working with male clients. Female therapists may be more likely to focus on self-nurturing and intimacy skills, reflecting the greater value that women in general place on relatedness and caretaking (e.g., Stewart & Lykes, 1985). On the other hand, even well-replicated gender differences occur in the context of substantial overlap between the responses of men and women (e.g., Stewart & Lykes, 1985).

These speculations about gender differences in therapist decision making raise a broader question about the place of values in cognitive-behavior therapy. Cognitive behaviorists have generally resolved value questions by appealing to the functional analysis, arguing that intervention targets should be based on an assessment of the practical impact on the client's functioning. On the other hand, it is widely recognized that therapists, including cognitive behaviorists, bring their own values to bear as they consider their clients (e.g., London, 1974). These choices may have serious implications. Davison (1976) argued, for instance, that behavior therapists should not agree to treat homosexual people who want to become heterosexual, because doing so "condones the current societal prejudice" against homosexuality (p. 57). In addition, for complex cases, there may be many views of what does and does not work in a client's life and of the central controlling conditions. Thus, case formulation, like other cognitive processing, involves construction rather than direct discerning of reality. The variables affecting this process ought to receive systematic empirical study. In particular, the effects of therapist and client gender on case formulation, in cognitive-behavior therapy and in other schools of therapy, are eminently researchable. In keeping with the cognitive-behavioral value on empirical investigation, we hope that our work encourages controlled study of this topic.

## NOTES

1. For ease of communication, *I* is used for the therapist in the case analysis.

2. Foreyt (1987) reviewed the literature on the controversy over abstinence versus controlled drinking.

## REFERENCES

Bandler, R., & Grinder, J. (1979). *Frogs into princes: Neuro linguistic programming.* Moab, UT: Real People Press.

Barbach, L. G. (1975). *For yourself.* New York: Doubleday.

Beck, A. T., Rush, A. J., Shaw, B. T., & Emery, G. (1979). *Cognitive therapy of depression.* New York: Guilford.

Brasted, W. S., & Callahan, E. J. (1984). A behavioral analysis of the grief process. *Behavior Therapy, 15,* 529–543.

Brown, S. (1988). *Treating adult children of alcoholics: A developmental perspective.* New York: Wiley.

Burns, D. D. (1980). *Feeling good.* New York: Morrow.

Charney, D. S., Heninger, G. R., & Jatlow, P. I. (1985). Increased anxiogenic effects of caffeine in panic disorders. *Archives of General Psychiatry, 42,* 233–243.

Davison, G. C. (1976). Homosexuality: The ethical challenge. *Journal of Consulting and Clinical Psychology, 44,* 157–162.

DeRubeis, R. J., & Beck, A. T. (1988). Cognitive therapy. In K. S. Dobson (Ed.), *Handbook of cognitive-behavioral therapies* (pp. 273–306). New York: Guilford.

Eisler, R. M. (1989). Gender role issues in the treatment of men. *The Behavior Therapist, 12,* 57–60.

Foreyt, J. P. (1987). The addictive disorders. In G. T. Wilson, C. M. Franks, P. C. Kendall, and J. P. Foreyt (Eds.), *Review of behavior therapy: Theory and practice* (Vol. 11, pp. 187–230). New York: Guilford.

Fremont, J., & Craighead, L. W. (1987). Aerobic exercise and cognitive therapy in the treatment of dysphoric moods. *Cognitive Therapy and Research, 11,* 241–252.

Glover, H. (1984). Survival guilt and the Vietnam veteran. *Journal of Nervous and Mental Disease, 172,* 393–397.

Goldfried, M. R., & Davison, G. C. (1976). *Clinical behavior therapy.* New York: Holt Rinehart & Winston.

Goldfried, M. R., & Hayes, A. M. (1989). Can contributions from other orientations complement behavior therapy? *The Behavior Therapist, 12,* 57–60.

Greenberg, L. S., & Safran, J. D. (1987). *Emotion in psychotherapy.* New York: Guilford.

Jakubowski, P., & Lange, A. (1978). *The assertive option: Your rights and responsibilities.* Champaign, IL: Research Press.

Keane, T. M., Fairbank, J. A., Caddell, J. M., Zimering, R. T., & Bender, M. E. (1985a). A behavioral approach to assessing and treating post-traumatic stress disorder in Vietnam veterans. In C. R. Figley (Ed.), *Trauma and its wake* (pp. 257–294). New York: Brunner/Mazel.

Keane, T. M., Fairbank, J. A., Caddell, J. M., Zimering, R. T., & Bender, M. E. (1985b). Structured interview for post-traumatic stress disorder. In C. R. Figley (Ed.), *Trauma and its wake* (pp. 424–438). New York: Brunner/Mazel.

Klass, E. T. (1990). Guilt, shame, and embarrassment: Cognitive-behavioral approaches. In H. Leitenberg (Ed.), *Handbook of social anxiety* (pp. 385–414). New York: Plenum.

Linehan, M. M. (1988). Dialectical behavior therapy: A cognitive behavioral approach to parasuicide. *Journal of Personality Disorders, 1,* 328–333.

Lipp, M. R. (1986). *Respectful treatment* (2nd ed.). New York: Elsevier.

London, P. (1974). *Behavior control* (2nd ed.). New York: Harper & Row.

Long, B. C. (1985). Stress-management interventions: A 15-month follow-up of aerobic conditioning and stress inoculation training. *Cognitive Therapy and Research, 9,* 471–478.

MacPhillamy, D. J., & Lewinsohn, P. M. (1982). The pleasant events schedule: Studies on reliability, validity, and scale intercorrelation. *Journal of Consulting and Clinical Psychology, 50,* 363–380.

Marlatt, G. A., & Gordon, J. R. (Eds.). (1985). *Relapse prevention: Maintenance strategies in the treatment of addictive behaviors.* New York: Guilford.

McCrady, B. S. (1985). Alcoholism. In D. H. Barlow (Ed.), *Clinical handbook of psychological disorders* (pp. 245–298). New York: Guilford.

Meichenbaum, D. (1985). *Stress inoculation training.* New York: Pergamon.

Safran, J. D. (1990). Towards a refinement of cognitive therapy in the light of interpersonal theory: I. Theory. *Clinical Psychology Review, 10,* 87–106.

Safran, J. D., & Segal, Z. V. (1990). *Cognitive therapy: An interpersonal process perspective.* New York: Basic Books.

Segal, Z. V. (1988). Appraisal of the self-schema construct in cognitive models of depression. *Psychological Bulletin, 103,* 147–162.

Sloane, R. B., Staples, F. R., Cristol, A. H., Yorkston, N. J., & Whipple, K. (1975). *Psychotherapy versus behavior therapy.* Cambridge, MA: Harvard University Press.

Smith, J. C. (1985). *Relaxation dynamics.* Champaign, IL: Research Press.

Stevens, J. O. (1971). *Awareness.* Moab, UT: Real People Press.

Stewart, A. J., & Lykes, M. B. (1985). Conceptualizing gender in personality theory and research. *Journal of Personality, 53,* 93–101.

Wachtel, P. L. (1978). *Psychoanalysis and behavior therapy.* New York: Basic Books.

Weiss, L., Katzman, M., & Wolchik, S. (1985). *Treating bulimia: A psychoeducational approach.* New York: Pergamon.

Zilbergeld, B. (1978). *Male sexuality.* Boston: Little Brown.

# IV

## EPILOGUE

# 14

# What Female Therapists Have in Common

## Laura S. Brown

## INTRODUCTION

At first glance, the question of what women therapists have in common seems simplistic and almost intuitively obvious. Our shared gender would seem to lead to shared experiences and thus common responses to clients and reactions from them. Having our womanhood in common seems to be so powerful a variable as to require little explication.

Yet this apparent simplicity is probably illusory. The social construct of "woman" is a complex and varied phenomenon, differing in its meanings and attributions across race, social class, age, sexual orientation, and interpersonal context (Brown, 1990). Our experiences of female biology are as individual and highly socially constructed as each of our lives. The simple fact of that biology does not lead to equally simple and similar experiences within it. What our gender represents to us as we live it, to our clients as they experience it, and as a phenomenon in the psychotherapeutic interaction will be equally diverse and will shift from client to client, from setting to setting, as the minute variables that transform the symbolic meaning of our gender also changes.

"Therapist" is not a static construct either. We change as therapists when we develop within the task. A female therapist in her first graduate-school practicum will not be the same therapist 10 years later, either as therapist or as woman. Our relationship to our work and the meaning that it has for our lives must be fluid, if only to reflect our movement through the developmental tasks of adulthood and the formation of our professional identities. Our sense of ourselves as women doing therapy—that is, the conscious gendering of our work—will also vary if it occurs at all, since for many women therapists the legacy of sexism has been a series of attempts to degender ourselves and to conform to an androcentric model of relating that is presented to us in our professional training. For lack of woman-identified models, we may lose access to our experiences as women and need to recover them in order to think of ourselves as "women therapists." Consequently, a woman therapist may have a conscious positive or negative identification with her gender, as well as a variety of nonconscious conflicts that will be subtly reflected in how she as a woman interacts with others, including clients.

Thus, the task of this chapter is to find a core in this diversity that will help to answer the question of what it is about being female that creates commonalities of style, approach, or perception of self among women therapists, across all the variables that create differences among us. My sense is that this process will raise as many questions as it answers and will in no way be a final word on the issue. Instead, what I hope to do is draw upon recent work in the psychology of women regarding the development of women's personality and the canon of women's autobiographical writings in order to raise some possible responses to the question of what women *qua* women may bring to the work of psychotherapy.

Interestingly, although many volumes have been written over the past two decades regarding the treatment of women, very little appears in this literature regarding women as therapists. Certain assumptions are made but rarely explored in any detail; for example, the assumption that women will be better therapists for women because of the likelihood of greater empathy but little analysis of how and whether empathy is different for women therapists than for men. Empirical research exploring questions of woman as therapist is scarce, the few studies that exist being often-cited but seldom replicated (see Orlinsky & Howard, 1980). This chapter will attempt to synthesize what has already been written about women as therapists and develop some new hypotheses that may be the catalyst for further empirical explorations of the impact of gender on the therapist.

A disclaimer is also important here. I wish to underscore that the diversity of race, class, sexual orientation, age, and able-bodiedness can and does profoundly influence what it means to be female. The theories that I will be referring to have been developed primarily in the context of studies of white, middle-class, relatively young, able-bodied heterosexual women. This deficiency in theory development must be reflected in any conclusions drawn from such theories. Whenever possible, I will draw upon literature that specifically speaks to the diversity among women to generate a more inclusive picture of the "female therapist" in this chapter.

## THE PHENOMENOLOGY OF BEING FEMALE

Gender identity—that is, the sense of oneself as male or female—is a phenomenological experience that is usually although not always linked with biological sex. The symbolic meanings of this identity are highly personal and individual, and often find expression in gender roles, the behavioral and attitudinal expression of gender identity taken on by the person.

What generalizations can we make about this experience of knowing ourselves as female? If we search both the psychological and autobiographical literature, several common themes emerge that have relevance for the work of women as psychotherapists.

First, the phenomenology of being female is a phenomenology of connection, the "self-in-relation" (Miller, 1976; Surrey, 1985). As elaborated primarily by the theorists working at the Stone Center at Wellesley College, this relational self, which may also be found in men in non-white, non-Western cultures (Bradshaw, 1990), leads girls and women to experience ourselves in terms of how we connect with another person. It is not that in healthy female development we are defined by the external parameters of relational roles per se (e.g., knowing oneself only as the "daughter of" or "wife of"); rather, we are likely to feel a greater sense of empathic attunement, a greater capacity to encounter another person at a level of emotional depth, an enhanced ability to be present with the intense feelings of another (Jordan, Surrey, & Kaplan, 1983).

Chodorow (1979) has presented one theoretical model for the development and the gendering of this enhanced capacity for empathic relating, linking it to the position of women as primary caregivers of young infants and to the impact of women-as-mothers on children's development of gendered identities. Empathy, which both Chodorow and others (Jordan, 1984; Jordan et al., 1983; Miller, 1984; Surrey, 1987) describe as a crucial aspect of the mothering role, becomes gendered because of the position of women in that role. Thus, women are likely to experience their capacity for empathy and comfort with the feelings of others as an expression of their gender identity.

Another common aspect to the phenomenology of being female in white Western culture is that of being the "other," the outsider (Daly, 1973). In patriarchal cultures, men and male experience are the common cultural referent, the norm against which other experiences are measured, and usually found wanting. This experience of otherness is of course ascribed not only to women; all people of color in a white culture (thus men of color, gay men, men with disabilities, old men, poor men) are ascribed "other" status by a dominant white-male culture. Yet this experience of otherness is not inextricably linked to gender; the "otherness" of these men is defined by cultural variables that are not as fixed and immutable as membership in the female gender. A gay man can "pass" for straight; the poor man can win the lottery; a man of color is male in relation to the women in his culture. Women are always and forever women. Our sense of otherness as women is unique because it is rooted in our biological difference from the dominant norm and thus in the most unchangeable aspect of who we are.

Otherness can carry varied meanings. One common aspect of this role is the position that it gives women as observers. To be outside is to be in the position of looking in, often unnoticed (Janeway, 1971). Because this otherness usually carries with it a loss of socially ascribed power, placing women in subordinate positions in relation to men, this observing may also entail the close sensitivity to the behaviors of the dominant that is necessary for survival. This acute attunement to what is happening with someone else—the long, often unconscious training in the skills of attending to the minutiae of someone else's expressions and movements that goes beyond empathic connection—has been trivialized by Western culture as "feminine intuition," robbed of the honor due the very specific repertoire of observational skills that this phrase represents.

Being an observer and an outsider may also enhance one's ability to see that "the emperor has no clothes." When women are not seduced by the illusory promise that if we act enough like men, we will be forgiven our gender and consequently into denying the insights that this perspective allows us (Dworkin, 1983), it often follows that the experience of being female is to be always quietly confronting the hypocrisies of the dominant culture (Johnson, 1987). Our "disloyalty to civilization," to use Rich's (1979) phrase, allows us a perspective unavailable to members of the dominant group. Women are thus likely to share the experience of being able to see through the roles and self-delusions of others, although we are rarely empowered to comment on what we observe and are often punished when we do so.

Finally, the experience of otherness that is embedded in knowing ourselves as women often comes with an enhanced ability to comprehend the experience of pain and alienation. The struggle that women in the United States have experienced in the past 200 years simply to be admitted to the institutions of society, from the voting booth to the bench to the civic organization, is concrete evidence of the experience of exclusion. Again, this is not solely the experience of women. Whites Only signs disappeared but two short decades ago, and rules, written or implied, continue to exclude men who are not fully within the dominant parameters from the institutions of power. However, for women, this experience of exclusion can and usually does transcend even those phenomena that confer privilege, such as wealth, education, or race (Bingham, 1988; Keller, 1983).

Yet another aspect common to the experience of being female is that of *empowering* others. Few women would describe what we do in this manner. After all, as culturally constructed, *woman* and *power* are contradictory terms, and the overt expression of power by women usually leads to women's further stigmatization and degradation (Brown, 1982; Smith & Siegel, 1985). Rather, this power to engender power and self-sufficiency in others is called by disguised, often gendered names; "raising children," "mothering," "the woman behind the man," "a good wife." The notion that women possess power that can be transformed and shared with others is alien to women's prescribed roles in a sexist society. And yet this caretaking position to which women are assigned is in fact a powerful and empowering one. In the "holding" role as mothers, women empower infants to know their feelings as real, meaningful, capable of being felt; in the caretaking role as wives, women empower their husbands by creating a base of support from which the world can be encountered (Luepnitz, 1988). In our relationships with one another, our caring and belief in other women have created revolutionary social movements in this century and long before, in addition to providing networks of emotional sustenance for each other (Raymond, 1986).

This role of caring empowerer, lacking visibility, validation, or acknowledgement as a powerful one, has often been carried out at great cost to women in energy, mental health, and well-being (Bernard, 1972). To take such power has been confused with the necessity of self-sacrifice, a theme that echoes from the lives of female saints and heroines (Noble, 1988) to the social roles of women in the present (Russ, 1982). Thus this position is one with which many women, struggling to empower ourselves, have had an ambivalent relationship. We have sought "real" (read "masculine") power in the place of the "powerlessness" of the nurturant person.

A final aspect of the phenomenology of being female in our culture is the experience of living in the shadow of violence. Not all cultures have been as violent against women, as overt in the expression of misogyny, as white, Western contemporary culture. Some have appeared to be even more so (Dworkin, 1974). But in speaking of the phenomenology of women raised in the past century, we must acknowledge that one of the social factors that is constantly interacting with our private sense of self is the public reality of violence against women.

This violence takes many forms and usually occurs repetitively in the context of intimate familial relationships. Russell (1986), studying a randomly selected nonclinical sample, estimates that 37% of girls are sexually abused prior to the age of 16 and describes most of that abuse as happening within the family. National crime statistics tell us that one-third of all women will be raped during their lifetime; increasingly, we know that rape is a crime committed by intimates and familiars, with the newly coined phrases *acquaintance rape* and *marital rape* being created to challenge the myth that sexual assault is perpetrated only by strangers (Finkelhor & Yllo, 1985; Russell, 1982). Between one-quarter and one-half of women are beaten at least once by their spouse or intimate partner (Walker, 1979). Sexual harassment in the workplace or academic setting, a more subtle yet quite damaging form of violence, is directed against as many as 70% of women, making this experience nearly universal (Institute for Research on Women's Health, 1988; New York Public Interest Research group, 1981). Nor is this violence against women a new phenomenon, as cultural historians have discovered (Gordon, 1988; Swift, 1987).

This violence is unlike other violence in that it is highly gendered. Although sexual assault can be perpetrated on a man, this act is seen as attaching a feminine gender to the victim. Often such violence is perceived by the individual woman or her social/cultural network as simply being "woman's lot," making the connection between being female and being violated explicit. The male victim of physical violence is usually not assaulted because of his social role (with the striking exception of gay men assaulted by heterosexual men) or relationship to his assailant, but for women, the most common source of violence is a parent or partner. Often the violence is perpetrated because the victim is a woman and is hated for being female. Thus for men, violence is construed as a random event, while for women, it becomes attached to their person in ways that lead both to victim blaming by the culture and self-blame by the victims.

While not every woman will be the direct target of violence, all women must create their sense of self in acknowledgement of the potential for violence. The role of example, myth, and threat have a powerful impact on how women construct their sense of safety and define the parameters of their actions. The image of women as fearful, cautious, and holding back that we incorporate into our sense of self is more than anything a reflection of the ubiquity of the violence around us. Again, we must note that there are parallels for members of other groups in our society; violence is the leading cause of death among black men, and insidious cultural genocide of Native Americans can be perceived as the root of high rates of self-destructive deaths in that population from alcohol-related causes.

In summary, I would argue that several themes emerge in female phenomenology (although not exclusively within that context) that are germane to the question of what women therapists have in common: the experience of empathic connectedness and self-in-relation; the experience of otherness, observer status, and exclusion; the experience of empowerment of others; and the necessity of integrating the presence and threat of violence into one's self-concept. In the following section, I will explore how each of these experiential components of female reality affect how women practice psychotherapy, how we perceive ourselves in that role, and how we are perceived by our clients.

## WOMEN AS THERAPISTS: TRANSLATING EXPERIENCE INTO ACTION

In endeavoring to translate the experience of being female in our current culture into its expression in the role of therapist, we must first examine the parameters and demands of the role and work of psychotherapy. It is my sense that in conducting such an analysis, the linkages between female experience and psychotherapeutic work will become more apparent, leading to answers to the question of what women therapists have in common.

What is it that therapists do? This question is an enormously complex one since a therapist is not a "therapist" is not a *therapist*. A cognitive behaviorist should, at least in theory, behave differently (and thus experience different demand characteristics in the role of therapist) than a psychoanalyst, a feminist therapist, or a family-systems therapist, to name but a few of the more than 100 systems of psychotherapy currently available (Corsini, 1981).

However, the experience of practicing as a therapist appears to engender behaviors and ways of being and feeling that transcend the theories;

at least, this appears to be the case when we read therapists' descriptions of their work. I would posit the following behaviors as essential to
the role and task of therapist, irrespective of one's system of
psychotherapy.

First, a therapist must demonstrate a capacity for empathy and flexibility of ego boundary in relationship to her clients. Without such empathy, a therapist is no more than a behavioral technician. Some of the
earliest claims of radical behaviorists that a relationship between therapist and client would be unnecessary as long as appropriate behavior-
change technologies were applied have been demonstrated empirically
to be without merit. Rather, even the most simple intervention loses
power when the therapist lacks the capacity to appreciate the feelings of
the client experientially (Surrey, 1987).

Second (and overlapping the ability to be empathic), a therapist must
be able to create a relationship with the client. Such a relationship may
be both real and symbolic, or may, in the therapist's particular theoretical perspective, operate only or primarily in one of those realms. However, without it, no therapy occurs. The brilliant student who can recite
the relevant literature but who lacks basic skills at relationship development will prove to be a weaker therapist than her colleague who is less
knowledgeable but more socially skillful.

A third requirement for therapists is a high tolerance for ambiguity
and the experience of powerlessness. Therapy is a complex endeavor.
The outcome of a particular session, the impact of a given action or in-
action on our part, may never bear visible fruit or may flourish so far
from their source to render the connection difficult to determine. As
therapists, we are confronted with never knowing precisely what it is
that we do that will engender insight, awareness, comfort, and change
for our clients, an ambiguity that may lead us to experience ourselves as
"imposters," not doing real work because we lack concrete evidence of
outcome (Gibbs, 1984). Yet to function effectively as therapists, we must
not only allow this ambiguity but (in some systems of psychotherapy)
encourage or promote it. Even when our approach leads us to a sense of
knowing the relationship between an intervention and its therapeutic
outcome, we are often left wondering. Did that cognitive reframe *really*
lead to that insight, or is the apparent causality illusory and simply a
source of ego gratification for the therapist? Clearly, the abilities to delay
gratification and to find one's work innately satisfying no matter what
the outcome are essential for therapists.

A fourth characteristic is the ability to be comfortable with feelings
that are often called primitive or regressed but that I prefer to describe
less pejoratively as young. These are the powerful affects of infancy:
rage, terror, adoration, grief, pain—all of which are likely to appear in

the therapy hour communicated through the adult who recalls them during treatment. Strong needs for being dependent, coupled with fear of engulfment and loss of boundaries, are often also present at these times. A skillful therapist must be able to be present with these young feelings without fear, disgust, or her own loss of sense of self. Rather, she must be able to allow and hold these affects, often before the client is capable of doing so. At the same time, the therapist must be able to respect the adulthood of the client and not strip her of her competency while acknowledging the presence of the affective child within.

Finally, the therapist exists to empower her clients. To be able to know oneself, to work productively, love intimately, say yes to life, set limits and respect, and know one's own boundaries—all of these are intensely powerful actions, and all are congruent with the goals for therapy outcome. We wish our clients to emerge from the process more fully human, more aware of and in overt possession of all their skills and talents, more appreciative of themselves and their survival. We must be able to give the credit to our clients for their growth, to place the locus of change in them rather than take primary credit for ourselves (Rosewater, 1987). We must be present at the recreation of a human being and then consciously and knowingly prepare to let them go. It is no accident that we use the word *termination* to refer to the ending of therapy; the finality of the word is a meta-message about the temporary nature of the therapy relationship, no matter how long or intense it has been.

In reviewing these characteristics of the generic therapist as I have described her, it becomes apparent that there is much about being female in this culture that overlaps with the requirements of being a therapist. Thus, I would argue that one thing that women therapists have in common is a greater preparedness for the tasks of therapy.

This is not an inconsequential difference. In the small amount of empirical research on differences between male and female psychotherapists, this increased aptitude for the role emerges in sharp focus. Orlinsky and Howard (1980) found that only the most experienced male therapists were perceived as equal in warmth, empathy, and skillfulness to women therapists of all experience levels. Jones and Zoppel (1982) had similar findings, with clients of both genders rating female therapists as more skillful at forming therapeutic alliances. Women's greater preparedness to work as therapists, and thus our apparent greater effectiveness at certain aspects of the therapist role, is likely to be an artifact of female experience. In reviewing those characteristics of female phenomenology that I have described above, several that translate directly into the work of therapy emerge.

If we accept for the sake of this argument the notion that in therapy a symbolic dynamic occurs that mirrors a parent–young child relationship in the power differential and the roles of the actors (a dynamic that need *not* be described in terms of "transference" since often these aspects of the therapy relationship are quite overt and conscious [Brown, 1984]), we can see that women are likely to find their role as therapists in this relationship a more ego-syntonic, better-rehearsed one. Women, whether mothers or not, have intrapsychically prepared themselves for the "mothering" tasks inherent in the therapist role (Chodorow, 1979). Our sense of self as women and our professional role as therapist fit more smoothly with each other than will be the case for men, who in becoming therapists must take on ways of being that have been rejected in other stages of personal development as "feminine" and thus ego-alien. Even a woman who consciously rejects the task of mother-parent may experience this sense of comfort and at-homeness in the work of a therapist.

Specifically, women therapists are likely to have in common a greater capacity for empathy with their clients, for several reasons. The first is the greater female capacity for empathy described above. Kaplan (1983) argues that true empathic communication in therapy mirrors to a large degree the experience of empathy felt by women, both as the female infant in the mother-infant dyad described by Chodorow and as the adult woman who has introjected the mother of that dyad into her own identity and style of interpersonal relating. The development of a relational self in women increases the capacity for empathy and ensures that this capacity will be central to the woman's sense of self. For the woman therapist, this leads to greater ease with those elements of therapy that are necessary for empathic relating. The therapy relationship, with its intense affect and blurring of ego boundaries, is likely to be familiar emotional territory for most women therapists to a far greater degree than for men.

The capacity for empathy is also enhanced by shared experience. Recent data suggests that large numbers of both women and men entering therapy have been victims of intimate interpersonal violence, with estimated rates ranging from 42% (Carmen, Reiker, & Mills, 1984) to 85% (Jacobson & Richardson, 1987). While the connection between surviving violence and development of psychiatric symptomatology is only beginning to be explored (Bagley & Ramsey, 1986; Brown, in press; Bryer, Nelson, Miller, & Krol, 1987; Root & Fallon, 1988), the picture that begins to emerge suggests that women therapists, who as women are more likely to have survived violence or experienced anticipating and fearing it, will be more capable of being attuned to the responses of their violated clients and more capable of validating the intensity of response to trauma. Such empathy is also likely to decrease the degree to which women therapists infer pathology in such clients, since to a greater degree than male therapists, women therapists will be able to reach into their own experience and discover feelings that are not unlike those expressed by such clients.

The comfort that women may have had to develop in the presence of young children as their caretakers may also be a source of women therapists' greater ease with young affects in the therapy session. Clients often comment on how difficult it was for previous male therapists simply to be present with their intense young affective expression, contrasting this with their women therapists' apparent lack of fear of or discomfort with such feelings. Women therapists are likely to be more skillful in working with such clients and thus more capable of conducting long-term treatment with severely wounded people.

Another aspect of female phenomenology that translates into the therapy setting and may lead to commonalities among women therapists is the capacity to be in, and utilize, the role of "other." Therapists, by virtue of their role, are given permission to act as a powerful observant other and to make comments, interpretations, and suggestions from that position. While women in general do not have this permission to comment, and many women therapists describe initial difficulties in giving voice to observations that feel intuitively correct, what women therapists may hold in common is greater practice in such observation and a more varied repertoire of observation skills. Women therapists are likely to be more acute and incisive in their observations and interpretations, and to be capable of attending to minutiae of word and action that would escape an equally well-trained man, who is likely to lack the years of vigilant attendance to others that comes with female experience. In that regard, one would expect that men from groups outside a dominant-white-male culture would function more like women in the therapeutic role. The woman therapist, by comprehending the experience of otherness, is also likely to experience greater empathy for the many clients who present with similar, but more paralyzing, feelings of alienation, disconnection, or devaluation.

Because the socially and emotionally constructed role of "mother," usually held by women, is one in which ambiguity and lack of control must be tolerated in order to facilitate the healthy development of children, women as therapists will be likely to deal more easily with this aspect of therapeutic work as well. As women, we have developed skills for coping with being rejected and devalued; thus our capacity as women therapists to handle anger, rejection, and resistance from clients will probably be more highly developed. The need to control, which is inimical to the process of therapy when expressed by the therapist, is less often a product of women's phenomenology of relatedness; women therapists will thus experience more ease in sharing power with clients and will be less likely to complain of experiencing power struggles in their work.

Finally, women therapists are likely to be more skillful at the empowerment of the people with whom they work. It is no accident that the emphasis on empowerment of clients as an explicit goal of psychotherapy emerged most clearly from feminist therapy, a system of psychotherapy developed almost entirely by women therapists (Douglas & Walker, 1988). Within many systems of psychotherapy, women therapists have taken the lead to critique and reframe approaches to treatment that disempower clients or rely too heavily on the exercise of therapist power for their effectiveness (Lerner, 1988; Luepnitz, 1988; Miller, 1976) placing new emphasis on the importance of restoring the client's lost or wounded sense of personal power instead of the client's ability to adjust well to the status quo (Greenspan, 1983).

Although much of the previous literature on women as therapists has emphasized the importance of the ability to make empathic connections as the predominant variable discriminating us from men, I would argue that while this difference exists and is important, it is the ability to empower our clients that is the more essential and impactful core of the work of women therapists.

I have come to this belief because of my sense that empathy per se, while facilitative of the development of the therapeutic relationship and helpful in creating a feeling of receiving nurturance and positive regard in the client, is only a first step in the practice of effective psychotherapy. If it is true, as I believe, that women therapists are more capable of empowerment, of sharing power with their clients, of engendering a sense of personal powerfulness in people who have believed themselves to have none, then what women therapists can do is be more effective in the healing work of therapy. We are at home within ourselves with being the supportive coach, the one how holds the hand as long as it is needed to support the toddler's first steps and simultaneously cheers those steps on when they occur. If therapy is to be productive of autonomous beings capable of interpersonal relatedness from within an awareness of their own power and strengths, women therapists have much to offer because of our lifelong training in becoming the facilitators of such growth.

The foregoing has stressed the positive in the factors common to women therapists. But as with other aspects of women's roles, women as therapists may experience profound ambivalence about the ease with which their experience as women blends into the demands of therapy. It is common for women therapists, like other women caretakers, to doubt the validity of their work or the genuine skill expressed therein (Gibbs, 1984). Ironically, this is often because so many of the complex interpersonal skills required for the work of therapy appear to come so "easily" to women, who forget the years of self-development that have gone into the creation of the female person taking on this task. Concurrently, such skills may have been overtly devalued during the woman's professional socialization in favor of a more androcentric, though less effective, approach to therapy that emphasizes therapeutic distance and control over empathy and relatedness (Kaplan, 1983). In consequence, women therapists may also have in common the need to heal ourselves from the internalized sexism and devaluation of female experience that was present during our personal and professional developments, to embrace and appreciate more fully the gifts that our experiences as women bring to our work.

## CONCLUSION

In this chapter, I have endeavored to create a workable set of hypotheses about what women therapists have in common. In reviewing what I have said, I find myself needing to fall back upon the strengths of my own woman's phenomenology to validate the intuitive rightness with which my ideas resonate back to me. Because as professionals we have failed to ask the questions in this chapter sufficiently to generate "hard data" of the sort that would satisfy the demands of an empiricist methodology, the information here reflects a methodology that Ballou (1990), in her description of feminist-therapy approaches to the creation of a research methodology, has described as that of "non-rational knowledge generation." Such methodologies, says Ballou, rely heavily upon the use of the intuition of the knower for the generation of knowledge. Reflecting this standard, I have relied heavily upon my own personal and clinical experiences, as well as those of many other women therapists who have written or spoken with me about their work, and clients who have described their experiences in treatment with both women and men.

Clearly, the generalizations made here bear close scrutiny. Not every woman therapist will find herself mirrored in my descriptions, precisely because of the great diversity among women therapists that I described at the beginning of this chapter. However, in attempting to rise to the challenge of this complexity, it is my hope that I will have stimulated movement toward the creation of different ways of answering this question.

## REFERENCES

Ballou, M. (1990). Approaching a feminist principled paradigm in the construction of personality theory. In L. S. Brown & M. P. P. Root (Eds.), *Diversity and complexity in feminist therapy*. New York: Haworth Press.

Bagley, C., & Ramsey, R. (1986). Sexual abuse in childhood: Psychosocial outcomes and implications for social work practice. *Journal of Social Work and Human Sexuality, 5,* 33–47.

Bernard, J. (1972). *The future of marriage.* New York: World.

Bingham, S. (1988). *Passion and prejudice: A family memoir.* New York: Alfred A. Knopf.

Bradshaw, C. (1990). A Japanese view of dependency: What Amae psychology can contribute to feminist theory and therapy. In L. S. Brown & M. P. P. Root (Eds.), *Diversity and complexity in feminist therapy.* New York: Haworth.

Brown, L. S. (1982, July). *Women and power: A paradigm shift.* Lecture presented at the University of Washington, Seattle, WA.

Brown, L. S. (1984). Finding new language: Getting beyond analytic verbal shorthand in feminist therapy. *Women and Therapy, 3,* 73–80.

Brown, L. S. (1990). The meaning of a multicultural perspective for theory-building in feminist therapy. In L. S. Brown & M. P. P. Root (Eds.), *Diversity and complexity in feminist therapy.* New York: Haworth.

Brown, L. S. (in press). Victimization as a risk factor in depressive symptomatology in women. *Proceedings of the Task Force on Women and Depression.* Washington, DC: American Psychological Association.

Bryer, J. B., Nelson, B. A., Miller, J. B., & Krol., P. A. (1987). Childhood sexual and physical abuse as factors in adult psychiatric illness. *American Journal of Psychiatry, 144,* 1426–1430.

Carmen, E. H., Reiker, P. P., & Mills, T. (1984). Victims of violence and psychiatric illness. *American Journal of Psychiatry, 141,* 378–383.

Chodorow, N. (1979). *The reproduction of mothering.* Berkeley, CA: University of California Press.

Corsini, R. (Ed.). (1981). *Innovative psychotherapies.* New York: Wiley.

Daly, M. (1973). *Beyond god the father.* Boston: Beacon Press.

Douglas, M. A., & Walker, L. E. A. (1988). *Feminist psychotherapies: Integration of feminist and psychotherapeutic systems.* Norwood, NJ: Ablex.

Dworkin, A. (1974). *Woman hating.* New York: E. P. Dutton.

Dworkin, A. (1983). *Right-wing women.* New York: Perigee.

Finkelhor, D., & Yllo, K. (1985). *License to rape.* New York: Holt Rinehart & Winston.

Gibbs, M. (1984). The therapist as imposter. In C. M Brody (Ed.), *Women therapists working with women: New theory and process of feminist therapy* (pp. 22–36). New York: Springer Publishing Co.

Gordon, L. (1988). *Heroes of their own lives: The politics and history of family violence.* New York: Viking.

Greenspan, M. (1983). *A new approach to women and therapy.* New York: McGraw-Hill.

Institute for Research on Women's Health. (1988). *Information packet: Sexual harassment and employment discrimination.* Washington, DC: Author.

Jacobson, A., & Richardson, B. (1987). Assault experiences of 100 psychiatric inpatients: Evidence of the need for routine inquiry. *American Journal of Psychiatry, 144,* 908–913.

Janeway, E. (1971). *Man's world, woman's place: A study in social mythology*. New York: Delta.

Johnson, S. (1987). *Going out of our minds: The metaphysics of liberation*. Freedom, CA: The Crossing Press.

Jones, E. E., & Zoppel, C. L. (1982). Impact of client and therapist gender on psychotherapy process and outcome. *Journal of Consulting and Clinical Psychology, 50,* 259–272.

Jordan, J. V. (1984). *Empathy and self boundaries*. Wellesley, MA: Stone Center for Developmental Services and Studies.

Jordan, J. V., Surrey, J. L., & Kaplan, A. G. (1983). *Women and empathy: Implications for psychological development and psychotherapy*. Wellesley, MA: Stone Center for Developmental Services and Studies.

Kaplan, A. G. (1983). *Empathic communication in the psychotherapy relationship*. Wellesley, MA: Stone Center for Developmental Services and Studies.

Kaplan, A. G. (1984). *Female or male psychotherapists for women: New formulations*. Wellesley, MA: Stone Center for Developmental Services and Studies.

Keller, E. F. (1983). *A feeling for the organism: The life and work of Barbara McClintock*. New York: W. H. Freeman.

Lerner, H. G. (1988). *Women in therapy*. New York: Jason Aronson.

Luepnitz, D. A. (1988). *The family interpreted: Feminist theory in clinical practice*. New York: Basic Books.

Miller, J. B. (1976). *Toward a new psychology of women*. Boston: Beacon Press.

Miller, J. B. (1984). *The development of women's sense of self*. Wellesley, MA: Stone Center for Developmental Services and Studies.

New York Public Interest Research group. (1981). *Study on sexual harassment*. Albany, NY: Author.

Noble, K. D. (1988, October). *The female hero*. Keynote lecture given at the third Women of High Potential Conference, Seattle, WA.

Orlinsky, D. E., & Howard, K. I. (1980). Gender and psychotherapeutic outcome. In A. Brodsky & R. Hare-Mustin (Eds.), *Women and Psychotherapy: An assessment of research and practice* (pp. 3–35). New York: Guilford.

Raymond, J. G. (1986). *A passion for friends*. Boston: Beacon Press.

Rich, A. (1979). *On lies, secrets, and silences*. New York: W. W. Norton.

Root, M. P. P., & Fallon, P. (1988). The incidence of victimization experiences in a bulimic sample. *Journal of Interpersonal Violence, 3,* 161–173.

Rosewater, L. B. (1987). *Changing through therapy*. New York: Dutton.

Russ, J. (1982). Power and helplessness in the women's movement. *Women's Studies Quarterly, 10,* 7–10.

Russell, D. E. H. (1982). *Rape in marriage*. New York: MacMillan.

Russell, D. E. H. (1986). *The secret trauma: Incest in the lives of girls and women*. New York: Basic Books.

Smith, A. J., & Siegel, R. F. (1985). Feminist therapy: Redefining power for the powerless. In L. B. Rosewater & L. E. A. Walker (Eds.), *Handbook of feminist therapy: Women's issues in psychotherapy*. (pp. 13–21). New York: Springer Publishing Co.

Surrey, J. L. (1985). *Self-in-relation: A theory of women's development*. Wellesley, MA: Stone Center for Developmental Services and Studies.

Surrey, J. L. (1987). *Relationship and empowerment*. Wellesley, MA: Stone Center for Developmental Services and Studies.

Swift, C. F. (1987). *Women and violence: Breaking the connection*. Wellesley, MA: Stone Center for Developmental Services and Studies.

Walker, L. E. A. (1979). *The battered woman*. New York: Harper & Row.

# Author Index

# Subject Index

Thematic Apperception Test (TAT),
  39–40
Theoretical orientation, 33–52
  adaptability factor, 35
  and resonance, 35, 36
Therapeutic alliance, *see* Alliance
Therapeutic errors, study of, 6
Therapist gender, impact of, 8
Therapist selection
  attitude similarity, 25
  competence and, 23, 24
  concern for client, 23
  empathy and, 23, 24
  expertise and, 23, 28, 29
  factors of, 28, 30–31
  female, 9, 21
  future research, 31
  gender of, 29, 160
  male, 9
  personality factors and, 22

qualities of therapist, 23
reputation of, 28–31
study of, 26–31
theoretical orientation and, 21–26,
  27, 30
Therapist-client relationship,
  219–220
  characteristics of, 25–26
*Three Essays on the Theory of
  Sexuality*, 155
Transference, 13, 24, 74, 159, 164
  asexual, 15
  and effect of gender, 9, 10
  eroticized, 10
  maternal, 9, 16, 159, 160, 164, 165
  paternal, 9, 159, 160
  and therapist gender, 159
  *see also* Countertransference

Understanding, significance of, 24,
  69